Gendered Insecurities, Health and Development in Africa

The concept of security has often narrowly focused on issues surrounding the protection of national borders from outside threats. However, a richer idea of human security has become increasingly important in the past decade or so. The aim is to incorporate various dimensions of the downside risks affecting the generalized well-being or dignity of people. Despite this rising prominence, the discourses surrounding human security have neglected to address the topic of gender, particularly how issues of poverty and underdevelopment impact women's and men's experiences and strategies differently.

Since its introduction in the 1994 UNDP Human Development report, the idea of human security has become increasingly influential among academics and international development practitioners. However, gendered dimensions of human security have not attracted enough attention, despite their vital importance. Women are disproportionately more vulnerable to disease and other forms of human insecurity due to differences in entitlement, empowerment and an array of other ecological and socio-economic factors. These gendered insecurities are inextricably linked to poverty and, as a result, the feminization of poverty is a growing phenomenon worldwide. The contributors to this volume rely on a gender-focused analysis to consider a number of issues central to human security and development in Africa, including food security, environmental health risks, discrimination within judicial and legal systems, gendered aspects of HIV/AIDS transmission and treatment technologies, neoliberalism and poverty alleviation strategies, and conflict and women's political activism.

The gender focus of this volume points to the importance of power relationships and policy variability underlying human insecurities in the African context. The insights of this book offer the potential for an improved human security framework, one that embraces a more complex and context-specific analysis of the issues of risk and vulnerability, therefore expanding the capacities of the human security framework to safeguard the livelihoods of the most vulnerable populations.

Howard Stein is Professor in the Department of Afroamerican and African Studies (DAAS) and also teaches in the Department of Epidemiology at the University of Michigan. His research has focused on foreign aid, finance and development, structural adjustment, health and development, industrial policy and rural property rights transformation.

Amal Hassan Fadlalla is Associate Professor of Anthropology, Women's Studies and African Studies at the University of Michigan. Her teaching addresses global perspectives on gender, health and reproduction, and gender, diaspora and transnationalism.

Routledge studies in development economics

Gendered Insecurities, Health and Development in Africa

Edited by Howard Stein and
Amal Hassan Fadlalla

LONDON AND NEW YORK

First published 2012
by Routledge

2 Park Square, Milton Park, Abingdon, Oxon OX14 4RN
711 Third Avenue, New York, NY 10017, USA

Routledge is an imprint of the Taylor & Francis Group, an informa business

First issued in paperback 2016

British Library Cataloguing in Publication Data
A catalogue record for this book is available from the British Library

Library of Congress Cataloging in Publication Data
Gendered insecurities, health and development in Africa / edited by
Howard Stein and Amal Hassan Fadlalla.
    p. cm.
    Includes bibliographical references and index.
    1. Women–Africa–Social conditions. 2. Women–Africa–Economic
conditions. 3. Women and human security–Africa. 4. Public health–
Africa. 5. Poverty–Africa. 6. Human security–Africa. 7. Economic
development–Africa. I. Stein, Howard, 1952– II. Fadlalla,
Amal Hassan.
    HQ1787.G454 2012
    305.4096–dc23   2012001188

ISBN: 978-0-415-59784-5 (hbk)
ISBN: 978-1-138-22497-1 (pbk)

Typeset in Times New Roman
by Wearset Ltd, Boldon, Tyne and Wear

For African women and their quotidian struggles

Contents

Illustrations

Figures

Tables

Contributors

Editors

Amal Hassan Fadlalla is Associate Professor of Anthropology, Women's Studies and African Studies at the University of Michigan. She teaches on global perspectives on gender, health and reproduction, and on gender, diaspora and transnationalism. Her recent work also focuses on issues related to human rights, humanitarianism and development discourses and practices in Africa and the diaspora. Her recent publications appear in *Signs: Journal of Women in Culture and Society,* 37(1), 2011; *Urban Anthropology,* 38(1), 2009; *Identities: Global Studies in Culture and Power*, 12(2), 2005; and in the School for Advanced Research edited volume *New Landscapes of Inequality: Neoliberalism and the Erosion of Democracy in America (2008). She is also the author of Embodying Honor: Fertility, Foreignness, and Regeneration in Eastern Sudan (*2007*).*

Howard Stein is Professor in the Center for Afroamerican and African Studies (CAAS) and also teaches in the Department of Epidemiology at the University of Michigan. He is a development economist educated in Canada, the US and the UK who has taught in both Asia and Africa. He is the editor or author of more than a dozen books and collections. His research has focused on foreign aid, finance and development, structural adjustment, health and development, industrial policy and rural property right transformation. His most recent books include *Beyond the World Bank Agenda: An Institutional Approach to Development* (2008), *Good Growth and Governance in Africa: Rethinking Development Strategies* (co-edited with Akbar Noman, Joseph Stiglitz and Kwesi Botchway, 2012).

Contributors

Sakiko Fukuda-Parr is Professor of International Affairs at New School University and has been an early and key contributor to the human security concept. She is a development economist working in the multidisciplinary framework of capabilities and human development, and is currently focusing her research on human rights and poverty, conflict prevention and global technology. From 1995 to 2004, she was lead author and director of the UNDP Human Development Reports. In 2000 she founded the *Journal of Human Development and Capabilities* which she currently co-edits. In addition to the Human Development Reports, her publications include: *The Gene Revolution: GM Crops and Unequal Development* (2007), *Readings in Human Development* (2003), *Rethinking Technical Cooperation: Reforms for capacity building in Africa* (1993), *Capacity for Development: New Solutions to Old Problems* (2002) and numerous papers and book chapters on issues of poverty, gender, human rights and technology.

Jayati Ghosh is Professor in the Division of Business at Dominican University in California. Her research interests are in the areas of economic development and health, with a special emphasis on women's health in Africa and Asia from an economic and social perspective. Dr. Ghosh has written a number of articles dealing with the AIDS epidemic and economic development in India and Africa. She also co-edited the book *HIV and AIDS in Africa: Beyond Epidemiology* (co-edited with Ezekiel Kalipeni, Joseph Oppong, and Susan Craddock, Blackwell Publishers,   2004). Her current research focuses on HIV/AIDS in India and Malawi. Some of her works have appeared in journals such as *Social Science and Medicine, Journal of Social Aspects of HIV/AIDS, Asian Profile* and *Geographical Review*.

Jok Madut Jok is Professor in the Department of History at Loyola Marymount University in Los Angeles and currently an undersecretary in the Ministry of Culture and Heritage in the new country of South Sudan. He received his Ph.D. in the anthropology of health from UCLA. He was born and raised in South Sudan. As a graduate student in Egypt and the United States, he worked on the impact of war on gender relations. He has conducted research in South Sudan and refugee camps in the neighboring countries where he chronicled how violence is reproduced within communities and families during times of violent political conflict. Jok has conducted numerous other studies on the impact of humanitarian aid in Sudan and is the author of *War and Slavery in Sudan* (2001), *Sudan: Race, Religion and Violence* (2007) *and Militarization, Gender and Reproductive Health in South Sudan* (1998).

Ezekiel Kalipeni is Professor of Geography at the University of Illinois at Urbana Champaign   and a population/medical/environmental geographer interested in demographic, health, environmental and resource issues in sub-Saharan   Africa. He has carried out extensive research on the population dynamics of Malawi and Africa in general concentrating on fertility, mortality, migration and health care issues. He is currently working on HIV/AIDS in Africa and population and environmental issues in Malawi. He is the author or editor of a number of books including *HIV/AIDS in Africa: Beyond Epidemiology* (2004), *Global Issues in Africa* (2008) *Women and HIV/AIDS in Africa* (2009). He also recently edited a special issue of AIDs and Gender in the journal *Social Science and Medicine*.

Zo Randriamaro is a gender equality and human rights activist from Madagascar. She is a development sociologist by training and has published several papers on gender, economic and trade issues. She has also served as an expert for the major international development organizations, including USAID and United Nations agencies. She was the former Regional Advisor on Feminized Poverty in Africa for the United Nations Development Fund for Women (UNIFEM). She is also a member of the Board of Directors of the Women's Environment and Development Organization (WEDO).

Lisa Ann Richey is Professor of Development Studies in the Department of Society and Globalisation at Roskilde University in Copenhagen. She conducts research on health, gender and international development in Africa. She is the author of *Population Politics: From the Policies to the Clinics* (2008), co-editor of *Women and Development (Women's Studies Quarterly Special Issue)* (2003) and co-author of *Brand Aid: Celebrities, Consumption and Development* (2011). Her current research focuses on therapeutic citizenship and the politics of antiretroviral treatment for HIV/AIDS in South Africa and Uganda.

Jacob Songsore is Professor Emeritus of Geography and Resource Development at the University of Ghana. Between 2003 and 2007, he was the Dean of the School of Research and Graduate Studies at the same institution. He is an urban, epidemiological geographer whose research has focused on environmental problems in urban households in Accra, the capital of Ghana. His many books and articles focus on rural and urban poverty, women and environmental care within urban households, proxy indicators for rapid assessment of environmental health status in residential areas, urban sanitation and sustainable global cities, structural adjustment and the urban poor and poverty and the burden of disease in African cities. His most recent volumes include *Urbanization and Health in Africa: Exploring the Interconnections between Poverty, Inequality and the Burden of Diseases* (2004), *Regional Development in Ghana* (2003), *State of Environmental Health Report of the Greater Accra Metropolitan Area* (co-authored, 2005) and *The Citizens at Risk: From Urban Sanitation to Sustainable Cities* (co-edited, 2001). He has taught and done research at the University of Port Harcourt in Nigeria, the Stockholm Environment Institute, the University of Frankfurt and the London School of Hygiene and Tropical Medicine.

Aili Mari Tripp is Professor of Political Science and Women's Studies at the University of Wisconsin-Madison and is President of the African Studies Association in 2011–2012. She is author of *Women and Politics in Uganda* (2000), which won the American Political Science Association's Victoria Schuck Award and a Choice Award. She has also authored *Changing the Rules: The Politics of Liberalization and the Urban Informal Economy in Tanzania* (1997) and co-authored, with Isabel Casimiro, Joy Kwesiga and Alice Mungwa, *African Women's Movements: Transforming Political Landscapes*

(2009). Her latest book is *Museveni's Uganda: Paradoxes of Power in a Hybrid Regime* (2010). Tripp has edited with Myra Marx Ferree *Global Feminism: Transnational Women's Activism, Organizing, and Human Rights* (2006) and three other volumes. She has published numerous articles and book chapters on women and politics in Africa, women's responses to economic reform and the political impact of transformations of associational life in Africa. Her publications draw on fieldwork carried out primarily in Tanzania, Uganda, Liberia and Angola.

Meredeth Turshen is Professor in the Edward J. Bloustein School of Planning and Public Policy at Rutgers University. Her research interests include international health and she specializes in public health policy. She has written four books, *The Political Ecology of Disease in Tanzania* (1984), *The Politics of Public Health* (1989), *Privatizing Health Services in Africa* (1999), and *Women's Health Movements: A Global Force for Change* (2007); she has edited five other books, *Women and Health in Africa* (1991), *Women's Lives and Public Policy: The International Experience* (1993), *What Women Do in Wartime: Gender and Conflict in Africa* (1998), which was translated into French (L'Harmattan, 2001), *African Women's Health* (2000) and *The Aftermath: Women in Postconflict Transformation* (2002). She serves on the Board of the Association of Concerned Africa Scholars, as Treasurer of the Committee for Health in Southern Africa, as contributing editor of the *Review of African Political Economy* and is on the editorial board of the *Journal of Public Health Policy*.

John Weeks is Professor Emeritus of Development Economics of the School of Oriental and African Studies of the University of London, and former director of the Centre for Development Policy and Research. He is author of numerous books and monograph length studies on African development covering countries such as Sierra Leone, South Africa, Kenya, South Africa and Tanzania and topics which include structural adjustment, macroeconomic policy, poverty reduction approaches, labor markets, agriculture and aid ownership. His most recent work on Africa includes two United Nations Development Programme studies of Zambia, one on macroeconomic policy and a second one on exchange rate policy. His latest book is entitled *Capital, Exploitation and Economic Crises* (2011).

Foreword

Sakiko Fukuda-Parr

As Mahbub ul Haq, who brought the concept of human security to global policy debates in the mid 1990s, put it in his 1995 volume *Reflections on Human Development*:

> Human security is a concept emerging not from the learned writings of scholars but from the daily concerns of people—from the dread of a woman that she may be raped in a lonely street at night, from the anguish of parents over the spread of drugs among their children, from the choked existence of prosperous communities in increasingly polluted cities, from the fear of terrorism suddenly striking any life anywhere without reason. A people's concept and a people's concern, human security is reflected in the shriveled faces of innocent children, in the anguished existence of the homeless, in the constant fear of the jobless, in the silent despair of those without hope.[1]

For women in sub-Saharan Africa, human security is a daily and chronic concern, for themselves and their households and communities. As elsewhere, women are the primary caregivers on whom other individuals rely for their own human security; women provide for the household's food needs, care for the sick, uphold the cleanliness of their home and their environments, and much more. Poverty is a pervasive threat to human security that affects virtually the entire population in many countries of the region, as each one of the chapters in this volume points out. This volume illustrates in graphic detail the multiple threats to human security that women face in different contexts, as well as women's agency in confronting the challenges.

The following collection of papers demonstrates the relevance of the human security concept. This volume highlights deprivations as downside risks that threaten lives and livelihoods through the rich array of papers that cover different threats related to food crises, HIV/AIDS, environment, peace negotiations, violence and economic policy. It emphasizes the multidimensional nature of threats to security, such as from illness, or war, or economic downturns, and notes how these different threats are inter-related.

Most importantly, this volume brings a unique contribution to the study of human security in two ways. First it focuses on gender and underscores structures of power as an essential factor in understanding threats to human security. As Aili Mari Tripp points out in her chapter on peace negotiations in Africa, "there are many aspects of the human security approach relating to agency that need to be sharpened in order to make the concept workable from a gender studies perspective." The volume draws attention to both power relations within the household and in wider society.

Second, this publication highlights models of economic growth as a determinant of human security. Amal Fadlalla and Howard Stein point out in their introduction that, "far too frequently proponents of human security fail to examine the insecurities, poverty and global economic disparities created by decades of neoliberal policies." Economic policies are an important factor behind the threats examined in the chapters.

The concept of human security has been controversial, and academics debate different definitions of the concept (broad and narrow). In particular, academics grapple with specific questions about the usefulness of relying on a broad definition of human security that encompasses both freedom from fear and freedom from want. Meanwhile, political negotiations to adopt human rights as a framework for security and development have made little progress. Yet despite such controversies, the concept continues to be used in policy debates and in research. The explanation for this recurrence lies in Mahbub ul Haq's insightful observation quoted at the beginning of this Foreword. Human security is part of the lived experience of people. It is a lived experience not easily reflected in other frameworks. Human security focuses on downward risks arising from both chronic and sudden threats to human well-being. Downward risks are not the central concern in the human development and capabilities approach, nor are such risks the primary concern in human rights; however, downward risks are part of these approaches to think about and act upon in promoting human dignity and freedoms.

Note

1 Mahbub ul Haq (1995) *Reflections on Human Development*, New York: Oxford University Press, p. 116.

Acknowledgments

In 2008, Amal Hassan Fadlalla and Howard Stein received a generous grant from the Institute for Research on Women and Gender (IRWG) to run a year-long speaker series in 2008–09 on "Gender, African Development and Human Security." The series was part of the African Development and Human Security Project, launched at the University of Michigan by Mamadou Diouf and Howard Stein with support from the Center for International and Comparative Studies in 2006. The project is administered in the Department of Afroamerican and African Studies in coordination with a student steering committee made up of graduate students from around the university. To date there are more than 200 graduate students and faculty affiliated with the initiative, representing every school in the university. The largest numbers are from the School of Natural Resources and Environment, School of Public Health, the School of Social Work, the Ford School of Public Policy and LSA. The chief aim of the project is to examine and explore new approaches to the study of human security and development in sub-Saharan Africa, while also building awareness within the University of Michigan community on these issues. To date the project has been involved with hosting outside speakers, organizing panels and conferences, showing films, sponsoring study groups and workshops and organizing a forum for graduate student papers.

The significance of a gender focus series on African development and human security was timely and was aimed at understanding the complexities surrounding African development, particularly how issues of poverty and underdevelopment impact women's and men's life experiences and strategies differently as they struggle to cope with the rapidly escalating violence, famine, wars and diseases. Women are disproportionately more vulnerable to disease and other forms of human insecurity due to differences in entitlement, empowerment and an array of other ecological and socio-economic factors. The speaker series attracted large audiences due to the prominence of the invited scholars, the breadth of their fields which sparked interesting interdisciplinary conversations and the broad interest in the subject. Papers came from the fields of political science, economics, geography, women's studies, anthropology, history and public health. All chapters except for the introduction were presented as papers during the speaker series.

We are grateful to many people that provided support for this initiative. We are particularly thankful to current and former DAAS colleagues and staff. Special thanks to Sean Jacobs, Elisha Renne, Adam Ashforth, Anne Pitcher, Kevin Gaines, Angela Dillard, Tiya Miles, Martin Murray, Kelly Askew, Sean Jacobs, Frieda Ekotto, Mamadou Diouf, Devon Adjei, Katherine Weathers, Don Sims, Wayne High and Beth James. From the beginning, Carol Boyd, Director of IRWG, was very gracious in her intellectual and financial support. The IRWG publicity coordinator Terri Torkko was instrumental in getting the word out. ADHS graduate student steering committee members Jennifer Johnson, Ted Lawrence and Cristy Watkins were very helpful in the organizational side of the speaker series. Anneeth Huddle commented on and edited a number of chapters. Emily Franchett and Madelynne Wager worked closely with us for many months in preparing the manuscript for publication. We are very grateful to the Routledge editorial staff for their patience and support as we worked our way through the inevitable delays and complexities associated with editing a volume of contributions from very accomplished and busy scholars. We would like to particularly thank Louisa Earls, Natalie Tomlinson, Emily Kindleysides and Tom Sutton.

We really appreciate the effort of the wonderful group of scholars we assembled for the speaker series and volume. They not only stimulated important discussions and debates with their provocative and insightful presentations but also carefully responded to comments as they drafted and redrafted their chapters. Finally, we would like to especially thank Sakiko Fukuda-Parr. She was the inaugural speaker who helped launch the University of Michigan African Development and Human Security Project in 2006 that ultimately led to this book project. We are very grateful for her feedback on this project and her very kind commitment to writing the foreword for the volume.

Abbreviations

ABC	approach to HIV prevention: Abstinence, Be faithful, use a Condom
ACORD	Association for Cooperative Operations Research and Development
AFL	Armed Forces of Liberia
AFSC	American Friends Service Committee
AGRA	Alliance for a Green Revolution in Africa
AIDS	Acquired Immunodeficiency Syndrome
ARV	antiretroviral drugs
AU	African Union
AWCPD	African Women's Committee for Peace and Development
AWPSG	African Women and Peace Support Group
CAADP	Comprehensive Africa Agriculture Development Program
CADF	China-Africa Development Fund
CDC	Centers for Disease Control
CDF	Comprehensive Development Framework
CEDAW	International Convention on the Elimination of All Forms of Discrimination Against Women
CEMIS	Community-based Environmental Management Information System
CO	Carbon Monoxide
CODESRIA	Council for the Development of Social Science Research in Africa
COPPWIL	Coalition of Political Parties Women in Liberia
CORN	Community Organizations Regional Network
CPRC	Chronic Poverty Research Center
DAWN	Development Alternatives with Women for a New Era
DFID	Department for International Development
ECOMOG	Economic Community of West African States Monitoring Group
ECOWAS	Economic Community of West African States
ESAF	Enhanced Structural Adjustment Facility
EU	European Union

FAO	Food and Agriculture Organization
FERFAP	Federation of African Women's Peace Networks
GAMA	Greater Accra Metropolitan Area
GDP	gross domestic product
GERA	Gender and Economic Reforms in Africa
GMO	genetically modified organism
GoNU	Government of National Unity
GOSS	Government of Southern Sudan
GSS	Ghana Statistical Service
HAART	highly active antiretroviral therapy
HDIS	High Density Indigenous Sector
HIPC	Heavily Indebted Poor Countries
HIV	Human Immunodeficiency Virus
HLTF	High-Level Task Force
HYVs	high-yield varieties
ICP	International Comparison Program
IFAD	International Fund for Agricultural Development
ILO	International Labor Organization
ILRIG	International Labor Research and Information Group
IMF	International Monetary Fund
INSTRAW	International Research and Training Institute for the Advancement of Women
IRIN	Integrated Regional Information Networks
ISI	import substitution industrialization
LISGIS	Liberia Institute of Statistics and Geo-Information Services
LPG	liquefied petroleum gas
LURD	Liberians United for Democracy
LWI	Liberian Women's Initiative
MAP	Multi-country HIV/AIDS Program
MARWOPNET	Mano River Union Women Peace Network
MDGs	Millennium Development Goals
MDIS	Medium Density Indigenous Sector
MODEL	Movement for Democracy in Liberia
MTCT	maternal-to-child transmission
NEPAD	New Partnership for Africa's Development
NGO	non-governmental organization
NPFL	National Patriotic Front of Liberia
OAU	Organization of African Unity
ODA	official development assistance
PEPFAR	The US President's Emergency Program for AIDS Relief
PMTCT	prevention of maternal-to-child transmission
PPP	purchasing power parity
PRGF	Poverty Reduction and Growth Facility
PRSP	Poverty Reduction Strategy Papers
RF	Rural Fringe

RSP	respirable particulates
SADC	Southern African Development Community
SAP	structural adjustment program
SPLM/A	Sudan People's Liberation Movement/Army
SSA	sub-Saharan Africa
TASO	The AIDS Support Organization
TSP	total suspended particulates
UNAIDS	Joint United Nations Program on HIV/AIDS
UDHR	Universal Declaration of Human Rights
ULIMO	United Liberation Movement of Liberia for Democracy
UNCHS	The United Nations Human Settlements Program
UNCTAD	United Nations Conference on Trade and Development (UN-Habitat)
UNDAW	United Nations Division for the Advancement of Women
UNDP	United Nations Development Program
UNEP	United Nations Environment Program
UNFPA	United Nations Population Fund
UNIFEM	United Nations Development Fund for Women
UNMIL	UN Mission in Liberia
WHO	World Health Organization
WID	women in development
WTO	World Trade Organization

Gendered insecurities, health and development in Africa

An introduction

Amal Hassan Fadlalla and Howard Stein

Since its introduction by the UNDP, the concept of human security has become increasingly popularized in academic and policy circles. The original formulation in the 1993 Human Development Report focused on the need to transcend a cold-war territorial preoccupation in a post-1989 world. In this new reality a people-centered approach could tap the resources from disarmament and the contraction of defense spending to enhance food, employment and environmental security at the heart of an unfinished social agenda (UNDP, 1993). The 1994 Report provided a fuller definition of the meaning and content of human security. Chronic dimensions of human security focused on the safety from long term threats like hunger, disease and repression. More immediate threats could also arise from sudden shifts in the normal patterns of daily existence in the home, in a place of employment or in a community. Threats can arise from human, natural or both sources (UNDP, 1994).

In reality causes of chronic vs. more immediate threats to human security can be common. Hunger can be protracted or occur suddenly if a flood destroys a crop of a subsistence farmer at harvest time or if a war drives them away from their land or storage facilities. Diseases like malaria or cholera can kill in a matter of hours. The key is to generate a human-centered construct that can incorporate various dimensions of the downside risks affecting the generalized well-being or dignity of people whatever the time dimension. The concept incorporates an array of different components focused on the safety from the threat of disease, hunger, conflict, repression, violence, environmental degradation, discrimination, loss of human rights, shifts in weather and climate, crime, and loss of employment and other forms of livelihood.[1]

Alkire, in one of the more trenchant essays on human security, defines the objective of human security as safeguarding "the vital core of all human lives from pervasive threats, in a way that is consistent with long-term human fulfillment"[2] (2003: p. 2). Safeguarding human lives involves institutionalizing early warning systems along with the capacities to protect in a way that is systematic not episodic and protective and preventative not reactive.

The scope of human security is limited to a set of basic functions linked to the survival (freedom from premature preventable deaths), livelihood and dignity of people. The definition also invokes the human as a central category to the provision of security, which does not exclude any group based on any distinguishing attributes like race, ethnicity or citizenship. Focus is on threats that are deemed to be pervasive in the sense that they are critical and of sufficient scale in their threat to core activities and are sufficiently repetitive and not anomalous or idiosyncratic. Any interventions to enhance human security then must be consistent with the enhancement of human dignity and fulfillment. Subjecting people to confinement while feeding them (e.g., refugees) might help their physical survival, but curtail their basic rights and freedom. The objective of such universal claims, however, should not be narrowly defined by strictly technical terms but should be a product of practical reasoning that arises from reflection of the experience, knowledge, needs and values of involved subjects.

It is evident both in the broader discussions of human security and the specificities of Alkire's definition of human security objectives that there is considerable overlap with Sen's capabilities approach, UNDP's human development and a host of human rights and humanitarian based approaches to development. What are the relationships between these different concepts? In what way does human security add value to the African development agenda? Why does this volume choose to privilege gender and health? What are the weaknesses and strengths of human security both relative to the literature and the issues addressed in the chapters in this volume? What are some of the concrete policy recommendations that come out of the contributions in this book? The contributors of this volume use multiple and interdisciplinary lenses to delve into these issues as they attempt to address such questions.

Human rights, humanitarianism, development and security: exploring analytical linkages

In its original formulation the concept of human security was differentiated from human development using choice set arguments (which reflected the influence of Sen's capabilities construct). In particular human development was seen as expanding the "range of people's choices." There were two dimensions to this, the formation of new human capabilities, such as improving health and skills, and the way the people utilize the acquired capabilities toward specific purposes, whether it is for leisure or work (UNDP, 1990: p. 10). Fukuda-Parr, for many years lead author of the UNDP's annual Human Development Report, takes it a step further and argues that human development is focused on the "search for freedom, well-being and the dignity of individuals in all societies," (2004: p. 119) where individuals are not just passive recipients of progress. Human development is also concerned with generating human agency with people actively participating in generating and shaping social and economic change.

In contrast, human security focuses more narrowly on whether people "can exercise these choices safely and freely" (UNDP, 1994: p. 23) and that the opportunities today will be available tomorrow. The report also pointed to an obvious link between the two that operates in both directions. For instance, human insecurity can lead to violence which can delimit human development opportunities while a lack of human development leads to a "backlog of human deprivation" (1994: p. 23) and with it fundamental challenges to human security like hunger and disease.

Alkire (2003) takes it a step further and points to four similarities. First, both human security and human development are people-centered in the sense that human beings are the end objectives of development not a means toward other goals such as the orthodox focus on economic growth. Second, both concepts are multidimensional addressing both material and psychological (e.g., people's dignity) needs. Third, they both have broad perspectives on the long term fulfillment covering all groups in society. Fourth, there is a considerable policy overlap on addressing the chronically poor since they lack the most capabilities in coping with chronic insecurities and improving their development prospects. For example, improving access to health care for the poor is fundamental to both objectives.

There are also differences of scope given that human security is focused on a more narrow set of objectives within a "vital core." Human security, in some ways, also deals with a more preventative level to impede the formation of new sources of insecurity to the vital core such as intervening to avoid new civil or international conflict. In addition, human security often has shorter time horizons, given the sudden impact of unforeseen events and the need to address them rapidly through interventions like emergency relief (Alkire, 2003: pp. 36–37). To this end, Busumtwi-Sam (2008) points out that human security is a relative condition while development is a process. It both affects and is affected by human development. Development is difficult to achieve where there is a high degree of insecurity since people are focused on struggling for the most basic dimensions of physical survival with little opportunity to enhance their capabilities to improve the quality of their life.

In this sense, human security concepts not only intersect with human development but also with the practices of neoliberal forms of humanitarianism and human rights that address the urgency of intervention, the emphasis on survival, and the use of right based practices and discourses to advocate for development in conflict zones. Many scholars working on neoliberalism in Africa have shown how the recent proliferation of non-governmental organizations (NGOs) working on development in Africa is linked to the retreat of the state, the fast growing communication networks, and the spread of humanitarianism and human right cultures. In her work on the neoliberalization of humanitarianism in the Sudanese contexts, Fadlalla (2008) shows how humanitarianism has been increasingly liberalized through NGOs' competition over global institutional and private funds (see also De Waal, 1997; Ferguson, 2006; Leebaw, 2007). Such humanitarian efforts work to save lives during conflicts, but do little to encourage sustainable development. Like human security, humanitarianism and human rights also focus on the category of the human as a site of scientific inquiry and the production of theoretical knowledge about development in Africa.

While discussions of human rights have been around for centuries (for example France's 1789 declaration of the rights of man), the human rights agenda was given full force with the UN's 1948 Universal Declaration of Human Rights. As an extension, in 1986, the General Assembly passed the Declaration of the Right to Development. The overlap between the two approaches is significant. For example, article 25 of the Universal Declaration of Human Rights states:

> Everyone has the right to a standard of living adequate for the health and well-being of himself and of his family, including food, clothing, housing and medical care and necessary social services, and the right to security in the event of unemployment, sickness, disability, widowhood, old age or other lack of livelihood in circumstances beyond his control.

Article 5 states

> No one shall be subjected to torture or to cruel, inhuman or degrading treatment or punishment.
>
> (UN, 1948)

There is little doubt that the promotion of human rights has been important in laying the ground for the acceptance of the human security agenda through the creation of legitimizing international norms. However, supporters of human security argue that norms and rights influence behavior but do not create sufficient obligations because no institution has the authority to enforce these rights (although the International Criminal Court is moving in that direction in some areas), and therefore rights can be juridical and somewhat ethereal. Moreover, rights tend to be indivisible without the criteria to set priorities. In contrast, human security focuses on concrete threats that can drive the international and national agenda to rapidly intervene to support human health and welfare (Alkire, 2003: pp. 39–40).

The human security concept is also closely linked to the capability approaches of Sen and Nussbaum. Alkire is explicit in recognizing that the vital core of her analytical approach is partly based on the capabilities approach with its focus on expanding the range of people's choices (2003: pp. 25–27). In particular it focuses on human beings as ends not means, raises the question of what people value, provides the basis for both human security and, ultimately, human flourishing which should not be impeded by human security interventions and is closely tied to human rights and development. Arguably the "vital core" used by Alkire in many ways reflects the idea inherent in Nussbaum's "threshold level of capabilities" (Nussbaum, 2000). The latter invokes the idea that certain functions are central to human life and that any threshold must allow people to exercise their dignity as human beings where they can utilize their "human powers of practical reasoning and sociability" (p. 72).

So where are the differences? Nussbaum (2000) points to 10 central human functional capabilities. For example, people should have a full life of normal length without dying prematurely. They also should be guaranteed bodily integrity including the ability to move securely from place to place without fear of violent or sexual assault. Other less physiological dimensions also include the access to education that can enhance their capacities to be imaginative and creative or being given sufficient time and space to be able to laugh, play and participate in recreational activities.[3] The overlap with Alkire's core is clear but not complete. "Not dying prematurely" (life) is pretty much the same as Alkire's "freedom from premature preventable death" (survival) which could involve everything from violent war to terrorism, natural disasters, economic crises, lack of health care access or facilities, criminal activities, environmental destruction, etc. However, capabilities such as "enjoying recreational activities" (play) or "being able to search for the ultimate meaning of life" (senses, imagination and thought) would not be considered part of a vital core (Nussbaum, 2000, pp. 78–81; Alkire, 2003, p. 27). Clearly, the emphasis is on protection and safeguards to a narrower set of core human functions not the enabling of human emancipation implied in the broader set of philosophical ideals embedded in Nussbaum's image of universal development. Arguably, Nussbaum's ideas are important in creating a society of great human potential and emancipation but seem somewhat ethereal and removed from the practical everyday challenges of dealing with the daily human security needs of the world's poor.

There is also considerable overlap in the concept of basic human needs and human security. There is little doubt, in its early formulations, the idea of basic needs arose from the work of Abraham Maslow (1943) on the hierarchy of needs where physical needs are at the bottom of the pyramid and other needs (safety, love, esteem and self-actualization) on top. Early work in the UN system laid the ground work for basic human needs. Drewnowski and Scott (1966), for example, built a level of living index, subdivided between physical needs (nutrition, shelter, health), cultural needs (education, leisure, security) and "Higher Needs," which are above some minimum level. There are obvious continuities between the two concepts. Above, Alkire refers to the vital core as focusing on a "minimal or basic or fundamental set of functions" (2003: p. 24), which seems little different than human needs.

However, as Gasper (2005) points out the main difference is the level of aggregation. Needs based approaches have tended to emphasize planning to supply a broad range of basic goods rather than in ensuring everyone has reached a minimum threshold. In contrast, human security approaches also incorporate a basic human right that no individuals are to be sacrificed for the greater good. To Gasper, the main advantage of human security is that it is a good "boundary object." A good boundary object is a construct that is able to generate a bridge between different intellectual and professional traditions.

Human security promotes analytical integration through an examination of the connection between disciplines and national boundaries. It helps unify four traditionally separated fields—humanitarianism, development, human rights and conflict resolution—while being imbued with the ethical imperatives of equity. It has greater policy relevance and prioritization since it focuses on basic needs, particularly compared to human development, which also promotes analytical integration and helps motivate action by focusing on the vulnerabilities of individual beings. Finally, human security has a structure of accountability through the UN system, which serves as a "boundary organization" that attempts to link the concerns of different stakeholders in turn both operationalizing and legitimizing the boundary object. In sum, human security incorporates crucial dimensions of development policy including ideals, concrete understanding of extant challenges and strategies to deal with them.

Criticisms of human security

The focus of human security on both the category of the human and the concept of security raises other critiques related to its impact on pressing questions of development and the enhancement of human life globally and in Africa in particular. The emphasis on human security as a set of practical agendas that transcend national borders suggests an emergent trend in a global mission to treat human life as both an asset and a threat. Humanitarianism and human rights as both cultural and political discourses and practices offer a platform for fostering global solidarity that carries such development agendas to fruition through the work of NGOs and other UN and civil society organizations. Many scholars, including contributors to this volume, view such transnational practices as hegemonic if they do not take into consideration the cultural practices and development priorities of the subjects whose lives are greatly influenced by these global development agendas. In her treatment of HIV in this volume, Lisa Richey suggests that the move to discuss AIDS as a global threat to humanity in the security council for the first time in 2000 suggests a move to a new authoritarian regime and authoritarian technologies that, although aimed at preventing the threat of AIDS, also push new agendas of global governance to the fore. Such agendas blur the boundaries between the national and the global and gloss over global disparities and class differences underlying the undifferentiated category of the human (e.g., Fadlalla, 2008).

Other criticisms have been aimed at the construct of human security both for theoretical reasons and as a guide to practical interventions. Jolly and Ray (2007) categorize five general areas of criticism. One area is that human security does not offer new directions for academics and policy makers and that the challenges addressed by the human security proponents are already handled well using other concepts. Instead human security complicates decision making in vital areas like climate change and health by competing for attention. Also the emphasis on securitization and intervention can involve the military in issues best handled by non-military interventions. Moreover, placing human security inside the UN raises false hopes given the limited capacity of the organization.

In response to such critics, proponents of human security along the lines stressed by Gaspar argue that threats today are interrelated and interconnected. Extreme poverty and infectious disease in the poorer areas of the world can spill over and affect the health and security of even richer countries. Development and security are inextricably linked and not easily understood within standard security studies nor within the usual parameters of international relations. The proof, to Jolly and Ray, is also in the utility of the human security issues identified in country specific human development reports.

Jolly and Ray also respond to the second area of criticism by arguing that the lack of fixed parameters is an asset not a liability.[4] Country analysis if done properly with proper local input is driven by what individuals identify as their main sources of insecurity rather than ones that are presumed by experts. In this manner human security represents the contextualized specificities of the security concerns of each country. For example, the Macedonia report on human development looks at human security concerns associated with the transition to a market economy which is very different than in Afghanistan where the issue is peace and military security, human security and development.

Busumtwi-Sam (2008) responds to such criticism in a slightly different manner. He delimits the scope of the concept by utilizing a deprivation-vulnerability approach. Within this context threats to human security mostly arise from anthropogenic risks which are a reflection of human action or inaction. The major problem with earthquakes is not the ground shaking itself but the failure to build structures of houses that could reduce human harm. The key element is to also identify vulnerabilities, which is a reflection of three indicators: exposure, sensitivity and resilience. Exposure measures the channels through which threats can lead to harm. Sensitivity focuses on the likely impact of any threat while resilience on the resistance, coping and recovery capabilities of affected populations. Sensitivity and resilience are closely linked to the resources and capabilities available to communities and individuals.

Understanding human insecurity requires not only examining vulnerabilities, which are "future states of adversity," but also comprehending deprivation, which reflects the "current state of adversity and dispossession" (Busumtwi-Sam, 2008: p. 22). Absolute deprivation is linked to poverty while relative deprivation is a function of inequality. Deprivation can also arise from barriers that impede individuals or communities from their economic, social, cultural and political right. Exclusion or the denial of access can situate deprivation in less individualistic and more systemic terms. For example, people are excluded from entitlements due to their poverty, landlessness or gender. In essence it is the deprivations and exclusions associated with their differentiations that make people vulnerable to threats to their security.

Jolly and Ray (2007) also doubt that human security will detract from pressing global issues like climate change and disease threats. In fact they argue the opposite. One can better comprehend climate change through the lens of human security with its focus on the fragile livelihoods of rural populations subject to the volatility of environmental changes. Recognizing the impact on the poorest and most vulnerable might better mobilize support for the global issue. A similar argument could be made on diseases with global implications.

They also believe the issue of the militarization of global development problems is greatly exaggerated. For example, the Afghanistan report on human security identifies the need for non-military responses to extant problems such as overcoming administrative malfunctioning, overreliance on expatriates and the need for more capacity building, addressing widespread inequality and injustice. Finally, the authors are content with the past record of the UN on human security related areas like health and disease control and see nothing in the structure of the UN to impede progress on human security.

Critics have raised issues other than those captured by Jolly and Ray. Human security studies also do not take into consideration anthropological interpretations of insecurity and threats which in many African communities are interpreted with reference to relational and spiritual understanding of belief systems. In his critique of human security, Ashforth (2010) argues that the concept ignores interpersonal relations including families and communities where some individuals can be perceived as accessing occult powers which can be deployed for good or evil. In the community he studied he shows how the relationship between substances and people include the ingestion of herbs in the search for effective solutions to health problems and the insecurities they induce. In such communities the connections between the perceived invisible spirits that inhabit the broader universe and individuals can have a marked impact on people's interpretation of the material world.

Like Ashforth, many anthropologists have argued that since security has both objective and subjective dimensions, humans have created mechanisms to recognize, avoid, master and manage dangers, often considering them to be the result of conscious purposive actions. Culturally, even if dangers arise from objective conditions, conceptions of security and insecurity are interpreted subjectively and frequently mediated through shared structures of belief. Such beliefs are not static however and they are constantly responding to realities of poverty, marginality and the modern transformation of postcoloniality (see for instance Stoller, 1995; Geschiere, 1997; Fadlalla, 2007). Efforts to promote human security, therefore, should not rest too strongly on external views of what creates real senses of danger and what is threatening to the globe without taking into consideration subjective ideation and communal strategies.

Arguments on the complexity of the individual and group self-conceptualization of insecurity are well taken. However, proponents of human security would argue that the effort is not really so much about generating freedom from fear alone and more about freedom from premature preventable deaths and loss of livelihoods which would help advance the freedom from both fear and want. Reducing real, palpable daily risks that increase morbidity and mortality would hopefully contribute to at least improving the objective dimensions of security while feeding into subjective aspects. As Busumtwi-Sam argues, absolute security is not possible and any human security agenda involves value choices about "whom to protect and from what" (2008: p. 19).

Gender, health and human security

The contributors to the volume engage with the concept of human security in various ways. They use gender as an analytical tool to examine how insecurities are located at the intersections of subjective and political nexuses that warrant closer attention to human security as a technical concept in order to advance debate surrounding development issues on both the academic and policy levels. By looking at gender disparities, the authors of this volume support Nussbaum's (2000) emphasis on a host of gender specific asymmetric risks. In the vast majority of African countries, women and girls are less well nourished, more prone to poor health, sexual abuse and violence and have less legal protection including fewer legally guaranteed property, contract and religious rights. They are frequently subject to the double burden of employment and household responsibilities, which can take a toll on their emotional and physical well-being. Girls are often wed at an early age compared to boys and receive disproportionately fewer family resources. Within male-headed families, and because of a host of cultural and economic reasons, women and girls are less likely to receive resources like food and medical care. Poor nutrition creates special health risks for pregnant and lactating women. On the national level there continues to be disparities in access to education and other public goods. Poverty also increases levels of male migration and forces women into high-risk activities that they use as survival strategies to feed their families. Africa has the highest rate of maternal mortality in the world (roughly 50 times higher than developed countries) and maternal mortality rates showed a rising trend over the 1990s (Kalipeni, 2000; Jamison *et al.*, 2006).

Gender inequality is strongly correlated with poverty, making women at the low end of income distribution at greater risk to sources of insecurity with implications for life expectancy. Poor women are more vulnerable to "poverty diseases" such as TB, diphtheria, yellow fever, malaria and cholera, many of which increased in Africa in the 1990s. The contributors to this volume focus on the overall socio-economic context that generates such bodily sicknesses, with greater emphasis on HIV/AIDS as a disease framed to be more threatening to global security and social well-being as discussed in the chapters by Kalipeni and Ghosh, and Lisa Richey.

Kalipeni and Ghosh offer an in depth gender analysis of HIV/AIDS transmission and risk in Malawi in the context of human security and gender inequalities. They show how HIV rates in Malawi are extremely high, particularly in urban areas, where around 23 percent of the adult population is HIV positive. Women are disproportionately more affected than men, and as a result it is necessary to examine why women are more vulnerable in this setting. Kalipeni and Ghosh rely on the vulnerability theory and a gender approach to assess the risk factors perpetuating HIV/AIDS transmission among women in Lilongwe, Malawi. Traditionally, HIV/AIDS interventions have relied on a behavior change model that targets the individual. This study's findings suggest that successful HIV/AIDS interventions should implement a multidisciplinary approach with a focus on altering the systemic factors contributing to the spread of the virus. They identify poverty as a significant risk factor in that it limits women's options and can lead to risky sexual behaviors. As a result of prevailing social norms regarding sexual behaviors and marital patterns, it is also common for men and women to have multiple sexual partners, which also leads to higher rates of HIV infection.

They show how a gender focused perspective to human security is important to allow women to access resources and information such as HIV/AIDS programs in order to combat the existing power and gender imbalances. Currently, many women have limited to no access to entitlements and education, and are often dependent on men for income generation. These inequalities lead to high-risk conditions and behaviors that make women more vulnerable to HIV infection. In addition, men generally have a monopoly on decision making powers, which further limits women's agency and their ability to protect themselves against risky situations. For this reason, it is important for men to be enlisted as partners in the intervention and policy design processes as well. In order to develop a sustainable HIV/AIDS prevention strategy, the issue of HIV/AIDS should be considered within the broader framework of human security as part of a larger effort to secure basic human rights and to reach the men and women in these societies.

Richey, on the other hand, offers a different treatment of HIV/AIDS in Africa and takes a more practice-focused approach. She examines HIV/AIDS as a global human security issue, specifically focusing on the importance of ARV regimens in combating the disease. Richey describes ARVs as "semi-authoritarian technologies" which are negotiated in local, national and global biopolitical settings. The dominant discourse surrounding HIV/AIDS treatment and counseling procedures is a neoliberal one that focuses on individualism and independent decision making. Richey notes that the policies surrounding ARVs reflect the prevailing gender relations that have often been established to uphold the interests of capitalist and patriarchal systems. As a result, the female perspective and women's needs tend to be ignored in such global practices.

Certain protocol established within this politicized framework is at times forced upon women, particularly in situations where family planning and reproduction are concerned. Among pregnant women receiving antiretroviral drugs, generally the priority is to prevent vertical transmission and to protect the health of the fetus, and at times this comes at the expense of the woman's health as an individual.

Relying on case studies from Uganda and South Africa, Richey examines the perspectives of health care workers, counselors and patients to determine the circumstances under which HIV/AIDS patients seek treatment. Although the basic outlines of ARV regimens are often determined on a global scale, the complexities arising from the social conditions surrounding the reproductive demands and desires of women with the rules and regulations of these semi-authoritarian technologies are negotiated by the treatment counselors on a daily basis. With regard to pregnancy, Richey notes a distinct shift from "prohibition to pragmatism" as it becomes apparent that denying African women their right to pregnancy and motherhood is unrealistic. Counselors must manage treatment regimens to appropriately fit the social conditions that women encounter in order to guarantee adherence to treatment guidelines. A major difficulty for these counselors is to simultaneously work with patients to prevent vertical transmission while continuing to uphold women's reproductive rights and decision making abilities in a society that honors and respects childbearing.

In her description of "African AIDS," Richey highlights that "African women's bodies are again at the center of the body politics as controlling viruses within bodies take a central role in political contestations and struggles over global resources and over local capital." Thus AIDS treatment occurs in a highly politicized context that has shaped the nature of ARV regimens. The result is a paradox in which efforts to address HIV/AIDS as a global threat to human security are simultaneously contributing to gendered insecurities regarding women's individual health, reproductive rights and family planning choices.

Neoliberalism and human security

Far too frequently proponents of human security fail to examine the insecurities, poverty and global economic disparities created by decades of neoliberal policies.[5] Arguably, this is a shortcoming that has allowed human security to more readily reinforce existing policy frameworks and to be integrated into mainstream security agendas (Chandler, 2008). As Franceschet (2006) points out human security has increasingly been dominated by legalism with its focus on conflict arising from legal violations to civil and political rights rather than the structural violence associated with the existing global order.[6] This is rather contrary to the original formulation which was inclusive of socio-economic threats to security.

Along these lines, poverty and neoliberal polices are discussed inextricably by the contributing authors of this book. Differential gender specific insecurities have taken their toll on female populations. In sub-Saharan Africa (SSA), the ratio of female to male population is around 101 : 100 compared to 104 : 100 in the highly developed countries in Northern Europe (UN, 2008). What is also disturbing is the decline in the ratio from 102.3 to 100 in 1980 (UN, 1980). The result is not entirely surprising since this represented a period of neoliberal polices where women increasingly became the shock absorbers of economies in extreme economic decline following structural adjustment packages (Sahle, 2008).

These policy packages of austerity through cuts in government spending, privatization of government assets and the deregulation of economic activity have contributed to human insecurity in multiple ways. One could include the retrenchment of government workers and the cutbacks in social safety nets, deregulation of financial markets, the privatization of state assets leading to large scale closures of companies, the introduction of user fees in health and education, the removal of food subsidies for the poor, the retraction of price supports for agricultural producers subjecting poor farmers to the vicissitude of prices and weather, etc. In response, women increased their participation in informal often high-risk activities to deal with rising expenses and lost income (Sahle, 2008; Randriamaro this volume).[7] As indicated by many of the authors in this volume, discussions about neoliberalism need to be embedded in the human security discourse if the term is to have real operational consequences for describing and dealing with the African realities of destitution and struggle.

As follows, Zo Randriamaro in her contribution to this book asks a salient question: "Whose human security?" In her discussion of the impact of neoliberalism on women in sub-Saharan Africa, Randriamaro argues that within the framework of human security, concerns such as economic rights and environmental integrity have been overlooked, and gender issues in particular have been largely ignored. The dominant framework for human security has embraced the neoliberal agenda for development. Such neoliberal policy prescriptions imposed by international financial institutions in many countries in SSA proved to enhance gendered and class inequalities, as well as global inequalities among countries. The neoliberal framework does little to reverse the norms and hierarchies that serve to marginalize and exploit women in many SSA countries. Violence against women in the public and private domains still runs rampant, and violations of sexual and reproductive rights, as well as economic rights, are still widely experienced by women.

SAPs and neoliberal policies have resulted in significant job loss in formal sectors, particularly the export and manufacturing sectors, and the work burden placed on women in low socio-economic classes has increased substantially. In addition, as formal sector work declines, more men are moving to the informal sector, traditionally occupied by women, such that women are experiencing higher levels of competition for their already limited workplace. In the wake of the financial crisis, remittance flows from family abroad have also declined, and this combined with rising food prices and a struggling agricultural sector has intensified the social and economic burdens experienced by women (see also Turshen in this volume). In addition, the elimination of social protection and welfare systems in these countries has also left women more at risk. Microcredit and microfinance programs may provide a certain degree of financial stability, but these programs contribute little to social development.

The concept of human security should be reconstructed to include the perspectives of poor women, since these are the people most threatened under the current system. Reform is needed at both the national and global levels. Within individual countries, public social protection mechanisms and state commitment to reforming women's rights are both necessary to improve the current state of human security for women. In addition, the global economic framework must be revisited so that developing countries are not forced to shoulder the bulk of the world's financial burdens. This would allow developing countries to improve the domestic socio-economic conditions contributing to human insecurities.

The neoliberal framework to alleviate Africa's economic problems relied heavily on anti-poverty relief development organizations and was characterized by a lack of government intervention and a reliance on "safety nets." Along these lines, Weeks and Stein argue in this volume that issues of poverty and insecurity should be closely investigated with reference to such liberal economic frameworks that often impact women negatively. According to the World Bank, the most cost effective route to alleviate poverty was by investing in women to expand their choice in economic activity. Researchers and policy makers in the World Bank also believed that the majority of the poor were self-sufficient farmers who were exploited by government policies that generated urban bias (the control of prices and marketing to keep prices low for urban populations at the expense of farmers). The best route out of poverty was the reversal of urban bias through the retraction of state intervention in agricultural markets.

The assumption behind these strategies is that individuals can lift themselves out of poverty with a certain amount of hard work and a reliance on the efficiency of the market. In addition, by treating the household as the unit of analysis the Bank policies ignored the intra-household distribution of resources that often worked against women and girls. This general approach has failed to generate adequate economic growth, particularly among poor populations, as evidenced by the period of economic stagnation and recession during the 1980s and 1990s and the continued high levels of rural poverty even after growth increased in the past decade. The assumption that market forces alone can lower poverty levels ignores the systemic social hierarchies and employment patterns that reinforce existing inequalities. A more effective policy framework should incorporate purposeful government action for short term poverty alleviation and long term poverty reduction.

According to Weeks and Stein, poverty alleviation and reduction strategies should refrain from attempting to distinguish between "poor" and "non-poor" populations and, likewise, the "winners" and the "losers" of the economic and social systems in place. One problem with such categorizations is that they are often based on income and means testing, a method that leads to inaccurate assessments of poverty levels due to flaws in the measures used and its inability to account for the existing structures of employment, remittances from abroad and non-marketed activities that often characterize the income sources of households in developing countries.

Weeks and Stein stress that an effective long term poverty reduction at the heart of human security will require a shift in the macroeconomic framework, such that fiscal policy is expansionary and aims to implement both short term poverty alleviation programs and public investment in the medium and long term. Orthodox macroeconomics assumes that there is a free supply of caring labor. Women's unpaid responsibilities are social assets that both markets and states fail to provide but are taken for granted by conventional measures of efficiency. Once care is seen as a crucial relational service that can be substituted by public or private sources then macroeconomic frameworks should incorporate strategies to lower the burden of household maintenance services aimed at reducing women's time constraints.

Such neoliberal polices, Meredeth Turshen argues, also threaten the fundamental basis of human life: food (one of the many facets of human security outlined by the United Nations Development Program). She evaluates the international food crisis and the related issue of land rights in Africa, specifically considering the impact of food security and existing land tenure policies on women. There are a number of factors contributing to the current food security crisis. First, structural adjustment programs imposed by international financial institutions served to destabilize agricultural sectors. In addition, there has been a rising emphasis on the production of crops for biofuels rather than food consumption, thereby limiting available food sources for local populations. Food speculation by financial investors and hedge funds has also created a significant increase in food prices, further inhibiting the ability of poor populations to afford adequate nutrition.

A recent international land grab has also led to land scarcity and continues to limit the representation of local interests in land deals in many developing countries. Climate change and political and economic instability have exacerbated the impact of all of these stressors. Although there have been considerable efforts to alleviate the food crisis through improvements in production technologies, a solution encouraging reforms in agriculture and land rights policy to promote food self-sufficiency and the protection of local rights may be more effective than a strictly technological fix.

Women are responsible for the majority of agricultural food production in Africa and are the main providers of food for the family unit. As such, women should be a primary focus of food security initiatives and land rights reform. However, this is generally not the case, as women have little to no representation in the policy formation and program development processes and also have limited access to land. Such social and economic marginalization, combined with women's increasing needs for nutritional requirements during childbearing years, makes women especially vulnerable during times of food crises. Development agencies and international financial institutions, such as the World Bank, have recognized the importance of protecting women's land rights for ensuring family food security; however, there is little evidence of these statements being applied in practice. Both customary and statutory legal systems continue to be driven by colonial and postcolonial corporate interests, and complications in securing gender equality in land tenure systems remain despite efforts for reform. Turshen provides a comprehensive overview of feminist critiques of existing land rights policies to assert that governments should focus on policy changes ensuring greater justice and equality of resource allocation for women in agriculture and land laws.

Poverty produced within the context of neoliberal policies is closely linked to environmental health hazards that affect more women than men. Poor women are more likely to assume roles, such as cleaning clothes and cooking, that put them in greater contact with water and associated water borne and water related diseases. Songsore examines these links in depth in his chapter about environmental hazards and risks surrounding the household and its environs in the low-income community of La in Accra, Ghana. He astutely notes that because it is mainly women in charge of the management and care of the family and home, the household can be considered an engendered domain. The environmental risks associated with the household tend to disproportionately affect women and children over men, largely because adult men spend less time in the household and therefore are less exposed to such threats. Examples of environmental health threats include respiratory problems from indoor air pollution and water related illnesses resulting from poor water supply and water sources, such as cholera, typhoid and diarrhea. In addition, the household environment in this community is characterized by differential power relations based on age, gender and kinship.

These power relations are strongly patriarchal, and men are considered the head of the house and family. As a result, men have greater access to financial resources. Men also hold the majority of the decision making powers, both within the household and at the government and policy making level. Because women have such limited representation in the policy design and resource allocation processes, it is difficult to accrue enough support to enact positive environmental changes addressing the burdens experienced by women and children in low socio-economic living conditions. Global pressures also impact household environmental conditions, either in the form of policy changes from SAPs or support from the international women's movement. However, despite the pressure from women's movements, changes in these conditions have been minimal. Songsore emphasizes the importance of working toward gender mainstreaming in environmental management in order to both alter gender relations in women's favor and improve environmental services to alleviate the domestic risks encountered by women.

Conflict, human security and peace

Africa's postcolonial realities are not disconnected from its remote colonial past. The creation of colonial boundaries in Africa solidified ethnic differentiation and socio-economic inequities perpetuated by national and international hegemonic regimes. Such inequities were the basis for the rise of armed political movements that called for democratization and equal inclusion in the rubric of national governance. The recent secession of Sudan into two northern and southern nation-states is an obvious result of a devastating long war that cost millions of lives and exacerbated realities of poverty and put both men and women at risk. Even after the secession, however, new realities of ethnic marginalization in both the north and the south threaten to fuel the war within and between the two nations. In such context of militarized ethnic conflicts, women's unequal access to resources makes them more susceptible to domestic violence, sexual harassment and rape. In this volume, Jok Madut Jok takes this discussion further by looking at the status of women's legal rights in post-war Sudan before the country's split on 9 July 2011.

Jok shows that after the end of the civil war in 2005, new legislation was enacted to protect women's rights and to increase women's participation in government. Despite the initial optimism among many that the new neoliberal state would guarantee national security and bring an end to violence against women, it is apparent that such legislation is not being adequately enforced or practiced by civilians and political and legal officials. Domestic and institutional violence against women continues to persist, and the existing legal system provides very little to counter such violence. Jok notes that the situation is complicated by the fact that government members continue to blame the war for the widespread gendered violence, thereby denying their individual roles in perpetuating this abuse and failing to guarantee legal rights for women. It is true that the war in Sudan did exacerbate violence against women. Women were often deliberately targeted during conflict, as rape was used as a military tactic and political tool. In addition, military violence often translated into domestic violence and abuse at home.

However, Jok emphasizes that gendered insecurities cannot be solely attributed to the civil war, and the reality is that violence against women is largely a result of deep-rooted cultural norms that reinforce social hierarchies which place women at the bottom rungs, thereby excluding women from the existing legal system and undermining their legal protection. Despite the widespread injustices and disempowerment that Sudanese women experience, Jok discourages the notion of women as voiceless victims. Sudanese women's groups and activists are gaining strength, asserting their demands for women's rights and inclusion in the government and legislature. Much of the progress is due to pressure from international groups and agencies, but as Sudanese women continue to become more involved in these campaigns, there may be hope for reforms in both protective legislation and customary practices in order to combat this gendered violence.

In the case of Liberia, another African country that has long been devastated by war and ethnic conflicts, the recent winds of peace may also require new gendered tools to understand women's social realities and their situation of social vulnerability. In the final chapter of this book Aili Tripp shows how the concept of agency can be refined and used conceptually to sharpen our understanding of human security and to address the prevailing power dynamics and gender relations in post-conflict societies. Instead of applying human security to gender, gender should be the main focus of analysis to understand how socio-economic insecurities are affecting women differently than men. Based on the prevailing gender dynamics within a specific setting, the definition of agency can differ for men and women, depending on how gender roles are defined and how the objectives and motivations of men and women vary. Tripp examines these differences and why they have developed.

Currently, women's peace efforts in Africa have largely been confined to localized peacemaking initiatives. These efforts have achieved some successes in furthering their agendas, and Tripp points out that 86 percent of peace agreements in Africa between 1989 and 2005 contain language about women's rights. Tripp traces women's engagement in peace movements, with specific attention to women activists in Liberia, to demonstrate that women's marginalization often shapes their political strategies and platforms. A common agenda for women's rights and political representation has unified women across political and ethnic divides, a phenomenon that facilitates the peacemaking process. Unlike the neoliberal frame of insecurity that focuses on individualism, Tripp shows how the women's peace movement in Liberia privileged collective work as a way of mobilizing to address women's economic and political rights. She notes that when women sought participation in peace negotiations during the 1990s, they did so on the basis of unity with women of different ethnicities and political parties, which was a strikingly different model from that of male negotiators. She highlights that this is not an essentialized "maternal politics of peace," but because the common pursuit of a gender equality agenda formed a unifying platform for women from which to negotiate. As a result of these differences in agentive practices, the roles that men and women have played in peacemaking activities have differed greatly. However, despite gains in some post-conflict countries, women continue to be left out of the more formal national and international peace negotiations. Therefore both the concept of agency and its relation to human security need to be reconfigured to address these types of gender dynamics and collective action.

Gender, for the authors in this volume, does not necessarily exclude men in vulnerable situations rather it aims to center the experience of women as a disadvantaged group to examine broader processes of power and socio-economic dynamics. Contributors to this volume show how gendered cultural and political decisions are essential to the analyses of the in/securities related to health and sickness (especially HIV/AIDS and treatment), unemployment, poverty, environmental pollution, and conflict and peace. They provide new insights on the political economy of human security and its connections with neoliberal policies, an area often neglected in the literature, and come up with important recommendations for concrete policy proposals to sharpen the human security concept for both academics and policy makers.

Notes

1 Since 1994 there has been a plethora of definitions of human security. Fukuda-Parr and Messineo (forthcoming) summarize some of these and place them in two different categories. Broad formulations point to vulnerabilities arising from all possible sources. Narrow formulations focus on insecurity arising only from violence. This volume follows the broader tradition which seems most pertinent to the gendered insecurities arising from the conditions of poverty, disease and violence prevalent in many African countries.

2 The overlap of Alkire's conception and the influential 2003 Ogata-Sen Commission on Human Security is very apparent. The commission defines human security objectives as the protection of "the vital core of all human lives in ways that enhance human freedoms and human fulfillment" (Commission on Human Security, 2003: p. 4). The commission came out of the 1999 Trust Fund for Human Security launched jointly by the UN Secretariat and the Government of Japan. The Commission arose out of the need to more clearly define the human security agenda and out of the MDGs meetings and the related call by the Secretary General to extend the UN agenda to advance the double freedoms from want and fear. Following the report the Trust Fund organized a human security unit in 2004 in the UN Office for the Coordination of Humanitarian Affairs to integrate human security in the UN system. The Trust Fund mainly operates by financing projects through UN agencies that are able to demonstrate the project's connection to human security. Among their stated goals are protecting people in conflict situations, supporting and empowering refugees, realizing minimum living standards, including assisting community-level efforts to establish mechanisms to protect

people exposed to extreme poverty, sudden economic downturns and natural disasters, enhancing health care and service coverage to those whom other initiatives have not reached successfully and improving educational opportunities, especially for girls (UN, 2011; interviews at the UN Secretariat and UNDP in New York in February, 2006). See Fukuda-Parr and Messineo (forthcoming) for a discussion of other initiatives including the Canadian and Norwegian sponsored annual meeting of the Human Security Network.

3 The other six include bodily health or reproductive health, nutrition and shelter; emotions or fulfilling attachments to people beyond each individual; other species or being able to express and act on concern with the living natural world; control of one's environment which means access to political and property right; affiliation or freedom of association without discriminations; and practical reasoning or the ability to engage in planning and thinking critically about the direction of one's life.

4 Fukuda-Parr and Messineo (forthcoming) concur with the view that the lack of fixed parameters is an asset. Human security should be seen as a goal which normatively and conceptually guides the formulation of policy and action. They are not meant to be a set of policies, a point which critics have often misunderstood when complaining about the absence of clearly ordered priorities.

5 Alkire (2003) mentions the issue only once in her lengthy paper on human security with a rather mild comment that where structural adjustment is used and poverty is increased even if it is unintended human security can be respected if safety nets are set up.

6 Structural violence is nicely defined by Paul Farmer (2003):

> Structural violence is one way of describing social arrangements that put individuals and populations in harm's way. ... The arrangements are structural because they are embedded in the political and economic organization of our social world; they are violent because they cause injury to people.

It should be noted that Franceschet (2006) also emphasizes that the legalistic approach to human security can allow stronger states to selectively impose their now morally justified will on weaker states which can help entrench existing hierarchical power structures.

7 Shoepf (2004), for example, documents the movement of women into sex worker jobs following the layoff of their husbands in Kinshasa in the 1990s.

Bibliography

Alkire, Sabina. (2003) A Conceptual Framework for Human Security, Center for Research on Inequality, Human Security and Ethnicity (CRISE) Working Paper Series, No. 2. (Online) Available at: www.crise.ox.ac.uk/pubs/workingpaper2.pdf [accessed 5 November 2011].

Ashforth, Adam. (Winter/Spring 2010) Human Security and Spiritual Insecurity: Why the Fear of Evil Forces Needs to be Taken Seriously. *Georgetown Journal of International Affairs*, XI (1), pp. 99–106.

Busumtwi-Sam, James. (2008) Contextualizing Human Security: A Deprivation-Vulnerability Approach. *Policy and Society*, 27, pp. 15–28.

Chandler, David. (2008) Human Security: The Dog that Didn't Bark. *Security Dialogue*, 39(4), pp. 427–438.

Commission on Human Security. (2003) *Final Report of the Commission on Human Security*. Washington, DC: Commission on Human Security.

De Waal, Alex. (1997) *Famine Crimes: Politics and the Disaster Relief Industry in Africa*. Bloomington: Indiana University Press.

Drewnowski, Jan and Scott Wolf. (1966) *The Level of Living Index*. Geneva, Switzerland: United Nations.

Fadlalla, Amal Hassan. (2007) *Embodying Honor: Fertility, Foreignness and Regeneration in Eastern Sudan*. Madison: University of Wisconsin Press.

Fadlalla, Amal Hassan. (2008) The Neoliberalization of Compassion: Darfur and the Mediation of American Faith, Fear and Terror. In: Jane Collins, Micaela di Leonardo and Brett Williams, eds. *New Landscapes of Inequality: Neoliberalism and the Erosion of Democracy in America*. Santa Fe, New Mexico: School for Advanced Research Press, pp. 209–228.

Fadlalla, Amal Hassan. (2011) State of Vulnerability and Humanitarian Visibility on the Verge of Sudan's Secession: Lubna's Pants and Transnational Politics of Rights and Dissent. *Signs*, 37(1), pp. 160–184.

Farmer, Paul. (2003) *The Pathologies of Power; Health, Human Rights and the New War on the Poor*. Berkeley: University of California Press.

Ferguson, James. (2006) *Global Shadows: Africa in the Neoliberal World Order*. Durham: Duke University Press.

Franceschet, Antonio. (2006) Global Legalism and Human Security. In: Sandra Jean MacLean, David Ross Black and Timothy M. Shaw, eds. *A Decade of Human Security: Global Governance and New Multilateralisms*. Aldershot: Ashgate, pp. 31–38.

Fukuda-Parr, Sakiko (2004) Rescuing the Human Development Concept from HDI: Reflections on the New Agenda. In S. Fukuda-Parr and A. K. S. Kumar, eds. *Readings in Human Development*. Oxford: Oxford University Press, pp. 117–124.

Fukuda-Parr, Sakiko and Carol Messineo. (forthcoming) Human Security. In: Arnim Langed and Graham Brown, eds. *Elgar Companion to Civil War and Fragile States*. Cheltenham: Edward Elgar Publishing.

Gasper, Des. (July 2005) Securing Humanity: Situating "Human Security" as Concept and Discourse. *Journal of Human Development*, 6(2), pp. 221–245.

Geschiere, Peter. (1997) *The Modernity of Witchcraft: Politics and the Occult in Postcolonial Africa*. Charlottesville and London: University of Virginia Press.

Kalipeni. Ezekiel. (2000) Health and Disease in Southern Africa: A Comparative and Vulnerability Perspective. *Social Science & Medicine*, 50, pp. 965–983.

Leebaw, Bronwyn. (2007) The Politics of Impartial Activism: Humanitarianism and Human Rights. *Perspectives on Politics*, 5(2), pp. 223–239.

Jamison, D. T., R. G. Feachem, M. W. Makgoba, E. R. Bos, F. K. Baingana, K. J. Hofman, and K. O. Rogo, eds. (2006) *Disease and Mortality in Sub-Saharan Africa*. 2nd edn. Washington, DC: World Bank.

Jolly, Richard and Deepayan Ray. (2007) Human Security—National Perspectives and Global Insights from National Human Development Reports. *Journal of International Development*, 19, pp. 457–472.

Maslow, Abraham. (1943) A Theory of Human Motivation. *Psychological Review*, 50, pp. 370–396.

Nussbaum, Martha C. (2000) *Women and Human Development: The Capabilities Approach*. Cambridge: Cambridge University Press.

Sahle, Eunice. (2008) Gender, States and Market in Africa. In Joseph Mensah, ed. *Neoliberalism and Globalization in Africa: Contestations from the Embattled Continent*. Basingstoke: Palgrave/Macmillan, pp. 71–92.

Shoepf, Brooke. (2004) Aids in Africa: Structure, Agency and Risk. In E. Kalipeni, S. Craddock, J. Opppong and J. Ghosh, eds. *HIV & AIDS in Africa: Beyond Epidemiology*. Oxford: Blackwell, pp. 15–28.

Stoller, Paul. (1995) *Embodying Colonial Memory: Spirit Possession, Power, and the Hauka in West Africa.* New York and London: Routledge.

United Nations. (1948) Universal Declaration of Human Rights. (Online) Available at: www.un.org/en/documents/udhr/index.shtml#a25 [Accessed October 10, 2011].

United Nations. (1980) Demographic Year Book, 1980. (Online) (2011) Available at: http://unstats.un.org/unsd/demographic/products/dyb/dyb2.htm [accessed October 10, 2011].

United Nations. (2008) Demographic Year Book, 2008. (Online) Available at: http://unstats.un.org/unsd/demographic/products/dyb/dyb2.htm [accessed October 10, 2011].

United Nations. (2011) United Nations Trust Fund for Human Security: A Brief History. (Online) 2007. Available at: http://ochaonline.un.org/trustfund/tabid/2107/default.aspx [accessed October 10, 2011].

United Nations Development Program. (1990) *Human Development Report.* New York: Oxford University Press.

United Nations Development Program. (1993) *Human Development Report.* New York: Oxford University Press.

United Nations Development Program. (1994) *Human Development Report.* New York: Oxford University Press.

1 The gender context of vulnerability to HIV/AIDS*

The case of men and women in low income areas of the city of Lilongwe in Malawi

Ezekiel Kalipeni and Jayati Ghosh

The HIV/AIDS epidemic in Malawi and other southern African countries has wreaked havoc with tragic demographic, economic and social consequences. In Malawi, HIV/AIDS prevalence in the urban areas of Lilongwe and Blantyre has been much more pronounced in comparison to rural areas. For example, in 2005 standardized urban prevalence rates for Lilongwe and Blantyre were 19.8 percent and 26.3 percent respectively, compared to 12 percent for rural areas (Weir *et al.*, 2008: p. 20). As Weir *et al.* note, although the high prevalence levels seen in previous decades have abated, both these cities suffer from an ongoing and unrelenting epidemic. These authors identify a number of community and individual based factors which have fueled the rapid spread of this epidemic, namely, HIV stigma, poverty, marital patterns, labor migration and mobility patterns, sexual norms, religion at the community level and education and knowledge about the disease at the individual level.

In a similar vein Lindgren *et al.* (2005) tease out these very same factors in a study they conducted through focus group interviews with Malawi women. Using a gender/power relationships approach, Lindgren *et al.* describe these factors which are poignantly characterized by the statement, "We are just vessels for our husbands" (p. 70). Their study offers a wealth of information relating to women's roles, power relations and the general disempowerment of women in Malawian society, all factors which have led to the rapid proliferation of HIV. They conclude that health education alone is insufficient to stem the tide of HIV in Malawi. If HIV is to be effectively tackled, then there is a need to shift the approach from a concentration on the "Abstinence, Be faithful, and use a Condom" (ABC) approach to a multidisciplinary and systematic approach that includes women's education and economic empowerment, as well as modifying legal and social structures that contribute to the spread of HIV/AIDS in Malawi.

Our study contributes to the unraveling of the community and individual level factors in low socioeconomic income areas of Lilongwe. Employing the gendered nature of vulnerability to HIV, we attempt to answer two basic questions: (1) what makes women in Malawi vulnerable to HIV? (2) How is this vulnerability configured differently than for men? Thus the central goal of this paper is to examine in greater detail the social and economic contexts of vulnerability to HIV among women in comparison to men in the city of Lilongwe. It is of great importance that we understand the socioeconomic and cultural contexts of HIV spread, particularly in cities such as Lilongwe where rates are two times higher than in rural areas. The standard biomedical/epidemiological model with its focus on behavior change alone needs to be reconsidered in the case of HIV/AIDS. Our argument is that HIV/AIDS is rooted in structural factors of history and poverty and in culture and society more than it is in biology and environment; that is, we explicitly link structure and agency. Therefore analysts have to consider HIV/AIDS, first and foremost not as a health issue or by invoking a biomedical epistemology, but rather as a development issue as several authors have argued. Consequently, moving beyond the health dimensions into broad development programs that diminish poverty and women's vulnerability to disease is required.

Unfortunately, biomedical and epidemiological models of inquiry and dealing with HIV continue to dominate and obtain an unfair share of the resources. This situation persists in spite of the fact that the prevention and treatment strategies for AIDS currently being employed, which focus on the individual as the locus of disease and prevention, have had limited success. By assuming that individuals can automatically change their behaviors through awareness and condom possession, interventions comprising educational outreach and access to condoms leave root causes of HIV untouched. We need to recognize that biomedical and epidemiological studies and the solutions these studies offer in terms of behavior change have been insufficient to explain the rapid proliferation of AIDS in Africa because they fail to address the root causes of vulnerability. It is in this context that our study concentrates on the gender dimensions of vulnerability by highlighting women's and men's insights on what they consider to be the root causes of the epidemic in the low socioeconomic income areas of Chinsapo, Area 25 and Area 29 in the city of Lilongwe (see Figure 1.1). It is our hope that this study will partially fill the gap left by biomedical and epidemiological studies. The results and discussion highlight the gendered nature of vulnerability, particularly how gender inequality and poverty influence the different ways that men and women become infected. We reiterate Lindgren's *et al.* (2005) study and Van Donk (2006) that any interventions that fail to address the broader issues of African social and economic life are bound to fail. This is because HIV in sub-Saharan Africa is a complex and regionally specific phenomenon rooted in local economies, deepening poverty, migration, gender, global economies and cultural politics (Kalipeni *et al.*, 2004a, 2004b).

Situating vulnerability in the human security framework

This chapter uses the vulnerability approach as the theoretical perspective to guide the discussion on gender and HIV/AIDS in low socioeconomic income areas of the city of Lilongwe. We place this perspective within the broader

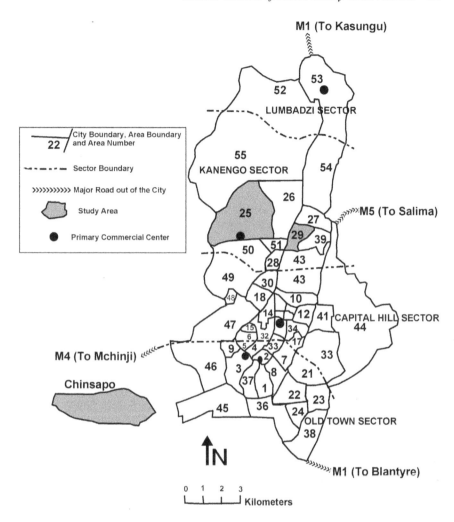

Figure 1.1 Location of study areas in the city of Lilongwe (source: authors).

human security framework. In the past, human security meant the protection of the state, which included its boundaries, people, institutions and values, from external enemies. Recently there has been a shift from this narrow definition of human security to a more holistic and all encompassing understanding of human security that is "human centered" rather than state centered, an approach that ensures "freedom from fear and freedom from want" (Alkire, 2003: p. 5). To this end, while realizing that the conceptions of human security vary widely, Alkire (2003) offers an interesting and innovative conceptual framework of human security that provides the basis for the vulnerability framework in this chapter.

According to Alkire (2003), the objective of human security is to safeguard the vital core of all human lives from critical pervasive threats, without impeding long-term human fulfillment (p. 2). In her framework she defines critical threats as those threats that cut into core activities and functions and pervasive threats as large-scale and recurrent dangers (p. 8). Alkire identifies a set of facets that together constitute human security. The foremost important aspect is safeguarding human lives through the identification of critical pervasive threats and prevention so that risks do not occur and, if they do occur, taking aggressive steps for mitigation to limit the damage. She notes that in doing so there is a need to respond in proper ways so that victims survive with dignity and maintain their livelihoods (p. 8). In her framework she also identifies what she calls the "vital core," which she defines as rudimentary but multidimensional human rights and human freedoms that all must enjoy, i.e., "people centered" with a clear focus on individuals and their communities (p. 3).

The human security framework and its definition offer an excellent broader theoretical framework within which to place our vulnerability approach in general and HIV/AIDS in particular. Indeed, throughout the discussion in her paper, Alkire (2003) identifies HIV/AIDS and other infectious diseases as pervasive threats to human security, alongside conflict, economic and financial instability and terrorism. She offers the spread of HIV/AIDS and the associated human costs of grief and caring for orphans as an empirical example of human insecurity, which has so far left indelible marks on communities (p. 12). There are a number of critical factors driving the wide proliferation of HIV/AIDS in sub-Saharan Africa, one of which is poverty, as identified by Alkire and other researchers. There is a direct link between gender, poverty and HIV/AIDS as we point out in the discussion in this chapter. The vulnerability approach suggests that lack of education resulting in limited marketable skills, poor health, inequality and low labor productivity render individuals susceptible to high-risk behavior (Oppong, 1998; Mabala, 2006; Kalipeni and Ghosh, 2007). Under the human security framework advanced by Alkire (2003) these are critical and pervasive threats that only serve to dramatically curtail the freedom from fear and freedom from want. The question therefore becomes, how do we mobilize policy makers to prioritize the prevention and mitigation of HIV/AIDS as indispensable to human, national and international security? Research results like those presented and discussed in this chapter can serve in one way or another to highlight the correlates of HIV/AIDS, including the precarious circumstances in which individuals might find themselves. In the spirit of Alkire (2003) and the UN Commission on Human Security (2003), we hope the results reported in this chapter will be helpful in further galvanizing governments and international bodies to maintain the broadest definition of human security, which comprehensively covers all the menaces that threaten human survival, daily life and dignity and strengthens efforts to confront these threats, particularly HIV/AIDS and the vulnerability it poses to Malawian people, especially women.

Structural adjustment programs and the threat to health and human security in Malawi

In the 1970s a recession hit a large number of countries worldwide causing many developing countries to face a host of problems such as increasing debt and declining terms of trade. In addition, rising protectionist attitudes led to limited access to markets in the developed countries. In response to the growing problems, since the early 1980s international institutions such as the International Monetary Fund (IMF) and the World Bank began to encourage developing countries to promote a set of programs focused on currency devaluation, import reduction and removal of state subsidies. Malawi implemented a series of Structural Adjustment Programs (SAP) over 1981 to 1994 (Kalipeni, 2004). These were geared toward reforming the agricultural and financial sectors and instituting budgetary and trade reforms. The aim was to reduce the role of the state and, in turn, increase the reliance on the private sector in critical areas such as education and health care. According to Chirwa (2005: p. iii) the vast majority of the reforms were implemented by 1995.

However, the implementation of SAPs has not translated into dramatic positive effects on price stability, reduction of poverty or growth in Gross Domestic Product (GDP). For example, in comparison to the 1980s, the Malawi Kwacha has, in recent years, experienced dramatic devaluations to the extent that in 2009 it was valued at MK141.1 : US$1 and is projected to be at MK175.3 : US$1 by 2011 (Economist Intelligence Unit, 2010). This greatly contrasts the value of the currency in 1990 when 2.5 Malawi Kwacha were the equivalent of US$1.00. As a result a large number of people, especially women, are highly vulnerable as today's incomes have shrunk, inflation is quite high and fees must be paid for all services including access to health care. While most of the work on structural adjustment programs has emphasized the economic rather than the social sector, a few works have examined the impacts of these programs on health and women's welfare (see for example: Kanji *et al.*, 1991; Loewenson, 1993; Asthana, 1994; Oppong, 1997; Turshen, 1999; Kalipeni, 2004; Kalipeni *et al.*, 2004a, 2004b). The consensus among these works is that structural adjustment programs have had serious consequences on the health of vulnerable groups, particularly women and children. For example, Kanji *et al.* (1991) argue that structural adjustment programs have exacerbated inequalities and threaten to reverse the social and health gains of the majority achieved through the struggle of independence. Loewenson (1993) and Potts (1995) offer irrefutable evidence which indicates that SAPs have been associated with increasing food insecurity and malnutrition, declining real incomes, rising ill-health and decreasing access to health care for both rural and urban populations. The lack of adequate health providers, facilities and fees for services limits the access to health care. The World Health Organization core indicator database shows that in 2004 there were about 7,000 nurses and midwifery personnel for the whole country of Malawi with physicians totaling only 266 (see WHO, 2006). This translates into less than one physician for every 10,000 people and about six nurses and midwifery personnel per 10,000 people.

Malawi depends heavily on agriculture as the main economic activity, employment and source of export earnings. According to the International Monetary Fund (2007), the agricultural sector employs nearly 80 percent of the work force and accounts for 80 percent of foreign exchange earnings. However, the agricultural sector is characterized by low productivity. Any decline in the share of agriculture adds to the existing problem of rural poverty and leads to increases in migration towards urban centers. Thus economic crisis in the rural areas disrupts stability and forces people, mainly men, to migrate to urban areas in search of jobs or to seek employment in more prosperous countries abroad, such as South Africa. As mentioned above SAPs and associated economic restructuring have fueled food and economic insecurity, which in turn leads to migration, increasing socioeconomic inequality and the spread of HIV/AIDS. Women are disproportionately impacted since considerable disparities exist between men and women, as indicated by the Gender Development Index of 0.49 (UNDP, 2009). Unequal access to education, health care and income increases women's security issues. Gender inequalities play a pivotal role in the spread of HIV as women are both physiologically and socially more vulnerable to HIV infection. Further, due to the privatization of education, women often have limited access to education, training and productive resources like land and credit. It is also important to note that gendered vulnerability not only depends on economic conditions, but also social position. Women in Malawi tend to have limited entitlements, and they generally earn low wages, are less likely than men to own land, do not receive any government assistance and do not benefit from international aid programs (Lele, 1990). All of these factors add the gender dimension to human insecurity. According to Schoepf *et al.* (2000) the devaluation of currency, which is the result of SAPs, limits a country's ability to commit resources towards HIV/AIDS prevention, treatment and care of the infected.

In short, increasing deterioration in the economy has meant little money for maintaining existing health care infrastructure. Poor countries such as Malawi have been hardest hit by the economic crisis that began in the early 1980s and was exacerbated by the imposition of SAPs. The proportion of funds allocated to health and education have seen a declining trend since the 1980s to the present. Cutbacks in health expenditure have resulted in large layoffs and significant salary reductions due to inflation. Most health workers have been compelled to take second jobs to make ends meet, resulting in absenteeism and poorer health care.

Recent reports from Malawi indicate a desperate situation with severe scarcities of medicines in government hospitals and health centers throughout the country. Generally speaking SAPs have meant the rise of poverty for the already impoverished, compromising human security and increasing the pervasive threats to well-being. In Malawi, poverty and malnutrition are now major national problems, and it is estimated that as much as 60 percent of the urban population lives below the poverty line. It is in this context that we use a gendered approach to examine vulnerability to HIV/AIDS in low socioeconomic income areas in the city of Lilongwe.

HIV/AIDS situation

Epidemic diseases such as HIV have profound economic and social effects. These effects differ from one country to another depending on a country's level of economic development. According to UNAIDS (2008a), worldwide the percentage of adults living with HIV has leveled off. During 2007 there were 2.7 million new infections and two million HIV/AIDS related deaths. Globally there are 33 million people estimated to be living with the virus (UNAIDS, 2008a: p. 32), of which 67 percent or 22 million are concentrated in sub-Saharan Africa (p. 39). In 2007 the annual number of new infections was estimated to be 2.7 million, which reflects a decline from three million in 2001. Over 2001 to 2007, the number of deaths due to AIDS related illness declined from 2.3 million to 1.7 million. The decline in the number of deaths may be attributed to the greater availability of treatments, which has increased the lifespan of HIV infected people. However, it is important to note that nearly 75 percent of AIDS deaths occurred in sub-Saharan Africa (p. 30).

The epidemic in sub-Saharan Africa varies greatly over space. In west and central Africa as well as the eastern part of the continent the adult prevalence rate is estimated to be less than 5 percent. The worst hit region is the southern part where the HIV prevalence rate is over 15 percent. Cameroon, Central African Republic, Gabon, Mozambique, Uganda and Tanzania reported HIV prevalence rates of over 5 percent (UNAIDS, 2008a: p. 39). In sub-Saharan Africa the main mode of transmission continues to be through heterosexual activities. In addition sex work is also an important factor in the spread of the epidemic. Drug use, although low, is attributed to be a factor in the transmission of HIV in the eastern and southern African region especially on the island of Mauritius and in the cities of Mombasa and Nairobi (p. 43).

Malawi, a country located in southern Africa, is no exception to the growing trend and severity in HIV prevalence. UNAIDS (2008b) reports that at the end of 2001 there were 850,000 adults and children in Malawi living with the HIV/AIDS virus, and this increased to 930,000 in 2007. It is also estimated that 12 percent of the adult population aged 15–49 in Malawi are infected with the HIV virus which is a drop from 13 percent in 2001 (UNAIDS, 2008b: p. 4). This may suggest that the epidemic has stabilized in the country. A closer look at the prevalence rate among women attending antenatal clinics in urban areas shows a declining trend too. Furthermore it is important to note that young women between 15 and 24 years are at higher risk of getting infected by the virus. According to UNAIDS (2008b: p. 5) the HIV prevalence rate for young women is about 9.1 percent, which is considerably higher than the 2.1 percent reported among men in the same age group. As one looks at the regional differences in prevalence rates it is worth noting that young women in the northern part of Malawi had an HIV prevalence rate of 9 percent compared to 0.7 percent for young men. In the southern region, young women reported a prevalence rate of 3.9 percent compared to 1.2 percent for young men, while in the central region the rate was three times higher, i.e., 13.4 percent for young women in comparison to 3.2 percent for young men (UNAIDS, 2008c: p. 8). It is therefore important to find the reasons behind these gender disparities in HIV/AIDS rates between men and women, particularly young men and women in urban areas where these differences are more pronounced.

Urbanization in Africa and its relationship to migration and HIV/AIDS

Overwhelmingly the world's population is undergoing a shift from being predominantly rural to urban. Due to an increase in the total number of urban inhabitants, different regions of the world are experiencing a rise in the number of cities and growth in the size of the cities, as well as in the proportion of people living in urban areas. In 2007 UNFPA stated that by 2008 about 50 percent of the world's population will be living in towns and cities. The same study reported that by 2030 the urban population will increase to 4.9 billion while the number of rural inhabitants will decline by 28 million (UNFPA, 2007: p. 6). Between 2000 and 2030 the urban population living in Africa is expected to double from 294 million to 742 million (Population Reference Bureau, 2007: p. 10). In 1950 about 15 percent of the African population lived in urban areas, a proportion which increased to 37 percent in 2000 and is projected to increase to 53 percent by 2030 (Cohen, 2006: p. 70).

According to UNFPA (2007: p. 7) the first wave of urbanization that extended over 200 years, 1750 to 1950, was centered in North America and Europe, during which the urban population increased from 15 million to 423 million. Over the second wave of urbanization, centered in the developing countries, the urban population is projected to increase from 309 million in 1950 to 3.9 billion in 2030. The second phase also coincides with the process of globalization. As cities of the developing world continue to be integrated into the global economy, it is argued that they must be benefiting from increased inflow of foreign direct investments, liberalization policies of governments, establishment of export processing zones, and others (UNFPA, 2007: p. 68). It is noted that these activities generate jobs for both skilled and unskilled labor, which in turn attracts migrants to the cities. However, the impact of globalization has proven to be a double edged sword in cities of the developing world. As the World Bank (2007) notes, globalization has not benefited all segments of the population, and many face increasing levels of poverty. This is particularly true of cities in sub-Saharan Africa.

The rate of urban population growth in sub-Saharan Africa has taken place without the attendant socioeconomic growth that comes with urbanization. As a result, the majority of the people living in urban settings live below the poverty line. Table 1.1 presents the demographic and urban growth rate in the different regions. It is estimated that the urban population will grow at 3.2 percent between 2005 and 2010, which is higher than the average population growth rate of 2.1 percent over the same period. It is precisely this phenomenal growth of urban populations that is frustrating any economic growth in these areas.

Table 1.1 Demographic and urban trends

Regions	Population 2007 (millions)	Projected population 2050 (millions)	Population growth rate (2005–10)	Percent urban population	Urban population growth rate (2005–10)
World	6,615.9	9,075.9	1.1	50	2.0
More Developed Countries	1,217.5	1,236.2	0.2	75	0.5
Less Developed Countries	5,398.4	7,839.7	1.3	44	2.5
Least Developed Countries	795.6	1,735.4	2.3	28	4.0
Africa	945.3	1,937.0	2.1	39	3.2
Asia	399.5	5,217.2	1.1	41	2.4
Latin America and Caribbean	576.5	782.9	1.3	78	1.7
Malawi	13.5	29.5	2.2	18	4.7

Source: UNFPA (2007).

In 2007, about 18 percent of the population of Malawi lived in urban areas and the urban growth rate over 2005 to 2010 was projected to be 4.7 percent. This is considerably higher than the overall population growth rate of the country. According to Rohregger (2006), in Malawi the level of industrialization has been low when compared to other countries in the southern African region. In general, in developing countries most industries tend to be concentrated in the few large cities. In the case of Malawi the limited role of industrialization may help to explain the relatively low level of urbanization (i.e., 18 percent urban population in 2007) (Rohregger, 2006: p. 1155; UNFPA, 2007: p. 90). During the colonial period, the country served as the source of labor for the neighboring mine-based economies of Zimbabwe, Zambia and South Africa. Under President Banda the country placed an emphasis on rural development strategies, which further explains the lower proportion of individuals living in the cities. According to the Central Intelligence Agency (2011), agriculture accounts for one-third of the gross domestic product (GDP) and 90 percent of the export revenues.

However, in recent years the rural economy has been facing the devastating impacts of deforestation, frequent drought, floods and famine. The lack of arable land and rural poverty has pushed rural inhabitants to the few urban areas of Lilongwe, Blantyre, Zomba and Mzuzu. Although Malawi is one of the least urbanized countries in Africa with only 20 percent of the population living in urban areas, the country is one of the most urbanizing in Africa at 6.3 percent per annum, three times the global rate and nearly twice the Africa rate of 3.5 percent (Phiri, 2004; Chome and Kithakye, n.d.). As shown in Figure 1.2, the cities and towns of Malawi are experiencing unprecedented growth rates with the absolute urban population expected to almost double by 2020. Chome and Kithakye (n.d.) note that sustainable urbanization is now one of the most pressing challenges facing Malawi. It is estimated that in the next 15 years 44 percent of Malawi's population will be living in towns and cities (Phiri, 2004). There is no question that rapid urbanization poses a number of critical challenges for Malawi, such as land and housing shortages, congestion, squatter settlements, crime, unemployment, but more importantly HIV/AIDS infection, a grave human security risk.

Needless to say that once in the city, the migrant population frequently experiences the stressful urban environment with many becoming destitute and detached from family, and the exposure of living in a totally new and strange environment (Englund, 2002, 2004; Ghosh and Kalipeni, 2005; Kalipeni et al., 2005; Kalipeni and Ghosh, 2007). In addition, the significant increase in circular migration results in a greater risk of exposing family members living in rural areas to HIV from returning circular migrants. As such, migration has become a major vector of HIV transmission from one place to another (Crush et al., 2006).

Within the past 20 years, HIV/AIDS infection has emerged as the most critical crisis to hit the urban areas. As noted earlier, Malawi's HIV infection prevalence rate is estimated to be anywhere between 12 and 15 percent. Of the one million people infected, the Malawi National AIDS Commission estimates that 25 percent, or 250,000, are in urban areas compared to 13 percent in the rural

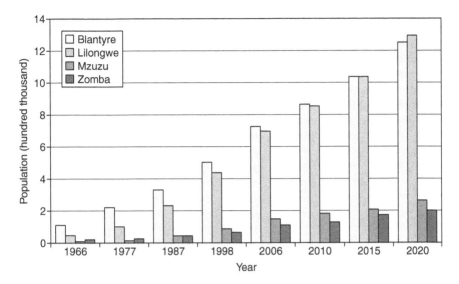

Figure 1.2 Population growth of major urban areas in Malawi (source: adapted from Chome and Kithakye, nd, used with kind permission from United National Malawi).

areas (Phiri, 2004). One major consequence of the epidemic has been the creation of over 600,000 orphans, many of whom have no one to take care of them. Most end up on the streets as commercial sex workers, beggars or thugs. It is therefore critical that we examine carefully the ways in which poverty in urban areas results in risky sexual behaviors, particularly for young females.

Research framework

The theoretical framework for this research focuses on economic, political, social and cultural aspects that make women more vulnerable to HIV in comparison to men. An important point that we would like to make is that economic vulnerability is not a root cause that pushes individuals to high-risk behavior. If that were the case then HIV infections would be confined to the poorest in the country. In fact HIV prevalence rates are high among doctors, lawyers, teachers and others. This goes to suggest that this group has adopted a lifestyle that renders them vulnerable to HIV.

The vulnerability approach suggests that lack of education resulting in limited marketable skills, poor health and low labor productivity renders individuals susceptible to high-risk behavior. According to UNDP (2007: p. 240), during the period from 1990 to 2004, about 65 percent of the population of Malawi lived below the poverty line. Poverty is widespread both in the rural and urban areas. Rural poverty and lack of employment opportunities compel individuals to migrate to the cities of Lilongwe and Blantyre. According to Englund (2002,

2004) many migrants assume that the cities will offer better economic opportunities. Such expectations are frequently not realized since the migrants do not bring with them adequate levels of education and training and thus have few marketable skills. Most migrants earn their living through small-scale trade or work as domestic help. In the formal sector they are employed as security guards, drivers or clerks. According to Englund (2004) wages are low both in the formal and informal sector, and the absence of labor unions increases the possibilities of exploitation of the workers by employers.

In addition to economic conditions, social and cultural norms increase an individual's vulnerability. According to Lele (1990) compared to men, women earn lower wages and are less likely to own land. The lower wages can be explained by the fact that women are less likely to study beyond the primary school level. The gender gap in schooling is pronounced between standard (or grade) five to eight. The reasons for the high levels of school dropout for girls include cost of schooling, demand for labor, early marriage and pregnancy, and fear of sexual harassment (Davison and Kanyuka, 1992; Kalipeni, 1997). In addition, society views Malawian women as homemakers and care givers and thus invests less in women's education and training. Such norms influence the unequal power structure by gender and make women more vulnerable to HIV. In such circumstances men are the decision makers both in and out of marriage.

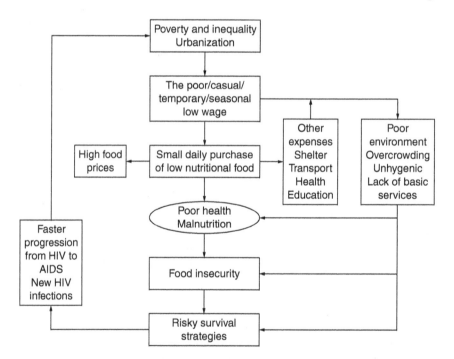

Figure 1.3 Linkages between urban food insecurity and HIV/AIDS (source: adapted from Crush *et al.*, 2006, p. 34, used with kind permission from the Southern African Migration Project).

The economic and social and cultural conditions make women vulnerable to exploitation and high-risk behavior.

With reference to urban areas the best way to view vulnerability to HIV and HIV as a security risk for Malawians living in urban areas is to employ a more recent framework proposed by Crush *et al.* (2006). In this framework Crush *et al.* conceptualize links between migration, HIV/AIDS and urban food security (see Figures 1.3 and 1.4). They note that the social and economic relationship between rural and urban areas is symbiotic, and at present food transfers to urban migrants appear to exceed urban cash remittances, although remittances remain crucial to rural production. Central to the framework is the insidious aspect of

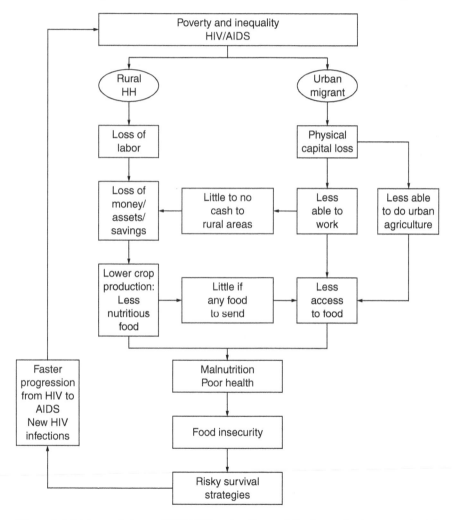

Figure 1.4 Linkages between HIV/AIDS, migration and food security (source: adapted from Crush *et al.* 2006, p. 35, used with kind permission from the Southern African Migration Project).

HIV/AIDS that is currently undermining and weakening physical and social capital in both rural and urban areas, especially for poorer households (Crush *et al.*, 2006). Although migration is a key element of the new social economy, it is also a significant vector of HIV/AIDS. Rural households are adversely impacted by HIV/AIDS in that HIV/AIDS compromises food security. As a result there is an attendant reduction in the flow of food from the countryside to the city, leaving the urban-based migrants more vulnerable to food insecurity. The framework developed by Crush *et al.* (2006) offers a compelling but complex web of causal connections and feedback mechanisms that result in the vulnerability of rural households and migrants to urban areas. Of significance to this study is Figure 1.4 in which Crush *et al.*'s framework shows a set of connections between poverty, urbanization, food insecurity, risky survival strategies and HIV/AIDS. In this chapter we examine the linkages between migration, poverty and vulnerability to HIV/AIDS in low socioeconomic income areas of the city of Lilongwe.

Methodology

During our fieldwork we focused on three areas in the city of Lilongwe, namely, Chinsapo, Area 25 and Area 29 (see Figure 1.1). In 1975 Lilongwe, located in the central part of the country, was declared the capital of Malawi (Mlia, 1975; Potts, 1995). Lilongwe is the administrative and commercial center of the country but does not have the level of industrialization usually seen in most capital cities of developing countries. According to Kalipeni (1999) at the onset Lilongwe was developed as an apartheid city which led to segregation of population. Native Malawians were assigned the eastern bank of the river Lilongwe while Asians were allocated the southeastern part of the same side of the river, while the British colonial administrators and other Europeans located on the other western bank of the river. The city has witnessed remarkable population increase from about 20,000 at the time of independence in 1964 to 99,000 in 1977, 223,000 in 1987, 434,000 in 1998 to the present 866,000 in 2008 (World Gazetteer, 2008). The population of Lilongwe is projected to surpass the population of Blantyre, currently the largest city in Malawi, some time in 2015 (see Figure 1.2) and is expected to reach a population of 1.3 million in 2020.

The communities in the three study areas of Chinsapo, Area 25 and Area 29 are largely composed of lower to middle income families (Englund, 2002, 2004). Chinsapo is the more rural of these communities, and its residents predominantly commute into the city center of Lilongwe to work in the informal sector. Residents of Areas 25 and 29 comprise both an urban and a peri-urban community and most inhabitants work in unskilled or semiskilled jobs. Each residential area is characterized by high population density and lack of building standards. The poor prefer to live in these areas because the rent is low, while the relatively well-to-do families prefer to live here because it is possible to build spacious houses without having to pay high land rents (especially in Areas 25 and 29). At the onset the areas lacked basic amenities and houses were built with limited attention paid towards access to roads. However, most houses have access to communal water points which have in turn greatly reduced the cause of disease and death among children (Englund, 2002: p. 143).

During 2003 and 2004 we carried out fieldwork in these areas to examine individuals' perceptions of their risks of HIV. We interviewed 60 women and 57 men who were selected randomly. We also conducted four focus group interviews: two with 20 women (10 women per focus group) and two with 20 men (10 men per focus group). We hired five interviewers in Lilongwe: two conducted interviews in Area 25, two in Area 29 and one in Chinsapo. Since the interviewers lived in the respective areas of our study, they were familiar with the localities and had the advantage of being able to speak the local language, Chichewa, understood by all of the residents in the areas. Participants were asked questions about religion, family background, economic conditions of the individuals, marriage history, family planning and social networks, fertility, sexual partnerships and HIV/AIDS. Each interview took about one hour to complete administering the structured questionnaires. For focus groups, the discussions were informal in nature. We asked about people's perceptions and understanding of HIV, what people thought about prevention of infections, and changing social and cultural practices. Also during the one on one administration of the structured questionnaires some of the participants volunteered more information about their history and their current circumstances in the city.

We selected the men and women from these communities for a number of reasons. First, these communities represent urban, peri-urban and rural areas. They attract migrants from the impoverished rural areas of Malawi. Upon arrival to the city most of these migrants continue to face economic hardship and absence of social cohesiveness. In rural communities social cohesiveness is central to daily life in that it maintains the sanity and supportive behavior for all members of a given village. Thus the absence of social cohesiveness and accountability make the residents more vulnerable to risky behavior and HIV infection. Second, we wanted to investigate the perception of risk among the male and female residents living in the three areas. Third, the population living in these communities represents a wide spectrum of occupations and family structures. This provided us an opportunity to interview various occupational backgrounds, members of married couple households, and divorced or single men and women.

Results of structured interviews

Gender relations

Overall we used similar questions when we interviewed women and men. However, the women's questionnaire had some questions that were pertinent to women only, such as family planning and birth histories. Keeping women's low socioeconomic status in mind we asked two central questions: (1) when would it be proper for a wife to leave her husband? and (2) what can a woman do without informing her husband? Physical abuse was cited as a reason for leaving a husband by the majority of the women, about 53 percent. The other reasons to leave the husband were sexual infidelity (33 percent) and if the woman thought her spouse might be infected with HIV (about 19 percent). Interestingly lack of financial support for the wife and the children was not considered to be a reason for leaving the husband, nor was the denial by the husband for her to use family planning. The reasons why these last two circumstances are not considered grounds for leaving a husband may be rooted in the social and cultural beliefs. Central Malawi, where Lilongwe is located, is characterized by a matrilineal system of descent in which the father is not obligated to support his own children but those of his sisters. Also in a high fertility rate society, having children is central to marriage; hence the low percentage scores on these two aspects. On the issue of mobility, women were asked if they could travel to the local market or to the local health center without informing their husbands, and the majority (over 63 percent) said they could not simply do so without informing the husband. These results suggest that a woman cannot necessarily leave a husband even when he does not provide economic support, is unfaithful and has HIV/AIDS. Furthermore a woman has to inform her husband about her activities outside the home, such as going to the local market or a health clinic, for fear of being accused of being unfaithful to the husband (see results in Table 1.2).

We asked the women several questions related to their reproductive rights. Table 1.3 presents the responses of the women on family planning issues. It is evident that most of the women depend on their husbands in terms of deciding whether or not to use contraceptive techniques and size of the family. For example, 81 percent of the women agreed that there was nothing much they could do to change the mind of their partner when he refuses the use of modern methods of child spacing. Over 35 percent of the women agreed that they had a say in the spacing of the next child's birth while 58 percent of the women

Table 1.2 Questions on gender issues: leaving husband or doing things without husband's knowledge

In your opinion, is it proper for a wife to leave her husband if:	*Yes (%)*	*No (%)*	*Don't know (%)*
He does not support her and the children financially?	6.5	88.3	5.2
He beats her frequently?	53.2	40.6	6.2
He is sexually unfaithful?	33.3	65.2	1.5
She thinks he might be infected with AIDS?	18.7	75.9	3.4
He does not allow her to use family planning?	11.0	86.4	2.6
Can you do the following without informing your husband:	33.5	66.5	0.0
Go to the local market	36.3	63.7	0.0
Go to the local health center			

Note
N = 60.

Table 1.3 Questions on gender issues: certain actions that can or cannot be taken by a woman

Action (State whether you agree, disagree, or have no opinion about the following statements)	Agree (%)	Disagree (%)	No opinion (%)
If your partner does not want to use modern methods of child spacing/family planning, there is nothing you can do to change his mind	81.3	16.6	2.1
If you decide that you want to delay the next birth, you will be able to have your way	35.6	57.8	6.6
If you decide that you want no more children, you will be able to have your way	44.0	54.1	1.9
Even if your husband does not want you to use family planning, if you want to you will use without his knowledge	57.3	38.6	4.1

Note
N = 60.

answered that they had no decision making role even if they wanted to delay the next birth. However, it was interesting to note that 57 percent of the women agreed that even if their husbands do not want them to use family planning, if the women wanted to, they would go ahead and use contraception without the husbands' knowledge. This is due to the fact that the family planning clinics in Malawi target only women. In such cases the women go to the clinics to obtain the information and learn the techniques without revealing it to the husbands.

Knowledge and attitudes about HIV/AIDS

The men who participated in the survey ranged from 15 to 44 years. About 54 percent had some secondary school education and 40 percent had some primary school education. Nearly 47 percent of the men were Catholics while the rest were Protestant, followers of Islam and other religions. About two thirds of the men, 64 percent, belonged to the Chewa ethnic group which is the predominant ethnic group in the Central Region of Malawi. The remaining 36 percent came from other ethnic groups such as the Ngoni, the Yao, the Tumbuka and the Lomwe. Weekly incomes ranged from MK1 to MK10,000, and the average weekly income turned out to be MK1,761 (US$16) with a standard deviation of MK2,274. This suggests that there were wide disparities in incomes earned with a few earning substantial amounts per week and the majority earning very little or nothing.

A number of specific questions concerning knowledge and attitude about HIV/AIDS were asked (Table 1.4). On the question of whether it would be acceptable to use a condom with a spouse for HIV/AIDS protection, over 52

Table 1.4 General knowledge and attitudes about AIDS and condoms

Question	Women			Men		
	Yes (%)	No (%)	Don't know (%)	Yes (%)	No (%)	Don't know (%)
Do you think it is acceptable to use a condom with a spouse to protect against AIDS?	20.0	80.0	0.0	52.6	35.1	10.5
Can you get AIDS if you have sex with someone who looks perfectly healthy?	100.0	0.0	0.0	89.5	3.5	3.5
Has your best friend slept with anyone other than her (his) husband (wife) in the last 12 months?	66.7	23.3	10.0	63.2	10.5	22.8
Do you suspect or know that your husband (wife) has had sexual relations with other women (men) apart from you since you were married?	67.0	33.0	0.0	14.3	25.0	60.7
Have you yourself slept with anyone other than your husband (wife) in the last 12 months?	0.0	100.0	0.0	35.1	58.3	–
Have you ever heard a talk at the clinic/hospital about how people can protect themselves against AIDS?	96.6	3.4	0.0	84.2	14.0	–
Have you ever heard a radio program about how people can protect themselves against AIDS?	96.6	3.4	0.0	100.0	0.0	0.0
Have you received information about how people can protect themselves against AIDS from a government or other official?	73.3	26.7	0.0	63.2	31.6	0.0

Notes
N = 60 women; 57 men.

percent of men answered yes while 80 percent of the women disagreed. This may suggest that women, due to their economic and social conditions, cannot ask for protection. The majority of the men (89 percent) and women (100 percent) agreed that physical appearance is no indication of someone having the virus or not. Questions regarding whether the respondents knew friends who were sleeping with someone other than their spouses showed that there was plenty of poly-partner sexual activities in these areas. The data indicates that over 63 percent of the men knew a friend who was sleeping with women other than their spouse. On the same issue, the women's responses were slightly higher at over 66 percent. When asked whether they suspected their spouses of having sexual relations outside their marriage, 67 percent of women answered yes while men generally reported that they were unaware of such relationships. The latter may reflect denial on the part of the men. As we probed further, women (100 percent) denied having sex with anyone other than their husbands while 35 percent of men answered yes. This may indicate reluctance on the part of the women to reveal the truth while men may not be as forthcoming as we had expected. We asked several questions related to knowledge about HIV/AIDS. Both men and women reported having heard about HIV/AIDS from health care personnel at clinics or hospitals. Overwhelmingly both groups (men and women) had heard about HIV/AIDS and how to protect oneself from contracting the virus from the radio.

Results of focus group interviews with women and men

The focus group discussions centered on themes, such as occupations and income generating activities, availability of health care facilities, knowledge and sources of information about HIV/AIDS, condom use and other preventive behaviors. To a greater extent, the results of focus group interviews complemented the findings in the structured interviews.

In response to the questions "What is AIDS?" and "What is HIV?" two of the participants offered the following answers:

FEMALE RESPONDENT 1: "AIDS has always been with us, my grandmother told me that in the past they used to call it kanyera or tsempho but it was not as bad as these days. Today it is extremely bad, people are dying of simple things such as flu, this AIDS is something else, nobody knows what it is!"

MALE RESPONDENT 1: "AIDS is a terrible disease, when you get it you die. The messages on the radio say that HIV is a certain small animal [kachilombo] in your body that you get from sleeping with women which then causes this terrible disease. I tell you, we are all going to die!"

One of the questions dealt with poverty and income generating activities in the area, and both women and men agreed that there are limited economic opportunities. This is illustrated by the following quotes:

FEMALE RESPONDENT 13: "I am sure you have seen for yourself that there is nothing much. The area is poor, there is no water, a few people can afford electricity for lighting, we have to walk a distance to the standing pipe to draw water, there are no schools here for our children to go to, crime and thievery are on the increase..."

FEMALE RESPONDENT 15: "Many of our husbands are self employed, selling second hand clothing or fixing kanyenya [grilled meat] and selling ziboli-bori [curios] at city center in Lilongwe, or selling goods by the roadside. You see the minibuses passing by, the drivers and conductors are likely to be our husbands in there. The income they bring home is too little to support the whole family. Many of us are lucky to have two meals a day. Just look at the kids running around, they are all malnourished."

Many of the women expressed concern about their income situation by discussing the employment of their husbands or boyfriends. The majority of the women were not gainfully employed. One woman noted that there are women in the communities who buy dried fish from the lake and bring it to Lilongwe and ask their children to sell it by the roadside. Other women travel to the surrounding villages to buy peanuts or maize, which they then sell to others in the area thereby supplementing their husbands' income. We further asked the women in the focus group if they were aware of any women sleeping with men for monetary gain. There was laughter from the women, an indication that this was a common practice. Here is a quote from one of the respondents:

FEMALE RESPONDENT 11: "What else can we do! Many of us never went to school, so no jobs for us. When the kids are starving at home and your husband has no income, well one has to do what one has to do to feed the children. So, yes, it happens and I know a few women who do that."

The presence of commercial sex workers in one of the locations (Chinsapo township) was confirmed in a one on one interview with a young woman (age 17) who had just migrated from a rural area to the city of Lilongwe. Indeed her story puts a human face on the factors that make people vulnerable to HIV/AIDS in a Malawian urban setting. She told us in great detail about her sad story:

FEMALE RESPONDENT 19: "I was in grade six when my father died in 2002. He used to grow tobacco to pay my school fees. Without him around, and coming from a family of six children, four boys and two girls, I was forced to drop out of school due to lack of school fees. I then migrated to Lilongwe to seek employment. But there is no employment here for an uneducated girl like me. So during the day we go to Lilongwe Market to sell second hand goods, but there is a lot of competition there. At night we try to do all we can do to get a little income. Sometimes we stand by the roadside to see if we can be picked, at other times we go to Lilongwe Hotel, Lingadzi Inn and other such places when there is a conference. If we are lucky in a night we might come back home with about K200 [US$1.50]. Some men just use us without paying us and we are too afraid of being beaten to ask for the pay. Life is tough here in the city, but it is even tougher in the village where I came from. From time to time I am able to send a little money to my mother but I don't reveal how and where I get it."

It is easy to see that poverty and women's low status have contributed to this girl's precarious situation. In further interviews with her, she revealed that she was scared that she might get infected with HIV. She indicated that some men use condoms and others don't, and she has to oblige in both instances since she needs the money badly. The HIV infection rate among commercial sex workers in Malawi is very high, estimated at 70 percent, since many of the clients are HIV infected and pass the virus on to the girls, and the girls in turn pass it on to other clients (Zachariah *et al.*, 2003; Weir *et al.*, 2008).

A married woman we interviewed clearly articulated her position in the marriage, particularly the factors that make it difficult for women to protect themselves against HIV/AIDS:

FEMALE RESPONDENT 22: "My husband died six months ago. He got so thin, began coughing, developed a rash, much like the rash that affects people with this disease they call AIDS. I know he died of AIDS because I too am losing weight and beginning to cough. I know I have it and I am soon going to die. I have three kids and I am worried as to who will take care of them once I am gone! It is very worrisome. I knew that my husband was moving around with these girls of low morals but I was afraid to ask him to take precautions. I wish I had left him immediately. I knew he was a cheater, but I am powerless, as I come from a poor family. The cattle he paid for the bride-price have all been slaughtered or sold by my parents."

This woman comes from the northern part of Malawi, where the patrilineal groups, such as the Tumbuka ethnic group, are predominant. They follow the patrilineal system in which bride-price or lobola is paid for women before marriage. Once a woman is married, divorce is almost impossible to effect, as the bride-price would have to be repaid to the man's relatives. This custom essentially puts women in bondage to men. Thus, married women, even if they are faithful to their husbands, are at risk of infection from unfaithful husbands.

Many such sad stories were recounted in our structured as well as focus group interviews. There were stories of young girls, as young as 13 years, giving birth to babies due to the fact that they had been orphaned. It was noted that in order to survive, young girls (sometimes as young as 10 years) sleep with many men, giving birth to babies whose fathers they do not know. In such cases, the probability is very high that these young orphaned females become HIV positive long before they reach adolescence.

With reference to knowledge about HIV and AIDS we found high levels of knowledge but great resistance to using the condom as a means of protection.

The focus group participants were aware of AIDS being a multi-symptom disease and knew someone who had faced AIDS. Some of the male participants expressed intense fear and worry about the disease. In the face of this tragedy respondents were asked several questions to prod them on how they and others were attempting to protect themselves. A number of respondents debated these questions intensely and below is an example of one man's response:

MALE RESPONDENT 10: "We have heard a lot about the rubber for men [condom] which President Muluzu introduced in 1994. But these rubbers are too thin, they often break during the action, and I don't think they protect you from the virus, they are just too thin, besides as one of us earlier noted, they are already tainted with the virus from the factory abroad. So why use them!"

An important concern raised by the men was the conflicting information given by the government and the Christian and Muslim religions.

MALE RESPONDENT 4: "We are also getting conflicting messages today. The government says use condoms! But the Catholic Church, the CCAP Church, the Muslims say if we use condoms we will go to hell, that they are immoral gadgets designed to make you sin. A year ago I heard Reverend [name withheld] on Radio Maria argue that the government is supporting promiscuity by handing out thousands of condoms every month. Let me also add that condoms are not 100 percent effective in preventing infection. The only sure way to protect myself is strict monogamy or abstinence. Which preaching should we follow? How do we protect ourselves?"

Discussion: urban poverty, gender and vulnerability to HIV

A number of studies have revealed that urbanization and HIV prevalence rates are intricately intertwined in countries of Southern Africa (Way, 1994; Dyson, 2003; Ngigi, 2007). Urban levels of HIV prevalence are known to be four to 10 times higher than those in rural areas. Another insidious aspect of HIV prevalence rates is that adolescent girls and young women in both rural and urban areas are the most affected in comparison to men. Indeed the rates are much higher among girls and young women in urban areas in comparison to rural areas (Mabala, 2006). While Dyson examines the impact of HIV on rates of urbanization, in this article we set out to understand people's perceptions of their knowledge, attitudes and other gender related factors that result in high rates of HIV in an urban setting. We were particularly interested in trying to understand why girls and young women suffer more from this epidemic.

    The results in our study indicate a very high knowledge of HIV even in the low socioeconomic income areas of the city of Lilongwe. Residents in these areas, both men and women, are aware that one can get infected through casual sex with many partners. They also indicate that the use of the condom in such circumstances can protect an individual from getting infected. There were of course misconceptions, misinterpretations of the facts, as well as confusion by a number of individuals, such as the rumor that condoms are tainted by the virus, that the Church says it is a sin to use a condom, and so on. These conflicting views and the presence of rampant poverty in these areas offered a fertile ground for the proliferation of the epidemic.

From the results of our focus group discussion and structured interviews, it was quite clear that there is a gender imbalance in low socioeconomic income areas of the city of Lilongwe. Women have little if any entitlements. The majority of the women in the sample were unemployed or underemployed, relegated to selling second hand clothing or foodstuffs by the roadside. Many women were totally dependent on the meager incomes their husbands were bringing into the household, which were inadequate to see the family through the month. It is in this context that we need to understand the data presented in Tables 1.2–1.4 which clearly shows that women have no recourse when their husbands are openly cheating. It is also fairly common for both men and women to have multiple sexual partners. For men having multiple sexual partners is a sign of their virility or masculinity, while for women, both married and unmarried, multiple sexual partners may act as a social security valve in which transactional sex may offer an extra income to feed their families.

The question is, what is it that needs to be done to curb the proliferation of the epidemic in the cities of Malawi? How can society protect vulnerable girls and young women? Indeed the results of this study confirm the presence of underlying factors which ultimately result in high rates of HIV in the city of Lilongwe and, for that matter, other cities of Malawi. These underlying factors include urban poverty, women's status, rural to urban labor migration, sexual norms and marital patterns. At the individual level factors such as low levels of education, knowledge and powerlessness for vulnerable groups all came up as major underlying factors that lead to or expose people to risky sexual behaviors. Unfortunately, these factors have been the least tackled in the fight against this epidemic. This calls for a need to rethink prevention strategies especially in urban areas. Over the past 20 years the focus of prevention strategies has been on individual behavior as the major factor driving the epidemic, and this has resulted in pouring millions of dollars into attempts to change individual behavior with reference to sexual activities (Zachariah *et al.*, 2003). While these efforts are commendable, evidence from all over the developing world has shown that this strategy has met little success in curbing the rapid proliferation of the epidemic (Lagarde *et al.*, 2001; Hearst and Chen, 2004; Kalipeni and Mbugua, 2005; Weir *et al.*, 2008; Mbugua, 2009).

As evidenced from the results of this study, adolescent girls and young women in low socioeconomic income areas of the city have suffered the brunt of the epidemic in the midst of rampant poverty, inequity, compromised social norms, sexual exploitation and other similar community factors. As Zachariah *et al.* (2003) and Crush *et al.* (2006) have argued, there is need for deliberate and systematic attention to be paid to the precarious circumstances faced by adolescent girls and young women in the city isolated from their familiar surroundings in rural areas. Some of the money being directed toward behavior change interventions needs to be diverted into programs that create a safe community environment that provides schooling and education, as well as livelihoods that guarantee vulnerable groups are protected from HIV infection. It is in this context that we end this section with the call to view HIV/AIDS not only as a disease, but a human rights and human security imperative.

We reiterate the UNAIDS recommendations with reference to HIV/AIDS and gender in Africa (UC Atlas of Global Inequality, n.d.). UNAIDS calls for the use of a gender approach by emphasizing the role of women and women's organizations in HIV/AIDS policy development, programming and implementations at all levels of government. The key here is female empowerment. In attempting to increase female empowerment there is also need to involve men as partners, a critical component in AIDS prevention and care, as shown in our study that men are the decision makers in matters relating to sexual and reproductive matters. Furthermore women's rights need to be strongly looked at as basic human rights which will certainly require a strong and unwavering will in instituting structural changes, including the transformation of social norms and practices that do not uphold these rights. The behavior change model is bound to fail, particularly in low socioeconomic income areas, if the underlying factors of gender inequality, poverty and current social norms are not tackled head on.

Conclusion

The increasing percentage of HIV infected population continues to have drastic consequences worldwide. In addition to the economic consequences related to rising medical costs, loss of labor, loss of investments, there are social and cultural consequences of unparalleled proportions. Using a vulnerability approach as the theoretical model, this chapter has examined the context of gender and risk to HIV among men and women in a low socioeconomic income area in the city of Lilongwe, Malawi. The major findings of the structured and focus group interviews in low socioeconomic areas of Lilongwe suggest that the rising epidemic, among women and men, is driven in part by poverty which restricts people's options, particularly those of adolescent girls and young females. It appears that the knowledge about HIV/AIDS has increased, yet this has not translated into behavior change patterns.

Malawi is among the countries hit hardest by the HIV/AIDS epidemic in southern Africa with anywhere between 12 percent and 15 percent of the population aged 15 and above infected by the virus. Urban prevalence is even higher with a 23 percent rate of HIV prevalence. In both rural and urban areas there is a preponderance of women who are HIV positive in comparison to men. It is therefore imperative that we understand the gender context of this disease, particularly in low socioeconomic income areas of towns and cities in Malawi. Poverty, gender inequality and asymmetrical sexual relations are keys to spreading HIV/AIDS among women by men. Women were unable to leave their husbands even when the men did not provide economic support, were unfaithful and had HIV/AIDS. Many of the women indicated that they were worried of being infected by their husbands. In short, in spite of women's awareness of the disease, women were unable to protect themselves, which increased their vulnerability to HIV infection.

Based on the findings in this chapter we conclude by highlighting that there is a need to use a vulnerability and gender approach within the broader conceptual framework of human security with reference to HIV. The concept of human security goes far beyond the traditional threats associated with war, forced movement of people and ethnic cleansing. It is important to note that economic, social and cultural factors do force people to live in abject poverty, create inequalities among genders, deny access to basic amenities and thus present risks to lives and long-term human development. Due to economic problems states become powerless and unable to provide for the people to whom they are expected to ensure security. Thus studies of HIV/AIDS should include hunger, natural disasters such as deforestation and desertification, and gendered security threats because, as in the case of Malawi, this epidemic has the potential to kill and present additional human security risks other than war. There is great need to empower both men and women in terms of their livelihoods. Men need to be engaged as partners, something which should be considered a critical component in AIDS prevention and care given that in many contexts men are the decision makers in matters relating to reproductive and sexual health. If socioeconomic conditions in these areas continue to remain the same, the behavior change model is bound to fail. A multi-pronged strategy that recognizes and tackles head on the underlying factors of poverty and gender inequality is urgently needed in the disadvantaged areas of the city.

Note

* This chapter is a derivative of two previously published papers that appeared in *The Journal of Social Aspects of HIV/AIDS (SAHARA)* in 2005 and *Social Science and Medicine* in 2007. The full citations of these two papers are: (1) Ghosh, J. and Kalipeni, E. (2005) Women in Chinsapo, Malawi: Vulnerability and Risk to HIV/AIDS, *The Journal of Social Aspects of HIV/AIDS*, 2(2), pp. 320–332; and (2) Kalipeni, E. and Ghosh, J. (2007) Concern and Practice Among Men About HIV/AIDS in Low Socioeconomic Income Areas of Lilongwe, Malawi, *Social Science and Medicine*, 64(5), pp. 1116–1127. This derivative chapter is published here by the kind permission of both *The Journal of Social Aspects of HIV/AIDS (SAHARA)* and *Social Science and Medicine*.

Bibliography

Alkire, Sabina. (2003) A Conceptual Framework for Human Security, Working Paper 2, Centre for Research on Inequality, Human Security and Ethnicity (CRISE), Queen Elizabeth House, University of Oxford. (Online) Available at: www.crise.ox.ac.uk/pubs/workingpaper2.pdf [accessed 5 November 2011].

Asthana, S. (1994) Economic Crisis, Adjustment and the Impact on Health. In: D. R. Philips and Y. Verhasselt, eds. *Health and Development*. London: Routledge, pp. 50–64.

Central Intelligence Agency. (2011) The World Factbook: Malawi. (Online) Available at:

www.cia.gov/library/publications/the-world-factbook/geos/mi.html   [accessed   16 October 2011].

Chirwa, E. W. (2005) Macroeconomic Policies and Poverty Reduction in Malawi: Can We Infer from Panel Data. Funded by and Submitted to Global Development Network. (Online) Available at: www.imf.org/external/np/res/seminars/2005/macro/pdf/chirwa. pdf [accessed 16 October 2011].

Chome, J. and D. Kithakye. (n.d.) United Nations Human Settlements Programme's: The Malawi Urbanization Challenge. United Nations Malawi. (Online) Available at: www. unmalawi.org/agencies/unhabitat.html [accessed 17 October 2011].

Cohen, B. (2006) Urbanization in Developing Countries: Current Trends, Future Projections, and Key Challenges for Sustainability. *Technology in Society*, 28(1–2), pp. 63–80.

Crush, J., B. Frayne and M. Grant. (2006) Linking Migration, HIV/AIDS and Urban Food Security in Southern and Eastern Africa. Southern African Migration Project, Renewal and International Food Policy Research Institute. (Online) 12 August 2008. Available at: www.ifpri.org/renewal/pdf/urbanrural.pdf [accessed 18 October 2011].

Davison, J. and M. Kanyuka. (1992) Girls' Participation in Basic Education in Southern Malawi. *Comparative Education R*eview, 36(4), pp. 446–466.

Dyson, T. (2003) HIV/AIDS and Urbanization. *Population and Development Review*, 29(3), pp. 427–442.

Economist Intelligence Unit. (2010) Malawi: Country Report. (Online) Available at: www.eiu.com/report_dl.asp?issue_id=1965137581&mode=pdf [accessed 11 February 2010].

Englund, H. (2002) The Village in the City, the City in the Village: Migrants in Lilongwe. *Journal of Southern African Studies*, 28(1), pp. 137–154.

Englund, H. (2004) Cosmopolitanism and the Devil in Malawi. *Ethnos*, 69(3), pp. 293–316.

Ghosh, Jayati and Ezekiel Kalipeni. (2005) Women in Chinsapo, Malawi: Vulnerability and Risk to HIV/AIDS. *Journal of Social Aspects of HIV/AIDS*, 2(2), pp. 320–332.

Hearst, N. and S. Chen. (2004) Condom Promotion for AIDS Prevention in the Developing World: Is It Working? *Studies in Family Planning*, 35(1), pp. 39–47.

International Monetary Fund. (2007) Malawi Growth and Development Strategy: From Poverty to Prosperity 2006–2011. (Online) Available at: www.imf.org/external/pubs/ft/ scr/2007/cr0755.pdf [accessed 16 October 2011].

Kalipeni, Ezekiel. (1997) Gender and Regional Differences in Schooling between Boys and Girls in Malawi. *East African Geographical Review*, 19(1), pp. 14–32.

Kalipeni, Ezekiel. (1999) The Spatial Context of Lilongwe's Growth and Development in Malawi. In: Ezekiel Kalipeni and Paul Tiyambe Zeleza, eds. *Sacred Spaces and Public Quarrels: African Economic and Cultural Landscapes*. Lawrenceville, NJ: Africa World Press, pp. 73–108.

Kalipeni, Ezekiel. (2004) Structural Adjustment and the Health-Care Crisis in Malawi. *Proteus: A Journal of Ideas*, Spring, 21(1), pp. 23–30.

Kalipeni, Ezekiel and Jayati Ghosh. (2007) Worry and Practice Among Men About HIV/ AIDS in Low Socioeconomic Income Areas of Lilongwe, Malawi. *Social Science and Medicine*, 6(5), pp. 1116–1127.

Kalipeni, Ezekiel and Njeri Mbugua. (2005) A Review of Prevention Efforts in the Fight against HIV and AIDS in Africa. *Norwegian Journal of Geography*, 59(1), pp. 26–36.

Kalipeni, Ezekiel, Sarah Zamor and Jayati Ghosh. (2005) AIDS and Intergenerational Communication Among Urban Women in Lilongwe, Malawi. In: Grace B.

Kyomuhendo, ed. *Women's Health: African and Global Perspectives*. Kampala, Uganda: Women and Gender Studies, Makerere University Press, pp. 122–142.

Kalipeni, Ezekiel, Susan Craddock and Jayati Ghosh. (2004a) Mapping the AIDS Pandemic: The Geographical Progression of HIV in Eastern and Southern Africa. In: Ezekiel Kalipeni, Susan Craddock, Joseph Oppong and Jayati Ghosh, eds. *HIV/AIDS in Africa: Beyond Epidemiology*. Malden, MA: Blackwell Publishers, pp. 58–69.

Kalipeni, Ezekiel, Susan Craddock, Joseph Oppong and Jayati Ghosh, eds. (2004b) *HIV/AIDS in Africa: Beyond Epidemiology*. Oxford: Blackwell Publishers.

Kanji, Najmi, Nazneen Kanji and Firoze Manji. (1991) From Development to Sustained Crisis: Structural Adjustment, Equity and Health. *Social Science and Medicine*, 33, pp. 985–993.

Lagarde, E., B. Auvert, J. Chege, T. Sukwa, J. R. Glynn, H. A. Weiss, E. Akam, M. Laourou, M. Carael and A. Buve. (2001) Condom Use and Its Association with HIV/Sexually Transmitted Diseases in Four Urban Communities of Sub-Saharan Africa. *AIDS*, 15, pp. S71–S78.

Lele, U. (1990) Structural Adjustment, Agricultural Development and the Poor: Some Lessons from the Malawian Experience. *World Development*, 18(9), pp. 1207–1219.

Lindgren, T., S. H. Rankin and W. W. Rankin. (2005) Malawi Women and HIV: Socio-Cultural Factors and Barriers to Prevention. *Women & Health*, 41(1), pp. 69–86.

Loewenson, R. (1993) Structural Adjustment and Health Policy in Africa. *International Journal of Health Services*, 23, pp. 717–730.

Mabala, R. (2006) From HIV Prevention to HIV Protection: Addressing the Vulnerability of Girls and Young Women in Urban Areas. *Environment and Urbanization*, 18(2), pp. 407–432.

Mbugua, Njeri. (2009) Cultural Attitudes and Ambivalence to the ABC Model in Sub-Saharan Africa. In: Ezekiel Kalipeni, Karen C. Flynn and Cynthia Pope, eds. *Strong Women, Dangerous Times: Gender and HIV/AIDS in Africa*. New York: Nova Science Publishers, pp. 171–184.

Mlia, Justice Ngoleka. (1975) Malawi's New Capital City: A Regional Planning Perspective. *Pan-African Journal*, 8(4), pp. 387–401.

Ngigi, M. M. (2007) Urbanization, Poverty and Culture in the Spatial Patterns of the HIV/AIDS Epidemic in Kenya. *Chigaku Zasshi–Journal of Geography*, 116, pp. 260–274.

Oppong, J. (1997) Medical Geography of Sub-Saharan Africa. In: Samuel Aryeetey-Attoh, ed. *Geography of Sub-Saharan Africa*. Upper Saddle River, NJ: Prentice Hall, pp. 147–181.

Oppong, J. (1998) A Vulnerability Interpretation of the Geography of HIV-AIDS in Ghana, 1986–1995. *Professional Geographer*, 50(4), pp. 437–448.

Phiri, F. (2004) Development-Malawi: Rapid Urbanisation Looks Irreversible. Inter Press Service News Agency. (Online) Available at: http://ipsnews.net/interna. asp?idnews=24810 [accessed 16 October 2011].

Population Reference Bureau. (2007) World Population Highlights, Key Findings From PRB's 2007 World Population Data Sheet. *Population Bulletin*, 62(3). (Online) Available at: www.prb.org/pdf07/62.3Highlights.pdf [accessed 16 October 2011].

Population Reference Bureau. (2009) World Population Data Sheet. (Online) Available at: www.prb.org/pdf09/09wpds_eng.pdf [accessed 18 October 2011].

Potts, Deborah. (1995) Capital Relocation in Africa: The Case of Lilongwe in Malawi. *Geographical Journal*, 151(2), pp. 182–196.

Rohregger, B. (2006) Shifting Boundaries of Support: Re-negotiating Distance and Proximity in Trans-local Support Relations in an Urban Fringe in Lilongwe City, Malawi. *Ethnic and Racial Studies*, 29(6), pp. 1153–1168.

Schoepf, B. G., C. Schoepf and J. V. Millen. (2000) Theoretical Therapies, Remote Remedies: SAPs and the Political Ecology of Poverty and Health in Africa. In: Jim Yong Kim, Joyce V. Millen, Alec Irwin and John Gershman, eds. *Dying for Growth: Global Inequality and the Health of the Poor*. Monroe, ME: Common Courage Press, pp. 91–125.

Turshen, M. (1999) *Privatizing Health Services in Africa*. New Brunswick, NJ: Rutgers University Press.

UC Atlas of Global Inequality. (n.d.) AIDS/HIV and Gender: In Africa HIV and AIDS Disproportionately Affects Women and Girls. (Online) 25 June 2011. University of California. Available at: http://ucatlas.ucsc.edu/health/aids/aids_gender.php [accessed 18 October 2011].

UNAIDS. (2008a) 2008 Report on the Global AIDS Epidemic, Status of the Global HIV Epidemic. (Online) Available at: http://data.unaids.org/pub/GlobalReport/2008/jc1510_2008_global_report_pp. 29_62_en.pdf. [accessed 12 October 2011].

UNAIDS. (2008b) UNAIDS/WHO Epidemiological Fact Sheet on HIV and AIDS, 2008 Update. (Online) Available at: www.who.int/globalatlas/predefinedReports/EFS2008/full/EFS2008_MW.pdf. [accessed 16 October 2011].

UNAIDS. (2008c) 2007 UNAIDS/WHO Sub-Saharan Africa AIDS Epidemic Update, Regional Summary. (Online) Available at: http://data.unaids.org:80/pub/Report/2008/JC1526_epibriefs_subsaharanafrica_en.pdf [accessed 16 October 2011].

UN Commission on Human Security. (2003) *Human Security Now: Protecting and Empowering People*. New York: United Nations.

United Nations Development Program (UNDP). (2007) Human Development Report 2007/2008—Fighting Climate Change: Human Solidarity in a Divided World. United Nations Development Program. (Online) 12 August 2008. Available at: http://hdr.undp.org/en/media/HDR_20072008_EN_Complete.pdf [accessed 18 October 2011].

United Nations Development Program (UNDP). (2009) Human Development Report 2009. (Online) Available at: http://hdr.undp.org/en/media/HDR_2009_EN_Table_J.pdf [accessed 11 October 2011].

United Nations Population Fund (UNFPA). (2007) UNFPA State of the World Population 2007, Unleashing the Potential of Urban Growth. (Online) Available at: www.unfpa.org/swp/2007/presskit/pdf/sowp2007_eng.pdf [accessed 16 October 2011].

Van Donk, M. (2006) Positive Urban Futures in Sub-Saharan Africa: HIV/AIDS and the Need for ABC (A Broader Conceptualization). *Environment and Urbanization*, 18(1), pp. 155–175.

Way, P. O. (1994) African HIV/AIDS and Urbanization. In: James D. Tarver, ed. *Urbanization in Africa: A Handbook*. Westport, CT: Greenwood Press, pp. 423–438.

Weir, S., I. Hoffman, A. Muula, L. Brown, E. F. Jackson, T. Chirwa, D. Zanera, N. Kumwenda, J. Kadzandira, E. Slaymaker and B. Zaba. (2008) *Final Report: Malawi Prevalence Study*. Lilongwe: University of North Carolina Project, Chancellor College of the University of Malawi and London School of Hygiene and Tropical Medicine.

World Bank. (2007) *Global Economic Prospects: Overview and Global Outlook*. Washington, DC: The International Bank for Reconstruction and Development, The World Bank.

World Gazetteer. (2008) Malawi: Largest Cities and Towns and Statistics of Their Population. (Online) (4 September 2008) Available at: www.world-gazetteer.com/wg.php?x

=&men=gcis&lng=en&dat=32&srt=pnan&col=dq&geo=-150 [accessed 18 October 2011].

World Health Organization (WHO). (2006) Core Health Indicators: Malawi. (Online) Available at: http://apps.who.int/whosis/database/core/core_select_process.cfm?countr y=mwi&indicators=healthpersonnel [accessed 11 October 2011].

Zachariah, R., M. P. Spielmann, A. D. Harries, W. Nkhoma, A. Chantulo and V. Arendt. (2003) Sexually Transmitted Infections and Sexual Behaviour Among Commercial Sex Workers in a Rural District of Malawi. *International Journal of STD & AIDS*, 14, pp. 85–188.

2 Treating AIDS in Uganda and South Africa

Semi-authoritarian technologies in gendered contexts of insecurity

Lisa Ann Richey

> The first debate on AIDS in the UN Security Council was in Jan 2000, chaired by the Vice-President of the US, Al Gore. This was the first time that a health issue was discussed in the Security Council and the formal moment where the notion of security was broadened beyond the absence of war or conflict to include what we now call "human security." Thus, while AIDS has perhaps been debated as a security issue, it has been at the absolute center of human security.
>
> (Piot, 2006)

The radical reconstitution of "global AIDS" (see Patton, 2002) "at the absolute center of human security" involved the imperative of expanding AIDS treatment in resource-poor settings. Within representations of global AIDS, Africa remains a "dark, untamed continent from which devastating viruses emerge to threaten the West" (Kitzinger and Miller, 1992, cited in Bancroft, 2001: p. 96). While it has become a common understanding that "African AIDS" has relied upon and perpetuated stereotypes of Africa as "Other," particularly in sexually exotic and exceptional ways (Stillwaggon, 2003), African women's bodies are again at the center of the "body politic" (see the classic text by Lock and Scheper-Hughes, 1996), as controlling viruses within bodies take a central role in political contestations and struggles over both global resources and local capital. Such contestations have pushed technological access to the forefront of political debates over global inequality among a wide variety of interest groups—from AIDS activists to global pharmaceutical corporations.

In high-income countries, treatment with antiretroviral drugs (ARVs) became widely available in 1996, and AIDS-related mortality dropped sharply. Over the past half-decade, and in contrast to conventional wisdom that such therapies would remain beyond the reach of most HIV positive people in developing countries, improving access to ARVs has become a global priority. While this goal has yet to be realized in most African countries, South Africa has undertaken the largest public ARV treatment program in the world, and Uganda's treatment figures are among the best in Africa. Despite such progress, ARVs can be described as semi-authoritarian technologies linked to controlled outcomes in both personal and political spheres. In addition, ARVs in Africa enter into, and are complicit with, highly contested gender relations. As Sylvia Tamale argues, women's subordination is predicated upon their sexuality, and the African state has a vested interest in controlling women's bodies and sexuality to ensure the survival of power structures of patriarchy and capitalism (Tamale, 2009). Although the HIV/AIDS epidemic in Africa has most affected people in their prime reproductive years, childbearing and parenthood remain paramount reproductive projects for people who live on ARV treatment or people who are married to ARV recipients. Thus, having children continues to be the most important signifier of a normal life (Smith and Mbakwem, 2007; Richey, 2011). This chapter focuses on the treatment side of living with HIV in Africa by charting some of the reproductive negotiations surrounding these semi-authoritarian technologies in clinics in Uganda and South Africa.

AIDS treatment is negotiated in highly gendered contexts that present formidable barriers for women who must adhere to treatment regimens. In Africa, women of reproductive age make up 20 percent of the general population, yet women aged 18–45 constitute 53 percent of the HIV infected population (Shelton and Peterson, 2004). Clinic level data suggests that it is worth explicit research consideration that women with AIDS continue to get pregnant, whether these women are on ARV treatment or not. Multiple studies have documented that sexual activity continues even after receiving a positive diagnosis for HIV across both so-called "developed" and "developing countries" (Myer *et al.*, 2007). Furthermore, many sexually active, HIV positive people continue to want to bear children (Cooper *et al.*, 2007; Myer *et al.*, 2007). In many African countries, motherhood is understood normatively, and the stigma of childlessness often rivals the stigma associated with being infected with HIV (Cooper *et al.*, 2007).

The combination of women's reproductive ambitions and the demands of ARV therapy produces an opportunity for negotiating both models and meanings of gender and health. Here I examine some of the complex and gendered issues that link vertical transmission of HIV to reproductive rights in the context of AIDS treatment counseling.[1] In the following sections of the chapter, I begin with an introduction to empirical case studies from Uganda and South African clinics. Then I describe the context of AIDS treatment counseling in regards to pregnancy and family planning. Next, I will trace the trajectory of counseling and the important shift that resulted from bringing AIDS into the counseling context. Then, I analyze examples of negotiations from Ugandan and South African AIDS clinics focusing on social issues, poverty and gender. Finally, I elaborate on conclusions surrounding the interplay between gender and human security, as AIDS treatment continues to expand in Africa.

In her (2004) study of African political regime change, Aili Tripp characterizes Ugandan President Museveni's rule as "semi-authoritarian." Such regimes are anti-democratic and deliberately combine the rhetoric of liberal democracy with illiberal rule. Semi-authoritarian regimes are propelled by popular support, but distribute their rewards through clientelistic channels. Key governance terms in this type of regime are "control," "management" and of course, "continuity." Control and management of resources, both human and material, must ensure continuity of the regime and an ongoing access to benefits. These semi-authoritarian regimes must embrace contradictory realities of both freedom and oppression.

In the neoliberal global economy, the relations between African states, development NGOs and the donors and lenders who fund them reflect these contradictory notions of global/local power dynamics, and these dynamics are reflected in accommodative bargaining (Tilly, 1999). Such bargains between donors and recipients at the policy level have felt implications for individual actors trying to negotiate issues of survival, production and reproduction (Richey, 2008a). Patients are never simply encountering local factors when they enter an AIDS clinic, but are part of a web of relationships, both economic and cultural, that link local clinics to global politics.

AIDS treatment in countries like South Africa and Uganda provides significant examples of the technological link between the biological and the political. Thus, in this chapter, I suggest that it may be useful to think of anti-retroviral drugs as semi-authoritarian technologies. This is because their influx into parts of Uganda and parts of South Africa can contribute to particular political outcomes due to the technological influence of ARVs. For example, treatment with ARVs requires stability of both individuals and communities. Their high cost makes them valuable commodities for consumption, trade, or as political spoils. Also, the global emphasis on patient adherence justifies international concern with the intimate behavior of Africans' pill-taking as a necessary part of global security. If "they" do not adhere to their pill regime, then "we," the global community, will suffer the consequences of more virulent strands of resistant HIV, which can develop in local bodies and potentially spread around the globe. Therefore, sufficient compliance to the regimen of ARVs is necessary to avoid "an emergency," thus producing the securitization of AIDS treatment. To understand the relationship between AIDS treatment and human security in Africa, this chapter will follow the analogy of the semi-authoritarian regime toward understanding semi-authoritarian technologies. Thus, it is critical to differentiate the opportunities, openness and life-giving powers from the constraints, barriers and limits to life that coexist under semi-authoritarianism. Questions of reproductive ambition by people living on ARV treatment call both sides into debate.

ARV's and pregnancy: management, control and cost-effectiveness

Since the Second World War, "legitimate" state intervention into the intimate and reproductive lives of its citizens primarily occurred through population policy and public health interventions. Thus the control of fertility signifies "modern," predictable, Westernized relations between the individual body and the body politic. In African countries, the technologies and practices of family planning are promoted as essential gestures for the performance of neoliberal modernity (see Richey, 2008a). Similarly, women's well-being is at the core of the management and control regimes of ARV technologies. Yet, it is not in fact women themselves whose well-being is the primary factor at stake, but the potential fetal "victim" of HIV transmission. Women who are pregnant are accorded special status in the global hierarchy of ARV allocation. Pregnant women are assumed to be the ones most in need of treatment—not for their own virus, but for the potential transmission of HIV to their fetus. Women are also helpful for the capture of their family into treatment regimes, and of course for providing care for their children or any dependent HIV positive family members. Thus, there are three points of intersection between ARV treatment and pregnant women: (1) pregnant women are to be given ARVs for the prevention of "maternal-to-child transmission"[2] (PMTCT) of HIV; (2) pregnant women are meant to provide an entry point to family care; and (3) pregnant women are entitled to ARVs as a means to extend their own lives for the sake of preventing AIDS orphans (see McIntyre, 2005).

ARVs as semi-authoritarian technologies are not democratic. This is illustrated in the conflicts around treating a pregnant woman as both a woman and as a mother. The individual woman on ARV treatment is conspicuously absent from much of the PMTCT imaginary. This rhetoric, which conceals the individual woman and focuses instead on preventing HIV complications and treating AIDS for both the fetus and the woman through the status of being a "pregnant woman," is politically efficacious. Holc (2004) draws on the discourses of abortion in Poland to argue that the construction of "fetal persons" is a process of subject formation that results in particular effects on other subjects. "The mythology of the personhood of the fetus gradually effaces another personhood—that which should be attributed to women" (Graff, 2001, cited in Holc, 2004: p. 766). Reinserting the woman as an individual into these discourses would create the possibility, and even likelihood, that AIDS-infected women will reproduce like other women. Embracing a more individual-centered approach within programs to prevent vertical transmission would also confirm that such programs have an ethically inherent responsibility for treating the mother, whether or not this is cost-effective in the public policy realm.

In developed countries, the near elimination of the risk of vertical transmission of HIV has been lauded as one of the indisputable successes of ARV treatment. The successes in African countries thus far have been limited. However, in South Africa, and in other places where such programs exist on sufficient scale and with adequate supplies and good management, pediatric HIV has become rare.[3] One reason we have little understanding of how HIV positive women negotiate treatment and reproductive dilemmas is because the mothers in Africa who are on ARVs[4] are most commonly limited to those on PMTCT[5] interventions. PMTCT interventions are considered the "trial run" for implementing full-scale ARV treatment programs. South African Ministry of Health officials explained that PMTCT programs are easier because they use the existing antenatal care infrastructure and personnel; thus, PMTCT programs are far less taxing on the health care infrastructure and more cost-effective than lifetime treatment. In the Western Cape, all public antenatal facilities offer dual therapy PMTCT, which has reduced vertical transmission rates to less than 10 percent.[6]

PMTCT is also the most cost-effective HIV/AIDS intervention (Nattrass, 2004). According to the then Deputy Director General for Health in the Western Cape in South Africa: "Just that single intervention saves our hospital system. When we calculate the cost of hospital admissions it would mean an additional Red Cross [large, specialized care] hospital at 100% of its operations." Yet, the Director also acknowledged that it is women who must accept the program and, disproportionately, women who pay the price of this intervention. "MTCT women are heroes—they do it to protect their babies and they lose a lot."[7] Indeed, these women are saddled with confronting the stigma of HIV together with the complex challenges of pregnancy. Anecdotally, pregnant women who test positive are usually left to deal with both their coming child and their disease alone when they disclose their status or are found out by their partners.

Additionally, research has confirmed that women who receive a single dose of the ARV drug Nevirapine to prevent the transmission of HIV to their child are much more likely to develop resistance to the drug afterward (Palmer *et al.*, 2006). The long-term persistence of the Nevirapine-resistant HIV is important for women who might need the drug again in subsequent pregnancies, when it will not be effective to control the vertical transmission of the resistant strain of the virus. Also, these women might need to take Nevirapine as part of their own regimen of ARV therapy, at which point it will not be effective for them. The conclusion of the Palmer *et al.* study's publication of results reaffirmed the centrality of the fetus as *a potential citizen* in the context of a state that does not prioritize ARV treatment for women:

> For the 90% of women in developing countries who do not have access to highly active antiretroviral treatment, there still may be a role for treatment with single-dose Nevirapine, due to the fact that it reduces the transmission of HIV from mother to child.
>
> (Rauscher, 2006)

The study thus argues that Nevirapine should be used if there is no other available regimen for preventing vertical transmission, even if the costs are high for the pregnant women. Thus, this sort of intervention pits the health of women against the health of their babies, assuming a meaningful distinction between the two can be adjudicated. It does not prioritize the political allocation of AIDS treatment in ways that do not discriminate on the basis of gender and mothers and non-mothers.

ARVs and the ethical dilemmas of treating both the mother and the fetus evoke historical feminist debates regarding the connections among the self, the fetus and the maternal relationship (Glenn *et al.*, 1994). Exposure to pregnancy necessarily risks exposure to HIV, as procreation involves unprotected sexual intercourse. As we will see from discussions of the clinic interactions, there is, in effect, an implicit separation between procreative sexual relations and all other types of sexual behavior. Yet, this separation between the mother and the sexually active woman is not only illogical, it represents a fundamental and gendered difficulty of AIDS treatment. Treatment counselors tell women that they must use a condom every time they have sex to protect themselves from re-infection with a resistant virus and to protect their partner, and at the same time, the counselors advise women on ARVs to plan pregnancies with their physician.

In spite of the fact that the "typical" ARV patient is a woman of childbearing age, very few studies have been done so far on family planning for women living with AIDS in the Third World. The existing ones emphasize the need to link contraceptive and AIDS interventions into a convenient service for women (Preble *et al.*, 2003; Best, 2004; de Bruyn, 2004, 2005). The understandings gained by in-depth research on reproductive decision making (Greenlaugh, 1995; Bledsoe, 2002; Johnson-Hanks, 2002; Fadlalla, 2007; Richey, 2008a) show that choices over childbearing and methods for its prevention are contingent upon women's perceptions of their physical and social situation, and that the cultural contexts of auspicious childbearing vary greatly across individuals and communities. This attention to both the particular, and the social, has not been incorporated at all into the new and more complex settings of AIDS treatment. Instead, as a recent study demonstrates, a development intervention matrix on "pregnancy status, HIV status and service delivery needs" with two separate columns for "wants future pregnancy" and "does not want future pregnancy" is still used (Preble *et al.*, 2003). If there is any reasonable hypothesis to be made on the reproductive decision making of women living with AIDS, it would be that the issues of contingency become even more pronounced in their lives than in the lives of women who are not currently struggling with the virus. These contingencies, often referred to by AIDS counselors as "social issues," fall outside the application of the semi-authoritarian technologies themselves and into the realm of AIDS treatment counseling.

Research setting: two case studies from Uganda and South Africa

My work on ARVs in Uganda and South Africa explores the contexts in which patients seek care for HIV/AIDS, including the perspectives of the health care providers, counsellors and patients themselves. The political context of both countries has shaped the character, scope and scale of the AIDS treatment that takes place in the clinics. The international context of donor aid committed to funding AIDS treatment is critical for both case studies. There is a global consensus that AIDS in Africa is a serious problem worthy of international attention. Sub-Saharan Africans made up 67 percent of the total people living with HIV across the globe and 72 percent of AIDS deaths in 2007 (UNAIDS, 2008).

By 2003, two global programs of unprecedented scale were being rolled out in Uganda and South Africa. The first, PEPFAR, was started by the then US President George W. Bush and stands for "The US President's Emergency Program for AIDS Relief." PEPFAR funds only selected countries, and it is administered through the US Department of State, signaling its strategic importance in contrast to typical health-related initiatives. It is the largest initiative by any country to combat a single disease in history (US State Department, n.d.). The initial PEPFAR commitment was a $15 billion program over three years. Since May 2009, it has expanded into the Global Health Initiative, supported by additional funding and intended to bring AIDS treatment beyond its emergency response. PEPFAR is reported as having directly supported ARV treatment for over two million people worldwide (The United States President's Emergency Plan for AIDS Relief, 2009).

The second, The Global Fund to Fight Aids, Tuberculosis and Malaria, is an independent, private foundation governed by an international board that works in partnership with governments, NGOs, civil society organizations and the private sector. It is an international mechanism to channel aid financing, and thus it is not an implementing agency. Of course, money travels with power, and The Global Fund controls the second largest pool of donor funds in the world (after the UN itself) (United Nations Global Compact Learning Forum, 2008). A comparative analysis of the activities of PEPFAR, the World Bank's Multi-country HIV/AIDS Program (MAP) and The Global Fund in three African countries found that resources from all these donors appear disproportionately focused on treatment and care at the expense of prevention (Oomman *et al.*, 2007: p. xii). The context of the global treatment response has been identified as promoting a sort of "government by exception" in which it is "lives saved" that count for promoting human security, and these lives saved are directly linked to notions of "asymmetrical conflict" and a "global war on terrorism" (see Nguyen, 2009). For instance, "African lives" become especially important since saving African women and children with AIDS becomes an integral part of "product value" among Western consumers with the initiation of "brand aid." Brand aid is a practice whereby one can buy a co-branded Product (RED) item and a percentage of the profits will go to support The Global Fund (Richey and Ponte, 2011).

In the Ugandan context, the provision of ARVs has played a significant role in recent national governance strategies. In the early 1990s, Uganda had the highest documented HIV infection rate in the world. However, it is now well known that the country managed to slow progression of the epidemic through a series of aggressive interventions. Uganda's multi-sectoral approach to AIDS engaged various sectors of the state and civil society, and thus it resonated with international donor interest in decentralization, civil society and public-private partnerships. In 1995, Uganda was the first country in the world to register a decrease in the number of new HIV cases each year. HIV prevalence declined from around 30 percent in the early 1990s to under 10 percent a decade later. The combination of political leadership from President Museveni, strong non-governmental organizations (NGOs) such as the well-known TASO, and a growing pool of homegrown AIDS expertise has given Uganda an advantage in its prevention and treatment of HIV/AIDS. Uganda was one of the first nations in Africa to distribute ARVs at a reduced cost in 1998, and since then the ARV program has expanded to become one of the largest on the continent.

In contrast, South Africa, until recently, was known for its national policy of "denialism" about HIV/AIDS.[8] In brief, South Africa probably has more than five million people living with HIV/AIDS—the highest number of any country in the world.[9] The national government was notorious for its lack of leadership on AIDS issues. Former President Mbeki questioned the link between HIV and AIDS, accused scientists of racism, claimed that ARVs were poison, and supported regimes of African potatoes and garlic as good alternatives to ARVs for AIDS treatment (see Nattrass, 2004). In spite of the historically problematic national policy stance, South Africa hosts the world's largest program for providing ARVs to treat its citizens as a result of decentralized health governance and international donor support. Monitoring South Africa's public ARV program has involved confrontations between civil society and the national government, with provincial ministries playing on various sides (Richey, 2008b). An assessment of the roll-out of ARVs on the basis of data collected by the country's premier demographic model argues that "South Africa may have one of the largest HAART [AIDS treatment] programs, however, given its resource endowments, this program should be even bigger" (Nattrass, 2006: p. 3).

I draw on two case studies of AIDS treatment counseling from Uganda and South Africa to show how ARV treatment settings are gendered within the context of ARVs as semi-authoritarian technologies. The Ugandan data comes from participant observation and a series of exploratory interviews with ARV treatment counselors at Upendo[10] clinic in urban Kampala. The author and/or a research assistant conducted semi-structured interviews with all of the eight ARV counselors at the facility in 2008. Upendo clinic is one of sub-Saharan Africa's most successful ARV provision facilities, and a large recipient of international development aid to provide treatment. Upendo has been an important partner in demonstrating the successes of donor aid to AIDS treatment, and its leader has been featured in important media performances highlighting the US's global AIDS policy. In the beginning of the Ugandan ARV treatment roll-out, most patients coming to Upendo for treatment were men, as drugs were available only for those who could pay for them or were enrolled in research studies with drugs. After the scale-up of ARVs in which they are now offered for free, using support from international donors such as PEPFAR and The Global Fund, the majority of the patients coming for treatment are women.

The South African data comes from a vertically integrated, multi-sited ethnography of AIDS policy conducted during six months of fieldwork in 2005. Heshima clinic is located within the oldest township in the Western Cape, dating back to 1927. In many ways, Heshima clinic is a "best case scenario" for ARV treatment in South Africa. Unlike most treatment facilities, Heshima is an integrated clinic, where ARVs are distributed together with primary health services, including family planning, nutritional counseling and limited psychological services. The clinic is well managed and mostly protected from huge NGOs and their accountability demands in order to enable staff to conduct clinic work with minimal disruption. The site is also groomed to demonstrate success in an ongoing sub-regional political feud in the health sector. Heshima has an ideal staffing ratio,[11] shared leadership instead of a hierarchical model, and is not a research setting but an operational setting, according to the Regional Director responsible for the clinic. At the Heshima clinic, approximately 15 people on average are considered for placement on ARVs each week. There are more women than men.[12] Most of the women are mothers; some are pregnant. In the province, at least one third of all HIV tests are done on pregnant women in the MTCT program and the other two thirds of those testing for HIV also include mostly women.[13]

Despite the differences in the political, social and historical trajectories of the two countries, I am interested in how the Ugandan and South African cases of AIDS treatment are linked together by the primacy of social reproduction: the importance of forming families and the complications that this poses for adhering appropriately to a semi-authoritarian treatment regimen. In the early days of AIDS treatment in Africa, pregnancy was not permitted as part of AIDS treatment. Yet, of course, practitioners discovered that there was no practical way to prevent HIV positive women from becoming pregnant. The doctors negotiate the appropriate drug choices to try to match stated reproductive ambitions, but it is the counselors who must negotiate the social issues around the adherence demands of these semi-authoritarian technologies. Thus, the ARV treatment regimens themselves bring about a shift in the power dynamics involving the possible negotiations around reproductive choice.

Reproductive rights, non-directive counseling and maternal obligations

The analogy of the semi-authoritarian characteristics of combining liberal democracy with illiberal rules is observable with the provision of AIDS treatment at the local level. Questions of rights, reproductive decision making and "social issues" are negotiated within the practice of AIDS treatment counseling. Counseling for reproductive decision making has historically been characterized as "nondirective" counseling. "Nondirective counseling" was meant to be "a type of social work entirely for the benefit of the whole family without direct concern for its effect upon the state or politics" (Reed, 1974: p. 336, cited in Bayer, 1990: p. 184). Globally, the trend toward "nondirective" counseling can be traced to the new forms of social work that developed in the 1970s to support genetic counseling. These new counseling forms were purposefully elaborated as distinct from, and in opposition to, the legacy of eugenics that had lost political and social approbation after World War II. Thus, "nondirective counseling" was one of the core practices involved in producing the neoliberal subject who, rather than being counseled to make a decision according to the demands of the system, the counselor or the state, was instead viewed as an individual subject whose "free choice" was critical for the agency required to act on her own behalf.

Despite its discordance with the traditions of clinical medicine at that time, nondirective counseling quickly became the hegemonic discourse. It profoundly shaped notions of counseling in the context of both US national policy and practice and in international health arenas (Bayer, 1990: p. 185). I refer to the US national context here because it has been the global public health hegemon for decades, and particularly in relation to reproductive health and HIV/AIDS (see Sharpless, 1997; Richey, 2008a). In Western family planning discourses there are politically charged debates over the extent to which the individual woman is responsible for her own reproductive decisions. An individual, who is autonomous to varying extents, is assumed to make decisions and thus "control" her sexual behavior, her actions during fetal gestation and the outcome of her procreative process. While this centering of reproductive control on the female body seems "natural," there is no necessary link between procreative possibility and reproductive decision making (Richey, 2008a: p. 4).

The notion of nondirective counseling for genetic disorders coalesced nicely with the foundational elements of neoliberal individualism and Western, liberal feminism. These ideologies support the notion that women must be permitted to control their own reproductive lives. Such liberty required a strong ideological attachment to notions of individual choice. Thus, nondirective counseling which focused on providing individuals with the knowledge necessary to make informed choices about their health was the standard that was meant to apply to family planning counseling, and to some extent to counseling for HIV testing and, later, AIDS treatment.

However, the cozy consensus on liberal choice was shattered by the problem of vertical transmission of HIV. As a result, the terrain of individual choice within reproductive decision making was littered with ideological shrapnel: explosive issues—such as what should take precedence, the rights of the woman or those of the fetus—had to be reconsidered from a different perspective. The issue of vertical transmission was first addressed at the US Centers for Disease Control (CDC) in December 1985 and it was recommended that "Infected women should be advised to consider delaying pregnancy until more is known about perinatal transmission of the virus" (Bayer, 1990: p. 189). This statement represented a dramatic break from all previous "nondirective" endeavors to support individual choice in the reproductive, private realm and instead it applied standard public health norms. It also emphasized the links between individual choices and the effects of these choices on the human security of others, not just the individual self, for example, decisions impacting the well-being of the fetus and the larger community at risk of HIV infection. Bayer emphasizes that the tentative language used conveyed a less drastic impression of what was happening, as women were advised to "consider" the "delaying" of pregnancy; yet the preventive orientation actually required a fundamental curtailment of their reproductive lives (1990: pp. 190–191).

The official shift in discourse here was no doubt shaped by US public opinion, and it had global repercussions. The March of Dimes, a US charity established in 1938 to combat polio, had an explicit policy against directive (persuasive) counseling of women at risk for bearing children with birth defects. Yet, when HIV was the possible defect, the entire perspective changed. Children born with AIDS were constituted as fundamentally different than children born with other birth defects. A television spot in the US showed a baby-like marionette whose strings are cut by a pair of scissors, while an off-camera voice announced: "A baby born with AIDS is born dying" (Bayer, 1990: p. 195). What is important here is that HIV radically altered the notions of reproduction, shifting the locus of reproductive decision making from the private toward the public domain. The possibility of bearing an HIV positive child shifted notions of the individual woman as rights bearer in ways that no other disease, defect or disorder had done. The difficulty of guaranteeing human security for the African woman living with HIV in a gendered context that privileges childbearing, while simultaneously acknowledging the risks of vertical transmission of HIV, is an area where policy has been slow to follow practice.

Gender and ARV counseling for women in Uganda and South Africa

The creation of value and evaluation of quality in a numeric, juridical and individualistic way is part and parcel of the discourse on neoliberal modernity and development (see Richey, 2008a). Such a discourse ignores how planning one's family or controlling aspects of human reproduction may have multiple meanings and differing local histories. Yet, successful reproduction, or "modern family planning," cannot be understood in local terms that ignore the global circulation of technologies and the concepts that accompany them. While the discourse of activists surrounding issues of global treatment would lead us to believe that universal human rights to ARV provision or reproductive choice are upheld through global covenants, national policies and local treatment protocols, the reality is that the ethics of treatment are manifested in the quotidian workings of clinic life. The psycho-social service providers, whether patient advocates, adherence counselors or occasionally, ARV physicians, are left to negotiate the complex biopolitical imperatives of ARV technologies with the "social issues" of life in contemporary urban Africa. Healthy procreation by HIV positive parents is a central part of this dilemma. Without neglecting the importance of the strictly biomedical realm of treatment for AIDS, my discussion will center on what local service providers refer to as the "social issues" and how these constitute integral challenges in the treatment process.

Although it is theoretically possible to remove HIV from the process of reproduction (there are three established methods for removing HIV from seminal fluid or from nonspermatozoal cells called basic sperm wash, density gradient centrifugation and the "swim up" method), these assisted reproductive technologies are practically unheard of in African or other developing countries (Thornton *et al.*, 2004; Cooper *et al.*, 2007).[14] In the absence of these technologies, couples could time ovulatory intercourse, assuming the partners' viral loads are undetectable and their CD4 counts are under 400 (ibid.; Gilling-Smith *et al.*, 2006). This would produce the highest likelihood of conceiving a pregnancy with each act of unprotected intercourse and would reduce the likelihood of HIV reinfection if both partners have a low level of the virus active at the time of the unprotected sex. Unfortunately, information on ovulatory regulation and laboratory tests is not easily accessible to HIV positive people in Africa.

In interviews with South African and Ugandan counselors, we asked if clients became pregnant while on ARV treatment, and all counselors reported that this was common. One Ugandan counselor joked, "Very many! If you want a book, I can write it for you." When we asked if it was acceptable for women to fall pregnant when on AIDS treatment, most counselors agreed, but elaborated that certain conditions must be met. Overall, whether a woman on treatment is entitled to pregnancy depends on the counselor's perception of her needs and abilities. Some of the legitimate needs as described by counselors are if a woman has no living children; if she has only female children; if her husband is pressuring her to have a baby; or if she will feel psychologically unhappy if she does not have another baby. Moreover, the ability to actually carry a successful pregnancy is linked to a complex series of negotiations and management of the demands of the technology and the complications of daily life. The ARV technologies, like the family planning technologies before them, enter the domain of client-provider medical practices in which reproductive decisions must be controlled, managed and guided by medical professionals, supporting individual "choices" made by the women themselves. In the following discussion I will draw examples from South Africa and Uganda to illustrate how these negotiations manifest in AIDS treatment counseling.

When a woman is being "worked up" for ARV treatment, hard-working adherence counselors take patients alone or with their "treatment buddies" into one of the counseling bungalows and try to counsel them on how to negotiate the terrain of treatment. This can involve the dissemination of information, the management of concerns and fears, and the transmission of values within the counseling context. One example of this process of counseling women comes from women's negotiations around family planning while on ARV treatment that we observed at Heshima clinic in South Africa. A young couple from the Eastern Cape, Nancy and her husband came in for their second counseling session with the female adherence counselor. They had been living in an informal (shack) camp for "temporary" housing since 1999 and have a seven-year-old child who lives with his grandparents in their home region. Despite this, their child entitles them to state-funded child support. The adherence counselor explained to Nancy and her husband:

The drugs are not forced on people ... the reason why we don't push people on these drugs is because it is a lifetime commitment. You are both young, and maybe one day you will want children. If the girl wants the drugs then she will have to hear all about what she must know. She must take her drugs every day. The virus is so clever that if you skip one day the virus will build resistance. The drugs suppress the virus ... you're rebuilding your body and it becomes strong and the patient will live longer. These drugs we're going to give her are three different regimens: two you take twice a day and one at night. But if you decide that you want to have children, we will take out the one at night and replace it with Nevirapine.

But you must stay together. Talk together and come and sit down with the doctor so that you can have the chances explained. If you [referring to the husband] are HIV negative again then your chances are higher to get a child. You can be referred to a fertility clinic, and they will explain your chances of getting a child. Nancy has told the doctor that she doesn't need a baby now, so it's OK to start her on these three regimens. She cannot fall pregnant taking Stavodine because it can affect the pregnancy. This is why she is supposed to use contraceptives. If she becomes pregnant, the child won't be normal.

Here, the counselor distinguishes that ARVs are not authoritarian—they are not "forced on people"—but that the treatments require a "lifetime commitment" from which there is no deviation. ARV treatment success requires choice, commitment, spousal communication and control of a woman's fertility. Implicitly, it is recognized that a healthy child could be the potential reward for such well-regulated reproductive decision making.

Similarly, in Uganda, a counselor explained how they have shifted from prohibition to pragmatism in counseling women for reproduction while on ARV treatment. She stated:

To get a child is a right of every woman. So long as you are mature, there is no way that you can prevent that right. However, we encourage them to see their doctor first before they get pregnant to see how is the viral load and the CD4 count, and can she maintain that pregnancy. ... If only both the husband and wife can come in together to see the doctor so that he can advise them.

In examples from both clinics, the meaning that ARV treatment provides to couples is that they can resume their lives, and in doing so, reproduction will mark success.

But the gendered negotiations around pregnancy involve more than just agreement between husbands and wives and their counselors and doctors. Linkages between local reproductive decision making and global discourses of procreative possibility are constructed in the following example. Pregnant, young Thandi came in for her second counseling session with the male adherence counselor, bringing her mother to act as her "treatment buddy" in hopes of getting quickly on ARVs to treat her own disease and protect her unborn baby. After explaining the virus and the drugs, the counselor advised Thandi's mother:

She can come for the PMTCT program so that the virus can be suppressed. The virus is in the blood so a child can be infected during pregnancy, labor and breastfeeding, so these drugs, they're made to prevent that. The results are positive so the Americans said, "So if this is working, why don't they give everyone the drugs so that the mother can raise her child on her own. At the same time, the English people said that this is good, now you are preventing [HIV in] the mother and child, but what about their fathers?" So in England they introduced these drugs to everybody, so now everyone can have a prolonged life.

The preceding quotation illustrates the central place of the pregnant woman in the global notion of security and regeneration (see Fadlalla, 2007). The notion is that increasing access to treatment begins with the pregnant African woman and then extends to her family, and ultimately to larger local bodies and global allies. The counselor's explicit linking of the drugs with international support may have been an attempt to reduce their stigma and build their associated credibility. Indeed, my own presence as a foreign observer in the room may have provided a silent complicity. It also provides an example of the external-orientation of the ARV program specifically and the Western Cape health department in general (see Richey, 2008b). When the national government cannot be counted on to support the ARV program, foreign alliances are constructed within the viable discourses of cost-effective childraising by poor African women.

The counselor continued to explain to Thandi and her mother, acting as "treatment partner," the regimen of childbearing on ARVs:

> Let's say you don't want only one baby, and maybe you'll get married. These days you must suppress the virus so if you want another baby and your CD4 count is high [you can have one]. The first few months when we start treatment, we will draw blood to see the progress of the virus in your body. If the CD4 is greater than 450 and the virus is suppressed, then you can have another baby. If the CD4 is over 450, the virus is undetectable, and the chances of the baby being affected are slim. It depends on your partner. If he is also positive and has a suppressed virus, then the doctor will agree that you can have another baby. Now your CD4 count is low, and after this baby is born you can go for contraception. Afterward you must use condoms all the time. You are on treatment and your boyfriend is not, so if you don't use a condom he will need treatment and your drugs won't do. It is dangerous to sleep with somebody not on treatment. We say to use condoms because the contraception is not 100% safe. Sometimes a condom can be torn, then you must also be using contraception—maybe Petogen or Depo Provera.[15] We always say to use contraception and condoms both. When you need another baby and both you and your partner have the virus undetectable then the doctor will arrange for you for that. This doesn't mean that if you are HIV positive you can't get a child, but if your CD4 is high we must protect the child.

The drugs themselves are conceived as semi-authoritarian technologies that bind together husbands, wives and doctors. The previous explanation by the counselor illustrates many of the complexities of reproducing while on ARVs. The use of conditional language, "if, then" implies a management strategy and a controllable outcome. *If*, both parties are able to manage their sexual encounters and their viruses, *then* they have the chance of achieving a healthy child. The clinic team is there to help protect the potential child through management of the virus. However, the corporeal sign, drawn through the blood, will tell if a patient can reproduce or not. Furthermore, the regime of recommended reproduction is quite complicated, using dual method protection of condoms and contraceptive injections, and it is made more so in the context of the patients' "social issues." In the lives of many of the clinic's clients, pregnancy is not necessarily the outcome of "choice," much less "planning." We are confronted by the paradox that the drugs that make "normal" life possible for HIV positive Africans by allowing them to reproduce, also threaten to produce an abnormal pregnancy through complications of the drug interactions.

In the counseling session described, after the extensive explanation of the possibility that she might want another child in the future, Thandi astutely ruptured the protocol discussing future possibilities. She interjected with her concerns for her immediate situation, as she herself was on ARV treatment and was already pregnant. Thandi asked the counselor: "Are those pills not going to cause any problems for my baby [currently in utero]?" While the professional counselor had been quite effectively explaining the protocol of how a woman on ARVs might continue with a "normal" reproductive life, the patient's response signals a pragmatism that brings forth the gendered contradictions in treatment. The protocols for planning between the counselor and the client are based on forethought, evidence-based planning and meticulous control of reproductive decision making. As such, the protocols are not necessarily relevant for the woman who finds herself pregnant with a low viral load and needs ARVs for the treatment of her own virus—and in addition for the vertical transmission of HIV to her child.

Discourses of liberal individualism, choice-making and reproductive rights frame the medical policies and practices at the clinics where I worked. Yet, at Heshima clinic, a doctor, expressing critical self-reflexivity, stated at a meeting that one of the patients had "just started on contraception two weeks before, because we forced her."[16] Others are described as "being on family planning specifically for the ARVs." In Uganda, counselors reported that the most difficult challenge facing their work was the negotiation of the complex "social issues" involving socio-economic problems of their poor clients. Counselors elaborated that these issues involved socio-economic problems, orphans, discordant couples and pregnant clients. Together with these "social issues," women on ARVs must add the dual possibility and complexity of an AIDS infected baby and one with birth defects attributable to the mother's treatment regime. ARV treatment further complicates the negotiating logics for realizing reproductive choice, a process that is already entangled by poverty and fertility desires.

The levels of both inequality and poverty in South Africa and Uganda present particular challenges for providing and receiving health care for AIDS. Smith and Mbakwem articulate clearly how "the drugs themselves, so valued for their physical effects, are reminders of the enduring difficulties and discrimination associated with HIV/AIDS" (2007: p. 24). Gendered relations of struggle and blame shape the way that these semi-authoritarian technologies are governed. The founder of one of South Africa's largest AIDS clinics summarized that "All programs are focused on the 'oppressed' and the 'innocent' ... all our programs are focused on women and children, men are guilty ... men are the perpetrators"

(Casey, 2005: p. 50). Within such a context, the technologies themselves are reminders of many levels of inequalities and the need to revisit constructions of human security that foster a neoliberal model of HIV/AIDS counseling and treatment at the expense of a deeper analysis of the root causes of these inequalities.

Conclusions

Treatment counselors provide most, if not all, of the non-medical assurance of ARV treatment success in the clinics of this study. With economic pressure for more task-shifting in which a greater number of responsibilities will be passed down to lesser-trained service providers to ease the impact of AIDS treatment on the health care system, this burden will become heavier. There are ongoing challenges in areas of poverty alleviation and gender relations that fall out of traditional public health interventions. As individuals are working through the processes of AIDS treatment, and counselors are expected to help women to become effective managers of their own bodies, viruses and fertility, the professional boundaries of counseling become difficult to maintain when medical and social needs intertwine. Clients request out-of-system support from their counselors, and counselors must respond to pleas for loans and gifts. Couples with discordant HIV status request help for dealing with stigma and with pregnancy. Local respondents insist that clear and pragmatic policies are needed on ARVs and pregnancy. Many of the issues raised are not part of the current constitution of medical treatment of AIDS, but exist elsewhere and are addressed through the piecemeal allocation of services by NGOs. Therefore, examples like nutritional support or psychological counseling may be critical for negotiating the realities of lifetime AIDS treatment, but they are not part of the ARV program. Thus, appropriate referral systems and institutions are necessary for handling the "social issues" of both Ugandans and South Africans living with AIDS. This would involve significantly more coordination and structure than the existing disparate interventions of NGOs and projects that underpin neoliberal development interventions.

The local provision of ARVs in Africa must be understood within the context of the global securitization of AIDS. Stefan Elbe (2006) opened the debate on the ethical dilemmas of the securitization of AIDS, which was taken further by O'Manique (2004) and others, but these debates underplay the local level of gender complexity surrounding biological and social survival. As Michael Williams (2003) argues, any issue can be "securitized ... if it can be intensified to the point where it is presented and accepted as an existential threat" (p. 516). This sort of securitization theory draws on classical realism's preoccupation with survival—the need for security, extreme necessity and essentialist threat (i.e., Muller, 2004: p. 283). ARV treatment comes sequentially after a large-scale creation of understanding by AIDS activists that HIV is a virus that will inevitably lead to AIDS, a deadly disease. Thus, decades of successful activism beginning in the US West Coast context and then expanding into what would become known as "global AIDS" (see Patton, 2002) had the unforeseen consequence of

opening up the possibility of securitizing AIDS. For AIDS to have become securitized, and for treatment to have been focused on survival, there had to have
been the precondition that HIV was a virus that led to AIDS and that AIDS
would lead to death. Hence, understanding the necessary precondition for constructing HIV as a "security threat," an existential threat to survival, helps to
explain why this premise was critical. Thus, the issues of the securitization of
AIDS helps to explain the magnitude of the polemics over any question of
whether HIV leads to AIDS which leads to death (i.e., Mbeki's denialism, see
Nattrass, 2006; Fassin, 2007; Richey, 2008a, etc.). If HIV did not lead to AIDS
and then to death, then AIDS would not be a legitimate threat to global security.

In order to understand the quotation that introduced this chapter, which suggests that AIDS exists at the absolute center of human security, we must consider the global and local negotiations around the social meaning of the drugs.
Susan Whyte has argued that ARVs are technologies of "popular exceptional-
ism" in the Ugandan context: the pills are more valuable, not used presumptively
for a variety of problems, under the guise of secrecy and confidentiality, and
kept in the home as precious objects. Unlike other medicines in Uganda, ARVs
possess singularity because they are used as part of a ritual framework. She
quotes one of her Ugandan informants who explained: "These meds have
rules!"[17] Furthermore, as this chapter has argued, "the rules" of ARVs are
embedded in gendered relations of power that treat African women's bodies as
the center of social and political debate about their efficacy and securitization.

Perhaps, ARVs as semi-authoritarian technologies in a postcolonial context
are part of a larger welfare technology with rules that allow for the administration and efficacy of ARVs on a large scale. At the same time, these rules also
regulate subject agency to fit a local and global biopolitical frame, lacking in any
inherently participatory compulsion. Thus, because the rules of ARVs are not
made up through local consultation, this set of rules does not, for the most part,
reflect the voices or perspectives of the African women who must depend on the
drugs for their physical survival and who negotiate the ARV technologies for
fertility and social survival. If this is the case, then we might argue that ARV
technologies fit well into Chatterjee's model of popular sovereignty in which

> the proliferation of modern state security and welfare technologies to meet
> these particular demands has created governmental bodies that administer
> populations but do not provide citizens with an arena for democratic delib-
> eration ... one in which democratic politics is shaped by governmentality.
>
> (Chatterjee, 2004: p. 4)

Clinic level data reminds us that it is worth explicit research consideration
that women with AIDS do get pregnant, whether the women are on treatment or
not. Most HIV positive Ugandans and South Africans report wanting children
for the same reasons that people without the disease want to have children: to
continue the family lineage, to have a child of a specific sex, and because they
do not have children already. There are now some policies and programs in place

to help with family planning integration, but these are primarily focusing on preventing pregnancy. For those who want children, counselors must refer to their own pragmatism without the guidance, support or backstopping of policy. As AIDS treatment is consolidated in developing countries, more attention is needed to how mothers and their children negotiate AIDS care and how those on ARV treatment negotiate motherhood. To do this we need a much better understanding of how their maneuvers can become less restricted by the limitations of semi-authoritarian technologies in contexts of poverty and the gendered expectations of being a good woman or a good man. Pregnancy prevention, reproductive ambition, and possible care and treatment of mothers and their children are integral parts of negotiating these semi-authoritarian technologies in gendered contexts.

Notes

1 However, I will not deal explicitly with the multiple issues of gender and power that make some individuals more susceptible than others to the HIV virus.
2 The term "mother-to-child transmission" is obviously problematic and epitomizes the discursive focus on motherhood, and the mother's ultimate failure to protect her child from harm by transmitting her own disease to an innocent victim. Unless I am referring to other discourses, I use the term "vertical transmission" in this paper to redirect the concept toward the actual process of viral transmission, not the responsible or irresponsible agents. The PMTCT program will be referred to by its name.
3 Although it is critical to reiterate that there are vast differences between regions in the provision and uptake of the PMTCT program, with the least-advantaged regions having the worst access and service provision.
4 Again, it is important to reiterate that most HIV-positive mothers in Africa are not on ARVs, as these services remain out of reach for most Africans who need them.
5 PMTCT ("prevention of mother-to-child transmission") interventions have focused on identifying women with HIV infection and then providing them with ARV prophylaxis to prevent the vertical transmission of the virus to the child in utero or during delivery.
6 From Department of Health interview 1, 8 September 2005.
7 Fareed Abdullah seminar held at the University of Cape Town, 23 September 2005.
8 The South African government's position on AIDS has reached the level of global caricature—the *New York Times* reports on "deadly quackery" (Moore and Nattrass, 2006); the *New Yorker* writes about "The Denialists" (Specter, 2007) and the *Financial Times* refers simply to the "chaos within" (Barber and Russell, 2007).
9 The HIV prevalence statistics are notoriously contentious; reputable statistics from different sources vary by more than a million people in their estimates of the number of South Africans living with HIV.
10 All names of individuals and clinics are pseudonyms.
11 There were four doctors working on site for most of the months I was working at the clinic.
12 Physicians interviewed in Cape Town estimated that at least 70–80 percent of their ARV patients were women because men do not come forward to receive treatment (Casey, 2005: p. 48).
13 Notes from Fareed Abdullah lecture, University of Cape Town, 23 September 2005; see also Abdullah, 2004.
14 Assisted reproductive technologies that can increase the likelihood of healthy reproduction for Africans living with AIDS made it into the newspapers, if not the clinics

in Kenya. Local papers reported the story of the "historic achievement of In Vitro fertilization" where it is now possible to "wash a man's sperm to rid it of the HIV virus before fusing it with a fertile embryo and implanting it in a womb" (*The East African Standard*, 11 May 2006).
15 Both are injectable family planning methods that provide contraceptive protection for 12 weeks.
16 Field notes 20 October 2005.
17 From a presentation at the Working Group on the Social and Political Aspects of AIDS Workshop, Kampala, Uganda, 4 January 2008.

Bibliography

Abdullah, Fareed. (2004) The Complexities of Implementing Antiretroviral Treatment in the Western Cape Province of South Africa. *Development Update: From Disaster to Development: HIV and AIDS in Southern Africa*, December; 5(3), pp. 245–264.

Bancroft, A. (2001) Globalisation and HIV/AIDS: Inequality and the Boundaries of a Symbolic Epidemic. *Health, Risk and Society*, 3(1), pp. 89–98.

Barber, Lionel and Alec Russell. (2007) Mbeki Seeks Ways to Limit Chaos to the North and Within. *Financial Times*, Comment and analysis, 2 April 2007.

Bayer, R. (1990) AIDS and the Future of Reproductive Freedom. *The Milbank Quarterly*, 68(Suppl. 2), pp. 179–204.

Best, K. (2004) Family Planning and the Prevention of Mother-to-child Transmission of HIV: A Review of the Literature. Family Health International Working Paper Series. Research Triangle Park, NC: Family Health International.

Bledsoe, C. H. (2002). *Contingent Lives: Fertility, Time and Aging in West Africa*. Chicago and London: University of Chicago Press.

Casey, Sean. (2005) Providing Highly Active Antiretroviral Therapy in Cape Town, South Africa: An Interview-based Case Study of Social Challenges to Treatment Provision. Masters Thesis, Faculty of the Humanities, Master of Philosophy in HIV/AIDS and Society. University of Cape Town. November.

Chatterjee, Partha. (2004) *The Politics of the Governed: Popular Politics in Most of the World*. New York: Columbia University Press.

Cooper, D., J. Harries, L. Myer, P. Orner, H. Bracken and V. Zweigenthal. (2007) "Life Is Still Going On": Reproductive Intentions Among HIV-positive Women and Men in South Africa. *Soc.Sci.Med*, Jul; 65(2), pp. 274–283.

De Bruyn, M. (2004). Living with HIV: Challenges in Reproductive Health Care in South Africa. *African Journal of Reproductive Health*, 8(1), pp. 92–98.

De Bruyn, M. (2005) *Reproductive Rights for Women Affected by HIV/AIDS: A Project to Monitor Millennium Development Goals 5 and 6*. Chapel Hill, NC: Ipas.

Elbe, Stefan. (2006) Should HIV/AIDS be Securitized? The Ethical Dilemmas of Linking HIV/AIDS and Security. *International Studies Quarterly*, Mar; 50(1), pp. 119–144.

Fadlalla, Amal. (2007) *Embodying Honor: Fertility, Foreignness, and Regeneration in Eastern Sudan*. Madison, WI: University of Wisconsin Press.

Fassin, Didier. (2007) *When Bodies Remember: Experiences and Politics of AIDS in South Africa*. Berkeley: University of California Press.

Gilling-Smith, C., J. D. Nicopoullos, A. E. Semprini and L. C. Frodsham. (2006) HIV and Reproductive Care—A Review of Current Practice. *BJOG: An International Journal of Obstetrics and Gynaecology*, Aug; 113(8), pp. 869–878.

Glenn, E. N., G. Chang and L. Rennie Forcey, eds. (1994) *Mothering: Ideology, Experience and Agency*. New York and London: Routledge.

Graff, A. (2001) *A World Without Women: Gender in Polish Public Life.* Warsaw: W. A. B. Publishers.

Greenlaugh, S. (1995) Anthropology Theorizes Reproduction: Integrating Practice, Political Economic, and Feminist Perspectives. In: S. Greenhalgh, ed. *Situating Fertility: Anthropology and Demographic Inquiry.* Cambridge: Cambridge University Press, pp. 3–28.

Holc, J. P. (2004) The Purest Democrat: Fetal Citizenship and Subjectivity in the Construction of Democracy in Poland. *Signs: Journal of Women in Culture and Society,* 29, pp. 755–782.

Johnson-Hanks, J. (2002) On the Modernity of Traditional Contraception: Time and the Social Context of Fertility. *Population and Development Review,* June; 28(2), pp. 229–249.

Kitzinger, J. and D. Miller. (1992) "African AIDS": the Media and Audience Beliefs. In: P. Aggleton, P. Davies and G. Hart, eds. *AIDS: Rights, Risk and Reason.* London: Falmer Press, pp. 28–52.

Lock, M. and N. Scheper-Hughes. (1996) A Critical-Interpretive Approach in Medical Anthropology: Rituals and Routines of Discipline and Dissent. In: C. F. Sargent and T. M. Johnson, eds. *Medical Anthropology: Contemporary Theory and Method, Revised Edition.* Westport, CT and London: Praeger, pp. 21–40.

McIntyre, J. (2005) Maternal Health and HIV. *Reproductive Health Matters,* 13(25), pp. 129–135.

Moore, John and Nicoli Nattrass. (2006) AIDS and South Africa: Deadly Quackery. *The New York Times,* Sunday 4 June 2006.

Muller, Benjamin J. (2004) (Dis)qualified Bodies: Securitization, Citizenship and Identity Management. *Citizenship Studies,* Sept; 8(3), pp. 279–294.

Myer, L., C. Morroni and K. Rebe. (2007) Prevalence and Determinants of Fertility Intentions of HIV-infected Women and Men Receiving Antiretroviral Therapy in South Africa. *AIDS Patient Care STDS,* Apr; 21(4), pp. 278–285.

Nattrass, Nicoli. (2004) *The Moral Economy of AIDS in South Africa.* Cambridge: Cambridge University Press.

Nattrass, Nicoli. (2006) South Africa's "Roll-out" of Highly Active Antiretroviral Therapy: A Critical Assessment. Centre for Social Science Research Working Paper, no. 158. CSSR: Cape Town, South Africa.

Nguyen, V. K. (2009) Government-by-exception: Enrolment and Experimentality in Mass HIV Treatment Programmes in Africa. *Social Theory and Health,* 7(3), pp. 196–217.

O'Manique, C. (2004) *Neoliberalism and AIDS Crisis in Sub-Saharan Africa: Globalization's Pandemic.* Basingstoke: Palgrave-MacMillan.

Oomman, N., M. Bernstein and S. Rosenzweig. (2007) Following the Funding for HIV/AIDS: A Comparative Analysis of the Funding Practices of PEPFAR. The Global Fund and World Bank MAP in Mozambique, Uganda and Zambia: HIV/AIDS Monitor and Center for Global Development.

Palmer, S., V. Boltz, N. Martinson, F. Maldarelli, G. Gray, J. McIntyre, J. Mellors, L. Morris and J. Coffin. (2006) Persistance of Nevirapine-resistant HIV-1 in Women After Single Dose Nevirapine Therapy for Prevention of Maternal-to-fetal HIV-1 Transmission. *PNAS,* 2 May; 103(18), pp. 7094–7099.

Patton, Cindy. (2002) *Globalizing AIDS.* Minneapolis and London: University of Minnesota Press.

Piot, Peter. (2006) Diverse Voices, Common Ground: Uniting the World Against AIDS, 7 March 2006, Georgetown University, Available at: http://data.unaids.org/pub/

SpeechEXD/2006/20060307_sp_piot_georgetownuniversity_en.pdf   [accessed   21 October 2011].

Preble, E., D. Huber and E. Piwoz. (2003) *Family Planning and the Prevention of Mother-to-Child Transmission of HIV: Technical and Programmatic Issues*. Arlington, VA: Advance Africa Project. Management Sciences for Health.

Rauscher, Megan. (2006) Persistence of Nevirapine Resistance After Single Dose Underestimated. Reuters Health Information, New York. (Online) 28 April 2006. Available at: www.pronutrition.org/archive/200605/msg00003.php [accessed 20 October 2011].

Reed, S. (1974) A Short History of Genetic Counseling. *Social Biology*, 21(4), pp. 331–339.

Richey, Lisa Ann. (2008a) *Population Politics and Development: From the Policies to the Clinics*. New York and London: Palgrave MacMillan.

Richey, Lisa Ann. (2008b) "Boundary Work" in the Provision of AIDS Treatment in South Africa: Science, Denial and Politics. *New Political Science*, 30(1), pp. 1–21.

Richey, Lisa Ann. (2011) Gendering the Therapeutic Citizen. In: Carole H. Browner and Carolyn F. Sargent, eds. *Reproduction, Globalization and the State*. Durham, NC: Duke University Press, pp. 68–82.

Richey, Lisa Ann and Stefano Ponte. (2011) *Brand Aid: Shopping Well to Save the World*. Minneapolis, MN: University of Minnesota Press.

Sharpless, J. (1997) Population Science, Private Foundations, and Development Aid: The Transformation of Demographic Knowledge in the United States, 1945–1965. In: F. Cooper and R. Packard, eds. *International Development and the Social Sciences*. Berkeley: University of California Press, pp. 176–200.

Shelton, J. D. and E. A. Peterson. (2004) The Imperative for Family Planning in ART Therapy in Africa. *The Lancet*, November27–December 3; 364(9449), pp. 1916–1918.

Smith, D. J. and B. C. Mbakwem. (2007) Life Projects and Therapeutic Itineraries: Marriage, Fertility, and Antiretroviral Therapy in Nigeria. *AIDS*, 21(Suppl. 5), pp. S37–S41.

Specter, Michael. (2007) The Denialists. *The New Yorker*, 83(3), pp. 32–38.

Stillwaggon, E. (2003) Racial Metaphors: Interpreting Sex and AIDS in Africa. *Development and Change*, 34(5), pp. 809–832.

Tamale, Sylvia (2009) Law, Sexuality and Politics in Uganda: Challenges for Women's Human Rights NGOs. In: Mutua Makau, ed. *Human Rights NGOs in East Africa: Political and Normative Tensions*. Philadelphia: University of Pennsylvania Press, pp. 51–74.

Thornton, A. C., F. Romanelli and J. D. Collins. (2004) Reproduction Decision Making for Couples Affected by HIV: A Review of the Literature. *Top HIV Med.*, May–June; 12(2), pp. 61–67.

Tilly, C. (1999). Survey Article: Power—Top Down and Bottom Up. *The Journal of Political Philosophy*, 7(3), pp. 330–352.

Tripp, Aili Mari. (2004). The Changing Face of Authoritarianism in Africa: The Case of Uganda. *Africa Today*, 50(3), pp. 3–28.

UNAIDS. (2008) *Report on the Global HIV/AIDS Epidemic 2008*. Geneva: UNAIDS.

United Nations Global Compact Learning Forum. (2008) Instituting a Whistleblower Policy in the Global Fund to Fight Aids, Tuberculosis and Malaria. In: *Business Fighting Corruption: Experiences from Africa Case Study Series*. South Africa: Pretoria, pp. 35–57. (Online) Available at: www.unglobalcompact.org/docs/news_events/8.1/bfc_web.pdf [accessed 20 October 2011].

US State Department. (n.d.) The United States President's Emergency Plan for AIDS

Relief. (Online) 7 January 2011. Available at: www.pepfar.gov/ [accessed 20 October 2011].

The United States President's Emergency Plan for AIDS Relief. (2009) World AIDS Day 2009: Latest PEPFAR Results. Available at: www.pepfar.gov/documents/organiza-tion/133033.pdf [accessed 20 October 2011].

Williams, M. C. (2003) Words, Images, Enemies: Securitization and International Politics. *International Studies Quarterly*, 47, pp. 511–531.

3   Whose human security?

Gender, neoliberalism and the informal economy in sub-Saharan Africa

Zo Randriamaro

The concept of human security has been the subject of extensive debates in academic and policy circles since the publication of the 1994 *Human Development Report* by the United Nations Development Program (UNDP, 1994) that championed the idea that human beings must be at the center of security concerns. At the international development policy level, 2003 also marked a significant milestone with the report of the Commission on Human Security established by the United Nations in 2001. The report was in response to the United Nations Secretary-General's call at the 2000 Millennium Summit for a world free of "deprivation," "want" and "fear." This report sought to re-conceptualize human security by shifting the agenda from the security of nation-states to the security of people, and affirming the connections between the protection of human rights, economic justice, environmental integrity and human development.

Six years after the publication of this report, however, ample evidence suggests that governments and accountable institutions at the national and international levels have tended to misuse the concept of security by paying little attention to economic justice, human rights and environmental integrity. Thus, millions of people in sub-Saharan Africa (SSA) and elsewhere are not free from the fear generated by war and conflicts. The recent food crisis was a dramatic reminder that millions of people in SSA are not free from hunger and want, and that the food price hikes have pushed an estimated 30 million additional persons into poverty (World Bank, 2008: p. 4). Feminist activists and gender equality advocates have underscored that even before the recent food crisis, women made up 60 percent of the chronically hungry in spite of their central role in agricultural production (Food and Agriculture Organization of the United Nations [FAO], 2006).

Based on my experience of more than a decade of engagement with gender and economic policy issues as both an activist and a professional with international organizations in Africa, I argue here that the human security perspective overlooked significant gender issues pertaining to the socio-economic well-being of sub-Saharan African (SSA) countries. The widespread tendency to treat the diverse SSA countries as one region has made matters worse at the policy level by institutionalizing "one-size-fits-all" neoliberal economic policy prescriptions and approaches imposed by international financial institutions on most indebted African countries.

Although the notion of security has been redefined as a new concept that counters nationalist and militarist interpretations, it remains a male-centered view of security, which has failed to deal with the security issues in women's lives. In SSA, these insecurities include the persistence of violence against women in both private and public spheres that includes unabated domestic and gender-based violence; the lack of sexual and reproductive rights; and economic violence, which is manifested in the continuing violation of women's economic rights. The ways in which such insecurities affect women are exemplified by the increasing or stagnant maternal mortality rates in most SSA countries, the feminization of poverty and the HIV/AIDS pandemic.

Another important feature of the new human security concept is that it seeks to build on and enhance human rights and development frameworks. As such, it locates the human security agenda within prevailing development frameworks, that is, the neoliberal framework, which has been a key factor in increasing poverty and inequalities between and within countries, as well as along class and gender lines (a discussion surrounding the definition and interpretations of "neoliberalism" will follow in the next section). Moreover, the human security concept is affected by the limitations of the human rights framework, due to the liberal tradition that it has inherited.

With regard to SSA countries, the major problem with this liberal legacy is the failure to address economic powerlessness in all its dimensions, particularly in relation to capitalism, colonialism and imperialism. As noted by Makau Mutua,

> the UDHR—the single most important human rights document— sanctions the right to private property. How plausible is a document that calls itself a "common standard of achievement for all peoples and all nations" if it does not recognize that at its writing the bulk of the global South was under European colonial rule and subject to the vilest economic exploitation by the merchants of capital?
>
> (Mutua, 2008: p. 1031)

In addition to the neglect of colonial and postcolonial realities by the human rights framework, the same author also underscores that the UDHR overlooks the cultural norms underlying ideas of group and community rights in the different postcolonial States.

Indeed, with respect to women's rights, the universal language of human rights has been unable to account for the gender-based prejudices and exploitation that women had suffered under the colonial and postcolonial regimes, and that they continue to suffer in different forms under the neoliberal globalization process. The patriarchal norms and traditional values underpinning this prejudice and exploitation are deeply entrenched at the community level, such that the recognition of group and community rights suggested by Makau Mutua would not automatically enhance women's rights.

In this regard, it is important to note that the language of human rights has been used effectively by women to challenge patriarchal norms and structures, resulting in the notable example of the adoption of the Protocol to the African Charter on Human and Peoples' Rights on the Rights of Women in Africa by the African Union Member States. The protocol, which became effective in 2005, has led to significant legislative developments for the protection and fulfillment of women's rights. The International Convention on the Elimination of All Forms of Discrimination against Women (CEDAW) has been ratified by 51 African countries and its provisions have been the basis for judicial decisions at the national level in countries like Botswana (Social Watch, 2010).

Most importantly, women's rights are about their freedom, influence and dignity, all of which are an integral part of their well-being. These issues deserve attention in their own right. Freedom, influence and dignity are key elements of women's status as citizens, defining their agency and capacity for collective action, as well as the way in which women relate to state and social structures.

The first part of this chapter discusses the concept of human security in the neoliberal framework and the impacts of neoliberalism on human security and development in SSA. The second part deals with the gendered impacts of neoliberalism on a "women's empowerment paradigm" and the informal economy. The last part focuses on some emerging issues that affect gender relations and women's livelihoods in the context of the crisis of neoliberal globalization, and points to the changes that should happen in respect to human security and women's rights in SSA.

Human security and neoliberalism in sub-Saharan Africa

The term "neoliberalism" used in this article refers to the set of neo-classical economic policies—also dubbed the Washington Consensus[1]—that became predominant at the global level since the 1980s, owing to the political alliances between the conservative governments in the US and Western Europe (George, 1999; Robbins, 1999). In economic terms, neoliberalism is essentially about the removal of all potential barriers[2] to allow for the free movement of goods, services, resources and enterprises to maximize profits and efficiency under the rule of the self-regulating market, with minimal interference by the state. Typically, neoliberal economic policies include macroeconomic stabilization (reduction of fiscal deficits, tax reform, market-based interest and exchange rates). Neoliberal economic policy also includes deregulation, the reduction of public expenditure for social services, privatization of state enterprises, securitization of property rights, liberalization and financialization of capital, and trade liberalization (Williamson, 1990; Martinez and Garcia, 2000).

Neoliberalism is also a political project that seeks to establish the primacy of market forces not only in the economic realm, but also in social life. As such, it aims to promote a market society through an ideology that privileges and supports specific social elites that control the market economy. As Pierre Bourdieu put it, the neoliberal program draws its social power from the political and economic power of those whose interests it expresses: stockholders, financial operators, industrialists, conservative or social-democratic politicians who have been converted to the reassuring layoffs of laissez-faire, high-level financial officials eager to impose policies advocating their own extinction because, unlike the managers of firms, they run no risk of having eventually to pay the consequences.

(Bourdieu, 1998)

The attitudes, ethics and culture of these social elites have greatly influenced neoliberalism. This is particularly so in American culture and, as I further discuss in the next section, in the context of the anti-poverty agenda and the rise of the poverty research industry.

In Africa, the history of neoliberal policies began around the mid-1970s, when a deepening socio-economic crisis confronted independent African states. This context of socio-economic turmoil called into question the sustainability of the dominant import substitution industrialization (ISI) development strategy that had been implemented in various forms[3] by African countries in the 1960–70 period in order to transform their economic structures. The implementation of this ISI strategy led to huge investments in socio-economic infrastructure, education and import-substitution programs to build the foundation for what is today the industrial sector in most African countries (Mkandawire and Soludo, 2003).

Most African governments, however, depended on revenues from a limited number of primary commodity exports and lacked the revenue base, including foreign exchange reserves, for the effective implementation of their development strategy. In addition, the continued economic dependence of postcolonial African states on the former colonial powers meant that

multinational firms extracted profitable concessions from fledgling African governments and continued to repatriate their profits, leaving relatively little surplus capital for national investment ... as much as 80 percent of loan funds are estimated to have remained in the hands of Western suppliers of capital goods, management and technical assistance.

(Schoepf *et al.*, 2000: p. 97)

This triggered the need for African governments to borrow heavily from international financial institutions as well as Western private banks. This in turn brought about soaring external debt. Externally, the increase in African foreign debt had been encouraged by the low interest rates applied by Western banks that needed to increase lending from the inflows of petro-dollars generated by oil price hikes.

In most African countries, this ISI development model was accompanied by the so-called economic nationalism approach, whereby the involvement of the state in major economic activities[4] was seen as a means to accelerate economic development. In the absence of a significant domestic private sector, the state ensured control over the economy through different processes of nationalization and regulation. In political terms, this approach translated into top-down and urban-biased policy processes through which the emerging political elite often subordinated national development goals to serve their own economic interests and to maintain their political survival, including through ethnic loyalty. In spite of the fact that the ISI has generally raised the living standards of citizens, it has been argued that its implementation has failed the agricultural sector, and further pauperized the rural and urban informal sector in several countries (Befekadu, 1994, and Olofin, 1995, cited by Mkandawire and Soludo, 2003).

Thus, the African transformation strategy relied heavily on flows of external financial assistance, mainly in the form of loans, private investment and aid, which marginalized the rural population. By the end of the 1970s, the results were stagnating income and productivity growth that did not outpace population growth, declining export market shares, deteriorating terms of trade, and chronic fiscal and external deficits. Combined with massive foreign debt, this situation paved the way for the structural adjustment of ailing African economies by Western institutions and the subsequent imposition of the neoliberal development paradigm.

As mentioned earlier, the neoliberal model for development emphasizes the promotion of a market-driven system along with the reduction of the role of the state in the management of the economy. It is based on a "consensus" that reflects the hegemonic influence exercised by powerful Western countries and the international financial and economic institutions which they control. The main components of the standard neoliberal policy package include export promotion on the basis of comparative advantage and currency devaluation to make exports more competitive. It also includes removal of subsidies to small subsistence producers, reduction or elimination of tariffs for the protection of domestic production, removal of price and capital controls, deregulation and liberalization of investment, together with tax incentives to attract foreign investors, privatization of public assets and services, cost recovery through user fees for health and education services, public sector reforms, mainly reduction of the civil service and public expenditure, reduction of labor protection and the flexibility of the labor force.

Thus, the economic, social and political landscape in SSA has been shaped by Structural Adjustment Programs, which have been the main instruments involved in the imposition of the neoliberal development model described above. The massive human costs of the programs in regards to health, education and other social indicators of well-being are well documented, including the gendered negative impacts that affect women disproportionately (Taylor, 2000; Tsikata and Kerr, 2000; Randriamaro, 2002).

The failure of the neoliberal model: gender and the global food crisis[5]

The food crisis facing millions of Africans is certainly the most striking illustration of the failure of the neoliberal model. The high proportion of the African population that faces hunger is bound to increase as a result of the global food and financial crises. After two decades of neoliberal policies, 200 million African people (28 percent of Africa's population) were chronically hungry in 1997–99, compared to 173 million in 1990–92. According to a recent assessment, "the proportion of people who suffer from hunger remains highest in sub-Saharan Africa, where one in three people is chronically hungry" (Food and Agriculture Organization of the United Nations [FAO], 2008: p. 12). In line with this rise in absolute numbers of the hungry, since 1980 food imports have increased faster than exports, reaching an estimated US$18.7 billion in 2000 alone (New Partnership for Africa's Development [NEPAD], 2003: p. 2). Thus, Africa is a net food-importing region.[6]

Such a food crisis is not new as far as the African region is concerned, since after all, chronic hunger and famines have been around for decades. Even though the recent global food crisis has affected many countries and people not usually affected by hunger, one could argue that this is a recurrent crisis within a "preexisting crisis" that has affected new communities and social groups in the poorest countries. This preexisting crisis, however, which is clearly rooted in the neoliberal development model, has been considered as marginal and subsequently neglected. Yet the rising numbers of hungry people indicate that its most recent crisis is indeed critical. Since the last major food crisis of the 1970s, as corporate control over the political economy of the global food system has increased, so has the number of hungry people, from around 415 million in 1990 to 862 million at present (FAO, 2008: p. 43). With respect to SSA, 20 million additional people—including a majority of women and girls—are likely to fall into hunger and poverty as a result of the food crisis (World Bank, 2008). One can also argue that this "marginal" crisis has gender-differentiated impacts that affect women disproportionately.

The food riots against rising basic food prices in many global cities, not only in parts of Africa, but also in nations such as Mexico and Haïti, are examples of the increasing discontent of people and their worsening livelihoods in both the global North and South. These riots are also warning signs of the fundamental flaws in a global food system whereby more than 860 million people are undernourished and over one billion are overweight (300 million of them obese). They are also a reminder that food has a social and cultural history shaped by different forces and trends, as well as by power relations. In the words of Henry Kissinger, "control oil and you control nations; control food and you control the people."

The food price hikes and shortages did not happen in a vacuum, but in a food system which operates as a subset of the global economic system and involves many agents with different interests and varying forms of political and economic power—from smallholder farms and families to government institutions and global corporations. This food system is affected by key trends such as:

1   The growing economic concentration of power among a handful of firms, which enables these bigger players to affect prices, reduce competition and set standards within agricultural and food sectors (Vorley, 2003; Murphy, 2006).

2   The shift from local to national, regional and global markets, with the above big players organizing actively to establish a "free global market" with the support of power-holders in global governance.
3   The search for and promotion of more effective tools to control the risks faced by the different agents and to protect their interests, including science, technology and information, as well as laws, rules and regulations.

The food crisis is due to the combined effects of short-term and structural factors and long-term trends linked to agricultural and trade reforms in SSA. On the supply side, the short-term factors involved in the food crisis include droughts, extreme weather conditions and erratic rainfall in major food-exporting countries (e.g., Australia and Ukraine) and some African countries; the depletion of food stocks, particularly of grains, resulting from the mismatch between production levels and the steady increase in demand for food; higher price volatility resulting from the rising costs of agricultural inputs (animal feed, energy and fertilizers) and speculation in commodity futures, as well as exports restrictions by major exporters of key food staples such as rice (e.g., India, Thailand).

While the 2.1 percent decline in world production of cereals in 2006 was due to extreme weather incidents in 2005 that were possibly related to climate change in major food-producing countries (High-Level Task Force on The Global Food Crisis [HLTF], 2008: p. 1), the expansion of biofuel production—mostly based on corn and rapeseeds oil crops—following the surge in oil prices in 2007, has contributed significantly to the increase in the costs of fertilizers and other inputs for food production. The transformation of land use from food to biofuel production has also played a significant role in the food crisis, as a growing number of African countries have engaged in biofuel production.[7] The Declaration on "Sustainable Biofuels Development in Africa" made by the African Union in conjunction with the United Nations Organization for Industrial Development and the Government of Brazil in August 2007 and the development of a 10-year action plan suggest that this trend is likely to continue.

The structural factors at the global level include the inequities in the existing global economic system and the organization of production and value chains, whereby African countries are contained in the production of (non-food) primary commodities and the low value-added end of global value chains, along with the failures in the international food market and distorted trade policies (HLTF, 2008). At the regional and country levels, as part of market-based reforms under SAPs and agricultural trade liberalization under the WTO Agreement on Agriculture, the affected African countries have applied reform measures that had negative impacts on food security and poor smallholders. These negative effects include the dismantling of marketing boards and the removal of guaranteed prices for farmers' products, along with agricultural subsidies and support and the reduction of tariffs on food products (ActionAid, 2008; Khor, 2008). Because they overlooked women's unpaid work for social reproduction, as well as gender differences in constraints and opportunities between men and women in trade, these reforms have mainly benefited men and have considerably hindered women's productive capacity and productivity (Randriamaro, 2006).

The long-term and structural causes of the food crisis are also linked to the inadequacy of the prevailing market-based model of agricultural policies, which are skewed in favor of the promotion of primary commodity exports and large-scale farming at the expense of food production and smallholder farming, within which the household is a key institution in the production system. This is despite the fact that "for the foreseeable future and the large majority of African countries, agriculture will remain the most important sector in the battle to reduce poverty and achieve food and nutrition security" (African Union, 2008: p. 1).

These issues are compounded by the erosion of the policy space[8] of African governments and institutions and the failure of technical solutions to support small-scale farmers, especially women, who play a crucial role in agriculture and food production. A related issue is under-investment in the agricultural sector, in spite of the commitment made by AU Member States in the 2003 Maputo Declaration on Agriculture and Food Security to increase their budgetary allocations to the agricultural sector by 10 percent by 2008. In addition, official development assistance (ODA) to primary agriculture declined from US$11 billion in 1990 to only US$7.4 billion in 1998 (NEPAD, 2003).

Whereas the global food crisis attracted increased attention to agriculture at the international level, in SSA countries the renewed interest in agriculture predates the global food crisis and led to the adoption of a Comprehensive Africa Agriculture Development Program (CAADP) in 2002 in order "to help African countries reach a higher path of economic growth through agricultural-led development which eliminates hunger, reduces poverty and food insecurity, and enables expansion of exports" (African Union, 2008: p. 2). This move partly stems from the growing consensus in policy and development circles around the failure of the Africa region to gain from globalization and the related reforms, in the face of numerous constraints that are clearly underlined in the CAADP document. These constraints range from:

> severe competition from industrial countries where total subsidies to agriculture (by OECD countries) were estimated at over US$311 billion apart from direct export subsidies on agricultural products totaling some US$14 billion; to dominance of developed country market opportunities for African agricultural exports; to continuing difficulties with conditions of access despite progress made in the implementation of the Uruguay Round of trade agreements; to generally low and declining prices for unprocessed products that dominate Africa's exports; and Africa's difficulties in meeting technical standards for export products in the context of the WTO Sanitary and Phytosanitary Measures (SPS) and Technical Barriers to Trade (TBT).
> (NEPAD, 2003: p. 14)

The few opportunities opened up by globalization—such as the growth in the production of non-traditional exports (e.g., cut flowers) and the establishment of large supermarkets in many SSA countries—have so far benefited consumers and producers who are well established near major urban areas, and who have better access to airports and storage facilities. The majority of smallholder farmers have not been able to seize these opportunities given the lack of transport infrastructure and access to credit, high-cost and variable input markets (e.g., fertilizer and seeds) and the difficulties in meeting quality control standards.

Underlying the trends described above, and cutting across the different sectors are persistent gender inequalities that have critical implications for food security, agricultural productivity and growth. For instance, agricultural production in Zambia could be increased by up to 15 percent if women and men had the same degree of capital investment in agricultural inputs, including land (IFAD, FAO and World Bank, 2008). In most African countries, gender inequalities perpetuate the marginalization of women and their access to productive assets, such as land, agricultural inputs, labor, technology, credit, markets, information and decision making. This marginalization occurs in spite of the multiple and central roles of women in food production, food security and natural resources management. Because women constitute the large majority of the rural labor force and dominate the subsistence subsector in SSA, women bear the brunt of the negative impacts of the food crisis.

Gender and human security in the neoliberal context

The discussion on the meaning of human security from a gendered perspective in SSA should be situated within a neoliberal context in order to account for the factors that shape the conditions under which women live and determine their "capabilities," that is the core set of basic human "functionings"—such as being alive, healthy and physically safe, the capacity to engage in a social community, to express compassion and not fear discrimination, and being able "to form a conception of the good and to engage in critical reflection about the planning of one's own life" (Nussbaum, 2000: p. 41). These central human capabilities build on basic constitutional principles that should be respected and implemented by all governments, as a bare minimum of what respect for human dignity requires (Nussbaum, 2000: p. 223).

While the challenges facing the implementation of this ambitious agenda are still to be effectively addressed in Western countries, the criticisms of the "capabilities approach to human security" as elaborated by Martha Nussbaum deserve special attention in the current African context. Some critics argue that because the capabilities approach narrowly focuses on individual liberation and access to public goods, it lacks an adequate understanding of interdependence— as opposed to independence—between men and women as an important factor in the construction of their interests as members of a social collectivity in different local contexts (Govindasamy and Malhotra, 1996; Malhotra and Mather, 1997; Kabeer, 1998).

Another serious criticism underscores the overwhelming focus of the capabilities approach on minimum necessary requirements, which "meshes with an almost universal shift in social-democratic politics, where the problem of poverty has supplanted the problem of inequality, and ensuring a humane minimum has taken over from worries about the overall income gap" (Phillips, 2001: p. 259). In substance, those critics point to the failure of the capabilities approach to divorce from the main tenets of the neoliberal agenda and to address the fundamental challenges of equal rights between social groups across and within nations, as well as between men and women. Anne Phillips' point about the focus of the capabilities approach on poverty is particularly relevant to the emergence of the anti-poverty agenda and the rise of the poverty research industry in SSA countries.

The anti-poverty agenda and the rise of the poverty research industry

One of the major impacts that resulted from the implementation of the human security agenda within a neoliberal economic and ideological framework is the shift from "development" to "poverty reduction." In SSA countries, this trend emerged during the structural adjustment period of the 1980s when fiscal constraints, combined with mounting criticism of the capture of resources by elites, forced many African governments to shift priorities and improve efficiency by focusing on targeting the poor. Social programs were reduced to targeted short-time interventions to cushion the worst effects of structural adjustment measures (Mkandawire, 2005).

In 1996, the deteriorating economic growth and dire social consequences of SAPs led to the launch of the Heavily Indebted Poor Countries (HIPC) initiative, which focused on reducing countries' debts while helping to spur growth and reduce poverty. Through this process, the World Bank-led Poverty Reduction Strategy Paper (PRSP) emerged as a framework aimed at ensuring that resources freed up by debt relief would be used for poverty reduction, alongside the IMF's Enhanced Structural Adjustment Facility (ESAF) lending framework. Given its lineage with SAPs, of which it retains an array of conditionality and cross-conditionality clauses to compel SSA countries to adopt the preferred options of the international financial institutions and creditor countries, the PRSP process has been key in the shift to the anti-poverty agenda.

By the end of the 1990s, the mandates of the IMF and the World Bank were seriously questioned as a result of the 1997 financial crisis in Asia and the mounting evidence of the failure of SAPs. This was against a backdrop of substantial external pressure building up around this issue, particularly from the NGO movement, such as Jubilee 2000, to make debt relief "broader, deeper, faster, better," and from the US administration to ensure that resources freed up by debt relief would be "well spent" (Christiansen and Hovland, 2003: p. 7).

The question of how to link debt relief to poverty reduction featured prominently in the 1999 Review of the HIPC Initiative, which led to the establishment of the IMF's Poverty Reduction and Growth Facility (PRGF) as the key instrument for providing loans to African governments. Poverty reduction was also the central focus of the 1999 World Bank's Comprehensive Development Framework (CDF) for aid and World Development Report on "Attacking Poverty." It also took center stage in the agenda of bilateral donors such as the UK Department for International Development (Christiansen and Hovland, 2003: p. 7).

Among other things, the narrowing down of the development agenda to a single focus on poverty reduction has led to the growth of a poverty research industry, which is dominated by a small group of experts. Most of these experts have been educated in American universities (Harris, 2007). These institutions are considered the predominant source of research and teaching models as well as of truth and norms about the development of SSA countries and the developing world (Escobar, 1988). This group includes an African minority whose ideas are shaped by neoliberal ideology, and in particular by American liberalism, that tends to view poverty as a phenomenon that has nothing to do with power relations and social inequities (O'Connor, 2001; Harris, 2007). Armed with these peculiar forms of knowledge, techniques and limited perspective, this African elite has contributed to institutionalizing the poverty research industry in SSA countries. The African elite has served as the springboard for promoting the "new consensus" on poverty and the ownership of the anti-poverty agenda across the continent, acting mainly as consultants for the international development institutions or auxiliaries to the foreign technical experts, and benefiting significantly from the returns of the poverty research industry in this process. Thus, in this hierarchy of poverty knowledge production, Africans continue to be adjudged "incapable of thinking for themselves and implementing policies" (Mkandawire and Soludo, 2003: p. 2).

The World Bank's neoliberal ideologies and methodologies are at the core of the mainstream "poverty knowledge production system." This system often glosses over the socio-historical contexts and experiences of poor countries and their knowledge production (Mkandawire, 1998; Mkandawire and Soludo, 1999; Olukoshi, 2001). As such, the poverty research industry has neglected the development of research tools and methodologies that are based on local experiences, indigenous and independent research, and continues to rely heavily on the policy analysis of a few Northern think tanks, the World Bank staff and international consultants. Moreover, although estimates of the costs associated with "technical assistance" related to anti-poverty programs are not readily available, the overwhelming focus on poverty by technocrats suggests that such costs are most probably similar to those incurred by SSA countries during the structural adjustment period, with "over 100,000 foreign technical experts costing over $4 billion annually to maintain" (Mkandawire and Soludo, 2003: p. 2).

Against this backdrop, and in spite of decades of research and activism by African women, the mainstream poverty research industry continues to ignore the theoretical and methodological approaches that women offer as alternatives to dominant and Northern-biased paradigms that have shaped conventional knowledge about poor women's lives, and what kind of policies would benefit them. As underlined by African women researchers and gender equality activists who initiated the first major research program on Gender and Economic Reforms in Africa (GERA[9])

> throughout the decades of debate, defenders of economic reforms ignored opponents' research on the basis that it lacked rigor or challenged opponents' research methodologies. Consistently, the World Bank has managed to dismiss the large body of evidence that demonstrates the negative impacts of economic reforms on women because of so-called methodological weaknesses.
>
> (Tsikata and Kerr, 2000: p. 11)

In the context of conventional neoliberal ideology, gender inequality tends to be conflated with poverty (Jackson, 1996; Randriamaro, 2002). According to this perspective, poverty is depoliticized in such a way that what is deemed important is the development of sophisticated poverty measurements that are based on the assumption that a scientific/technological approach is the magic cure for "solving" poverty (O'Connor, 2001; Harris, 2007). This approach neglects deeper understandings of the ways in which poverty is a result of unequal power and social relations; it also neglects gendered processes of accumulation and distribution of wealth within the neoliberal state and the free-market economy.

A case in point is South Africa (one of the best "reformers" according to Bretton Woods institutions' standards), where trade liberalization has led to increased unemployment and informalization of work (Taylor, 2000; Randriamaro, 2006). Because trade liberalization policies ignored the differences among citizens based on age, class, race, geographical location or ethnicity, it is generally poor and marginalized groups of women who are negatively affected by unemployment and the restructuring of labor markets. For instance, the liberalization of tariffs (from 41.2 percent in 1995 to 28.9 percent in 1999) in the South African footwear and leather subsectors has led to multiple retrenchments and dramatic changes in production processes in local factories that have had disproportionate impacts on women (Randriamaro, 2006).

In addition, there has been a direct relationship between company restructuring in the footwear industry and the growth of the informal sector. Indeed, the informal sector has become the last resort not only for the increasing number of retrenched workers, but also for factories through the sub-contracting of some factory functions to the informal sector in order to cut on labor costs. In this process the interaction of gender, class and race inequalities has meant that African women form the large majority of retrenched workers who joined the informal sector, especially as compared to white, colored and Indian/Asian women (International Labor Research and Information Group [ILRIG], 2001, cited by Randriamaro, 2006).

Furthermore, trade liberalization and free-market policies have major implications for social reproduction, which is defined here as "the work involved in biological reproduction, the reproduction of human labour, including education and training, and the reproduction of provisioning and care needs" (Bakker, 2003 in Braedley, 2006: p. 216). In addition, "this work, whether performed as wage or unwaged labor, is performed primarily by women. Unwaged labor is particularly interesting in that women perform unwaged labor in addition to their waged employment" (Braedley, 2006: p. 216). Mainstream poverty knowledge has downplayed the role of social reproduction in both the formal and informal economy, as evidenced by mainstream approaches and strategies for poverty reduction. The conventional economic models and indicators consistently ignore the contribution and value of women's unpaid work for social reproduction and treat it as an input that is not only free, but also renewable and infinitely elastic (Elson *et al.*, 1995).

Gender, neoliberalism and the women's economic empowerment paradigm in SSA

In recognition of the high incidence of poverty among women in SSA countries, the new consensus on poverty reduction has brought about heated debates on the feminization of poverty. This has resulted in the "institutionalization of compassion for women" (Randriamaro, 2003), leading to approaches to women's economic empowerment that do not fundamentally question structural gender and class inequalities. Although the consensus around the multi-dimensionality of poverty in the recent period has reduced the tendency to view women as helpless victims of poverty, by and large, the prevailing approaches to women's economic empowerment are market-based. These approaches overlook the basic reality of poor women's paid work, most of which takes place in the informal economy, as well as women's unpaid work for social reproduction. In a practical context, one of the consequences of such approaches is the fragmentation and contradiction of policy options for women's economic empowerment.

For instance, some African governments (like Senegal and Kenya) have used resources from debt relief to increase their budgetary allocations to the health and education sectors; however the ongoing privatization of these services has kept such services out of reach for poor women who cannot afford to pay user's fees and who continue to bear the burden of unpaid care work to compensate for the services that governments no longer provide. In addition to the infringement of women's rights to health, the strain on women's time budget does not allow them to engage in remunerative economic activities that can help lift them out of poverty.

Therefore, from a gender perspective it is important to note that neoliberal policies have led to "a gendered reconfiguration of responsibilities between citizens and the state," whereby the burden of social service provision has been shifted decisively onto poor women and community level "civil society organizations" (Hawkesworth, 2006: p. 121). Furthermore, the responsibility for providing economic opportunities and security to poor women has shifted away from the state onto these women themselves. Notably, this shift has occurred through microcredit programs and microfinance activities (Rankin, 2001), as well as women's income-generating activities and entrepreneurship programs.

A key feature of such neoliberal development policies is the emergence of the image of the "good woman" (Cornwall *et al.*, 2008) who abides by the rules of microcredit programs; who is engaged in income-generating activities; and who is entirely devoted to the care and well-being of her family under all circumstances. Although some of the anti-poverty programs are meant in part to address the negative impacts of neoliberal policies, "they have a marked tendency to reproduce and reinforce deeply conservative notions of womanhood and of women's roles within the family" (Molyneux, 2006 in Cornwall *et al.*, 2008: p. 2).

Thus, in the recent period, the main architects and promoters of neoliberal economic reforms such as the World Bank and the Department for International Development of the UK (DFID) have begun to champion the role of the woman as a "weapon" in the fight against poverty (DFID, 2007: p. 31) and to invest in women entrepreneurs as a way to promote "smart economics" (Buvinic and King, 2007). While these developments have been welcomed by many as a sign of women's increased integration into the mainstream development agenda, the increasing instrumentalization of women's economic empowerment raises major concerns about the predominance of the efficiency argument over issues of equity and economic rights.

Moreover, the implementation of the anti-poverty agenda has depoliticized the concept of women's economic empowerment, which has come to mean poor women's survival in the globalized economy. The operationalization of this concept in mainstream development practice has very little to do with addressing the structural gender inequalities that account for women's subordination and challenging the existing economic and social order. Instead, it accommodates women within this order.

The changes entailed by the anti-poverty agenda implemented through debt relief mechanisms[10] must also be examined against the background of the contradictory outcomes of the inflexible macroeconomic conditionalities built in the PRSPs; the privatization of social and essential services; the introduction of regressive tax policies; the liberalization of the agricultural sector; and the deregulation of the financial sector, all of which undermine women's livelihoods as well as the little progress in social expenditures that has been made in some SSA countries[11] due to the liberation of resources from debt relief.

Feminist economists who advocate a gendered perspective have underlined that the issue of gender equity goes well beyond simply increasing social spending and that women's economic security and rights should not be de-linked from the macroeconomic policies that determine the resource flows and investments required to address public poverty. These policies have mainly benefited men and a minority of women who have better access to productive assets than the large majority of poor women who are concentrated in the informal economy.

Gender and the informal economy

The cumulative impacts of SAPs and neoliberal globalization on production structures and the labor market in SSA have brought about high levels of unemployment and the increasing informalization of work, which continues to add to women's economic insecurity. One of the most important characteristics of the labor market in Africa is the prevalence of informal employment, which accounts for 72 percent of non-agriculture employment in sub-Saharan Africa (International Labor Organization, 2002).[12] This informal labor market is also highly feminized and characterized by low wages and inflexible market conditions.

Because of their concentration in the informal economy, women constitute a major part of the working poor, which means that they do not earn enough from their work to lift themselves out of poverty. It goes that "... the vast majority of women involved in informal and parallel activities are confined to low-income activities with little opportunity for accumulation of wealth. Furthermore, these activities are among the hardest hit by crisis in the official economy" (Beneria, 1991, Meagher and Yunusa, 1993 cited in UNIFEM, 2006).

The informal economy in SSA is dominated by trade-related activities, with services and manufacturing accounting for only a small percentage of this sector (UN, 1996 cited in International Labor Organization [ILO], 2002). For example, in Angola, Nigeria, South Africa and Uganda, a majority of informal sector workers are active in retail trade (ILO, 2002). Of these workers, 70 percent are self-employed, with the remainder in wage employment. Street vending is one particular informal activity that is prevalent on the continent. According to 1992 figures, street vendors represented 80.7 percent of all economic units surveyed in urban areas in Benin, with women making up over 75 percent of vendors (Charmes, 1998). The analysis of more recent data on the informal sector in SSA points to the predominance of informal cross-border trade, which has increased in conjunction with formal trade since the 1990s due to a number of factors[13] (UNIFEM, 2006).

Country case studies across SSA[14] show a gendered pattern in both formal and informal trade activities, whereby high entry costs and high returns activities are dominated by men because women often lack access to productive assets and are confined to businesses that require little start-up capital and yield relatively low returns to labor (Reardon, 1997; Baden, 1998; Bryceson, 1999; Dolan, 2002; UNIFEM, 2008). It has also been found that the large majority of women informal traders are mainly involved in small-scale trade activities, especially of fresh agricultural produce with a high degree of perishability (Baden, 1998; UNIFEM, 2008). Thus, men's and women's location within the trade sector is determined by the entry costs to trade, with a clear gender segmentation between male-dominated high entry costs-high return activities, and low entry costs-low returns activities where women preponderate.

These case studies referenced above confirm that the involvement of poor women in SSA's economic diversification has mainly consisted of the addition of trading activities which produce little income and poor returns to labor. As noted by Whitehead, "although there are some women who are diversifying into better incomes, for the vast majority of rural women, diversification is more of a survival strategy than a route out of poverty" (Whitehead, n.d.). Moreover, analysis of household expenditures in case studies and across SSA reveals that in most cases, poor women spend their income from trade and other income-generating activities on food, basic necessities for their households and children's needs (UNIFEM, 2008). These findings point out that for many women, the level of their trade income and their patterns of consumption do not allow for an accumulation of assets that can lift them out of poverty (UNIFEM, 2008).

In this context, it is important to note the increased competition between women and men in informal trade in agricultural products, which might be due to the fact that trading in agricultural products has become more profitable.[15] Recently, newspapers have reported the displacement of women from their share of the informal markets by male and foreign actors in countries like Senegal and the Democratic Republic of Congo, where the inflows of Chinese investments have been accompanied by the entry of Chinese immigrants.

It is interesting that most of the attention of commentators and media has focused on the emergence of China both as a global economic powerhouse and an alternative source of development assistance to SSA countries, yet there is little attention paid to the nature of Chinese investments and their implications. Compared to the "traditional" donors from Western countries, China does not carry the historical baggage of colonialism, neocolonialism and structural adjustment, however this does not preclude that China's investments should be evaluated against their implications for the development goals of SSA countries. It is also important to analyze whose interests are served by investment agreements with China. The fact that Chinese investments come from a country that is officially socialist does not guarantee that they are immune to the influence of neoliberalism, nor that these investments will have a benign impact on the lives of African men and women. In the case of Sudan, for example, Fadlalla points to the Chinese as part of "eastern competitors" to Western liberalism,

> acting as proxy capitalists, these countries directed the movement of capital through the Sudanese urban landscape and defined economic development in terms of khaskhasa (privatization), serving the interests of local-global investors dealing in oil, telecommunications, construction, and fast-food businesses and providing neoliberalization with an eastern Islamic façade.
>
> (Fadlalla, 2008: p. 212)

Thus, the informal sector, which used to be traditionally dominated by women, and was once considered as the last really "free" market,[16] has become the site of intensifying competition. It also appears that it has attracted a lot of attention from financial capital holders.

Whose human security? "Smart economics," microfinance and the new poverty market

In SSA, poverty continues to be a salient product of neoliberal policies, as evidenced by the fact that most SSA countries are among the most chronically deprived,[17] with about 199 million people living in chronic poverty (Chronic Poverty Research Center, 2009). Among these, the working poor, most of whom are women, constitute the majority. Furthermore, poverty reduction strategies, which are the main vehicles for the implementation of an anti-poverty agenda, provide little evidence of specific analysis of persistent poverty, while issues of gender equality and women's empowerment remain marginal (Chronic Poverty Research Center, 2009).

Unsurprisingly, neoliberal responses to the fact that poverty levels have been increasing instead of decreasing in many African countries are market-based, and gender equality has become a key strategic element of these responses. As World Bank promoters of gender equality as a form of "smart economics" propose, reducing poverty will depend on "women's ability to compete in [four] markets," mainly, product, financial, land and labor markets (World Bank, 2006: p. 5). Thus, market access and competitiveness have become the central goals, with the ultimate goal to maximize the returns to investments in women's labor force and human capital.

Since "smart economics" would have it that resources should be invested where the returns are highest, this market-oriented conception of poverty reduction and women's empowerment has justified the growing interest in small and micro enterprises in the informal sector among policy makers since the last few years. Furthermore, the conception of women and the poor as independent agents who should be able to compete on the neoliberal market and be responsible for their own well-being has justified the removal of social protection and safety nets from the responsibility of the State.

Microcredit and microfinance have also become the main arms of neoliberal development policy for promoting women's and the poor's entrepreneurship, in spite of widespread contestations of their results in SSA. These approaches, which sought to remedy the failure of the mainstream formal financial system to reach poor women, have undoubtedly played a positive role in women's survival strategies, especially in regards to income. However, the extent to which access to microfinance empowers women is questionable, as there are critical limits to income gains for women. In fact, the overemphasis on microfinance as the solution to women's economic empowerment has trapped poor women in the "microfinance ghetto" (Randriamaro, 2001) due to the prevailing view that while women are worthy recipients of microcredit programs, women are not credit-worthy clients of mainstream financial markets. This is despite the unanimous recognition that women rarely default on their loans and the potential of their long-time demand for services from mainstream financial markets to spur domestic investment and growth (Randriamaro, 2001).

Nevertheless, in the past, microfinance organizations have been able to reach poor women because these organizations have specifically addressed the constraints women face. This is likely to change, as a result of new developments in the financial sector: as the 2009 World Survey on the Role of Women in Development points out,

> microfinance organizations are under considerable pressure to become financially sustainable, in part because the potential for mobilizing the savings of poor people around the world has attracted the attention of international investors. Data from several regions suggest that commercialization will lead to declining access for women.
>
> (UNDAW, 2009: p. ix)

Thus, microcredit and microfinance schemes no longer belong to the domain of social development, which used to be their main goal, and their main preoccupation has become "financial sustainability." As happened in social services such as health and water, the private sector is expected to take the lead in the provision of financial services to the poor, and the implicit priority for lending is no longer to reduce poverty, but to ensure profitability. A growing number of commercial banks have been attracted by the huge potential of expansion of the microfinance market, which is commensurate with the number of poor people that is bound to increase in SSA,[18] and these commercial banks have engaged in the provision of microcredit and microfinance services, using new information technologies to provide more density of coverage, while reducing risks and delivery costs. As a result, several SSA countries[19] have engaged in the development of microfinance policies to regulate this new poverty market that has emerged alongside the poverty knowledge industry.

Just like other markets, this poverty market is also gendered. Women constitute the majority of the borrowers and are praised for their high repayment rate. While the promoters of microcredit lament the fact that the volume of women's loans is smaller than men's, there is very little consideration for the hidden costs of these repayment rates in their analysis of the costs and benefits of microcredit. An example of these hidden costs is that many women—in SSA as well as in other regions of the world—often repay a loan with other loans from other microcredit providers and are trapped in a cycle of increased indebtedness.[20]

The neoliberal insecurities generated by poverty reduction programs point to a policy obsession with the targeting of so-called "economically active" poor women and men, leading to the exclusion of those who need assistance most. As such, this approach overlooks the basic reality that poor people cannot afford to not work and that poor women are often unpaid family workers. It reproduces institutional discrimination and gender biases that account for women's exclusion from formal financial institutions by ignoring the value of women's unpaid work and the gender-specific constraints facing them.

Conclusion: the crisis of social reproduction and human security in sub-Saharan Africa

In SSA, the demand for poor women's work has increased sharply to compensate for falling household incomes due to job losses in export and manufacturing sectors and the reduction in remittance flows from migrant family members working abroad (Seguino, 2009; World Bank, 2009). Falling household incomes in turn compound the negative impacts of the high food prices and the prolonged crisis of SSA agriculture.[21] As happened with SAPs, the social costs of the crisis of neoliberal globalization are being shouldered by women who serve as "shock-absorbers" in the face of rising unemployment and costs of living (Fukuda-Parr, 2008).

While women are confronted with increased risks and insecurities, the recommendations from economists and experts on both food and economic crises focus on necessary cuts in public expenditure and the crucial need to maintain macroeconomic stability (African Development Bank, cited in AllAfrica.com, 2008; World Bank, 2008). As studies on the gender impacts of SAPs have demonstrated, such orthodox prescriptions were part of the causes of the SAPs' massive human costs. Such prescriptions are also most likely to increase the feminization of poverty and women's unpaid work burden (Elson, 1992; Randriamaro, 2002) in the absence of public social protection systems in most SSA countries.

Furthermore, a basis for major concern is that women who were involved in the food riots that took place in several SSA countries[22] went in the streets not only to protest against the rise in food prices, but also to voice their concerns about the fact that they can no longer cope with the overwhelming stress on their capacity to act as a buffer against the deleterious impacts of the economic crisis on their households. This is an alarming signal about the emergence of the crisis of social reproduction, which affects women in SSA disproportionately because of their ascribed gender roles and exclusion of their voices in policy and decision-making processes. It is very telling that according to the media reports,

> the answer from ordinary men and women who were asked what they think about the financial and economic crisis was predominantly "what crisis?" Such an answer from people who have been living in poverty for decades comes as no surprise and points to the fact that before this crisis, there was an underlying crisis rooted in the contradictions of the current global development paradigm.
>
> (Randriamaro, 2009: p. 5)

Similarly, some newspapers have designated the food riots that erupted between February and May 2008 as the "housewives' revolt" (Napon, 2008) because ordinary women led and constituted the majority of the participants in some of these riots. These women went in the streets with empty cooking pots and bags to show that they had nothing left in their homes. In Burkina Faso, one woman employed by a private enterprise explained that, "the majority of Burkinabe workers are low paid. With a monthly budget of FCFA40,000 [about €60], I do not know how I can possibly make do with it. We only eat once a day and the children cannot understand." In Côte d'Ivoire, women shouted that they were tired and mobilized for two full days to demonstrate against the degradation of their living conditions.[23]

The developments discussed throughout the paper describe the context within which the concept of human security should be reconstructed from the perspective of poor women in SSA. These women do not have the power to set the human security agenda and do not benefit from it, in spite of their vital role in shielding the lives of their families and communities from the threats and insecurities generated by neoliberal globalization and free-market economies. Such reconstruction is intricately related to governance and citizenship issues at the national level and the extent to which SSA countries will have the necessary policy space and resources.

While many view the global financial and economic crises as an opportunity for these countries to move away from the neoliberal orthodoxy, the recent developments in SSA in the aftermath of the economic crisis suggest that the expansionary and counter-cyclical economic policies adopted by some SSA countries (such as South Africa and Mozambique, among others) represented only a temporary retreat from the standard neoliberal policy package (Randriamaro, 2010). Sadly, there is every reason to believe that most SSA countries will return to "business-as-usual" policies and that the struggle for holding them accountable for women's rights is far from being over.

Because the control of women's labor has taken center stage, the priority of a new human security agenda should be to ensure that women are no longer treated as resources to be controlled and exploited by male-dominated structures and institutions and that the burden of social reproduction is distributed more equally. In this regard, the role of institutions at the national level, and in particular the State, is critical in mediating the impact of the human security agenda on poor women. Public social protection mechanisms, State regulations in line with international conventions and commitments to women's rights, and supportive domestic institutions and policies are instrumental in guaranteeing that the changes enacted by the State and national institutions are both lasting and beneficial to poor women.

The reconstruction of a human security agenda that truly enforces women's rights and their connection to economic justice and environmental integrity depends on fundamental changes in global economic governance and the regulation of global financial markets, including the restructuring of "the current system [which] in fact shifts the burden of global financial risks from players in global markets to poor countries and poor households" (Fukuda-Parr, 2008: p. 6).

Notes

1 The list of concrete policy proposals articulated by John Williamson, which gained consensus among the international financial institutions based in Washington, especially the US Treasury.
2 Such as tariffs, certain domestic standards and regulatory measures, and controls on capital and investment flows.
3 The socialist model and variants of the "mixed economy" model, both of which shared common approaches categorized as follows by Charles C. Soludo: "the capital formation centered approach; the economic nationalism centered approach; the socialist development approach; and the basic human needs approach" (Mkandawire and Soludo, 2003: p. 21).
4 Such as the "domestic production of capital goods, development of domestic scientific and technological capacity, and domestic-resource based industrial production" (Mkandawire and Soludo, 2003: p. 21).
5 This subsection draws heavily on the interim draft of a study commissioned by ACORD on Food Sovereignty, Gender and Agricultural policies in sub-Saharan Africa. I am solely responsible for the views expressed in this draft paper.
6 Except for some countries such as South Africa.
7 Including Mali, Togo, Niger, Ghana, Senegal, Madagascar, Malawi, South Africa, Zambia, Uganda, etc.
8 I.e., the range of available policy options.
9 I happened to be the first African manager of the GERA Program during its second phase which focused on Gender, Trade and Investment in Africa.
10 Such as the Poverty Reduction Strategy Paper (PRSP) processes in many SSA countries.
11 Such as Mozambique, Uganda, Tanzania, Sénégal, Mali, Malawi and Benin.
12 Seventy-eight percent excluding South Africa.
13 These factors include population growth, urbanization, changes in subsidies (national and international) under trade liberalization; retrenchments in civil service under SAPs and high rates of unemployment, especially among women and youth; devaluation of local currencies and chronic shortages of foreign currency; increased demand for imported goods and commodities; decline in household income and related increase in poverty levels among urban households; and increased demand for cash as prices rise (WIDTECH, 2000, Meagher, 2003, CORN and AFSC, 2004, cited in UNIFEM, 2006).
14 Including a series of baseline studies undertaken by UNIFEM in 2007 on gender and informal cross-border trade in the sub-regions of Francophone and Anglophone Western Africa, Eastern Africa, Southern Africa and Central Africa that I have coordinated.
15 In the case of Cameroon for instance, the availability of lucrative markets in the oil-producing countries on its borders is an important push factor.
16 In the sense that it is the last resort for disenfranchised women and men.
17 These countries are "[c]haracterized by low initial levels of welfare (relatively low GDP per capita, and relatively high mortality, fertility, and undernourishment), and by relatively slow rates of progress over time across all available indicators" (CPRC, 2008: p. 14).
18 As mentioned in the reports on the achievement of MDGs and other reports on poverty, the number of poor people in SSA will increase by 2015.
19 Such as The Gambia and Malawi among others.
20 Personal observations during field missions in SSA countries.
21 Women account for an average of 70 percent of agricultural production across SSA.
22 Namely in Burkina Faso, Niger, Sénégal, Côte d'Ivoire, Cameroun.
23 It is interesting to note that they sent messages via their mobile phones as an effective

way of mobilization. As underlined by one commentator, "this is an extreme manifestation of the paradoxes of neoliberalism: access to technology, but empty stomachs" (Direnberger, 2008: p. 1).

Bibliography

ActionAid. (2008) Failing the Rural Poor: Aid, Agriculture and the Millennium Development Goals. (Online) Available at: www.actionaid.org.uk/doc_lib/failing_the_rural_poor_actionaid_report.pdf [accessed 1 November 2011].

African Union (AU). (2008) Progress Report on Implementing the Comprehensive Africa Agriculture Development Program (CAADP-Sirte): Agricultural Growth, Poverty Reduction and Food Security in Africa. From the 4th Conference of African Union Ministers of Agriculture, Addis Ababa, Ethiopia, 26–27 February 2008. (Online) Available at: www.africa-union.org/root/ua/Conferences/2008/avril/REA/01avr/Experts_CAADP_Progress.pdf [accessed 1 November 2011].

AllAfrica.com. (2008) African Countries Endorse Measures to Mitigate Impact of Global Financial Crisis. African Development Bank. (Online) 12 November 2008. Available at: http://allafrica.com/stories/200811130144.html [accessed 2 November 2011].

Baden, S. (1998) Gender Issues in Agricultural Liberalisation. Report No. 41, BRIDGE, Institute of Development Studies, Brighton.

Bakker, I., ed. (1994) *The Strategic Silence: Gender and Economic Policy.* London: Zed Books.

Bourdieu, P. (1998) Utopia of Endless Exploitation: The Essence of Neoliberalism. *Le Monde Diplomatique.* (Online) December 1998. Available at: http://mondediplo.com/1998/12/08bourdieu [accessed 1 November 2011].

Braedley, S. (2006) Someone to Watch Over You: Gender, Class and Social Reproduction. In: Meg Luxton and Kate Bezanson, eds. *Social Reproduction: Feminist Political Economy Challenges Neo-liberalism.* Montreal: McGill-Queen's University Press, pp. 215–230.

Bryceson, D. F. (1999) Sub-Saharan Africa Betwixt and Between: Rural Livelihood Practices and Policies. African Studies Centre, Working Paper 43, De-Agrarianization and Rural Employment research program, Leiden University.

Buvinic, M. and E. M. King. (2007) Smart Economics. *Finance and Development,* 44(2), pp. 7–12.

Charmes, J. (1998) Micro-enterprises in Africa: The Need for a Follow-up Survey of their Dynamics and Role in Job Creation Within the Continuous Expansion of the Informal Sector. Presentation at the Conference on "Enterprise in Africa: Between Poverty and Growth." University of Edinburgh, Centre of African Studies. Edinburgh. 26–28 May 1998.

Christiansen, K. and I. Hovland. (2003) The PRSP Initiative: Multilateral Policy Change and the Role of Research, ODI Working Paper 216, London.

Chronic Poverty Research Center (CPRC). (2009) The Chronic Poverty Report 2008–2009: Escaping Poverty Traps. (Online) Available at: www.chronicpoverty.org/uploads/publication_files/CPR2_ReportSummary.pdf [accessed 2 November 2011].

Commission on Human Security. (2003) *Final Report of the Commission on Human Security.* Washington, DC: Commission on Human Security.

Cornwall, A, J. Gideon and K. Wilson. (2008) Reclaiming Feminism: Gender and Neo-liberalism—special issue. *IDS Bulletin,* 39(6).

Department for International Development (DFID). (2007) Gender Equality at the Heart of Development. London. (Online) Available at: http://webarchive.nationalarchives. gov.uk/+/http:/www.dfid.gov.uk/Documents/publications/gender-equality.pdf[accessed 1 November 2011].

Direnberger, L. (2008) Genre et sécurité alimentaire: les inégalités face à la faim, Approche sexospécifique des émeutes de la faim en Afrique, *Genre en Action*, Bulletin no. 7, July 2008.

Dolan, C. (2002) Gender and Diverse Livelihoods in Uganda (draft). UEA, LADDER Working Paper 10, Norwich.

Elson, D. (1992) Male Bias in Structural Adjustment. In: H. Afshar and C. Dennis, eds. *Women and Adjustment Policies in the Third World*. New York: St Martin's, ch. 3.

Elson, D., N. Cagatay and C. Grown, eds. (1995) *World Development*. Special issue on Gender, Adjustment and Macroeconomics, November; 23(11).

Escobar, A. (1988) Power and Visibility: Development and the Invention and Management of the Third World. *Cultural Anthropology*, 3(2), pp. 428–443.

Fadlalla, Amal Hassan. (2008) The Neoliberalization of Compassion: Darfur and the Mediation of American Faith, Fear and Terror. In: Jane Colins, Micaela di Leonardo and Brett Williams, eds. *New Landscapes of Inequality: Neoliberalism and the Erosion of Democracy in America*. Santa Fe, New Mexico: SAR Press, ch. 11.

Food and Agriculture Organization of the United Nations (FAO). (2006) The State of Food Insecurity in the World 2006: Eradicating World Hunger—Taking Stock Ten Years After the World Food Summit. (Online) Available at: www.fao.org/docrep/009/ a0750e/a0750e00.htm [accessed 1 November 2011].

Food and Agriculture Organization of the United Nations (FAO). (2008) The State of Food Insecurity in the World 2008: High Food Prices and Food Security—Threats and Opportunities. (Online) Available at: www.fao.org/docrep/011/i0291e/i0291e00.htm [accessed 1 November 2011].

Fukuda-Parr, S. (2008) The Human Impact of the Financial Crisis on Poor and Disempowered People and Countries. Presentation at the Interactive Panel on the Global Financial Crisis, UN General Assembly, New York, 30 October 2008.

George, S. (1999) A Short History of Neoliberalism: Twenty Years of Elite Economics and Emerging Opportunities for Structural Change. From the Conference on Economic Sovereignty in a Globalising World, Bangkok, 24–26 March 1999.

Govindasamy, P. and Malhotra, A. (1996) Women's Position and Family Planning in Egypt. *Studies in Family Planning*, 27(6), pp. 7328–7340.

Harris, J. (2007) Bringing Politics Back into Poverty Analysis: Why Understanding Social Relations Matters More for Policy on Chronic Poverty than Measurement, CPRC Working Paper 77, Vancouver.

Hawkesworth, M. (2006) Feminists v. Feminization: Confronting the War Logics of the Bush Administration. *Asteriskos*, 1(2), pp. 117–142.

High-Level Task Force on The Global Food Crisis (HLTF). (2008) Comprehensive Framework For Action. United Nations. (Online) (July 2008) Available at: www.un.org/issues/ food/taskforce/Documentation/CFA%20Web.pdf [accessed 1 November 2011].

IFAD, FAO and World Bank. (2009) *Gender in Agriculture Sourcebook*. Washington DC. (Online) Available at: http://siteresources.worldbank.org/INTGENAGRLIVSOU-BOOK/Resources/CompleteBook.pdf [accessed 1 November 2011].

International Labor Organization (ILO). (2002) The Informal Sector in Sub-Saharan Africa, Working Paper on the Informal Economy, Geneva.

Jackson, C. (1996) Rescuing Gender From the Poverty Trap. *World Development*, 24(3), pp. 489–504.

Kabeer, N. (1998) Money Can't Buy Me Love? Re-evaluating Gender, Credit and Empowerment in Rural Bangladesh, IDS Discussion Paper 363, Institute of Development Studies, Brighton.

Khor, M. (2008) Food Crisis, Climate Change and the Importance of Sustainable Agriculture, Presentation at FAO Food Security Summit, Rome.

Malhotra, A. and M. Mather. (1997) Do Schooling and Work Empower Women in Developing Countries? Gender and Domestic Decisions in Sri Lanka. *Sociological Forum*, 12(4), pp. 599–630.

Martinez, E. and A. Garcia. (2000) What is "Neo-Liberalism?" A Brief Definition for Activists. (Online) 26 February 2000. Available at: www.globalexchange.org/campaigns/econ101/neoliberalDefined.html [accessed 7 October 2010].

Maxwell, S. (2003) Heaven or Hubris, Reflections on the "New Poverty Agenda." *Development Policy Review*, 21, pp. 5–25.

Mkandawire, T. (1998) Thinking about Developmental States in Africa. Study No. 9 within the UNCTAD series on African Development in a Comparative Perspective, Geneva: UNCTAD.

Mkandawire, T. (2005) Targeting and Universalism in Poverty Reduction, Social Policy and Development Program, Paper Number 23, Geneva: UNRISD.

Mkandawire, T. and A. Olukoshi, eds. (1995) *Between Liberalisation and Repression: The Politics of Structural Adjustment in Africa.* Dakar: CODESRIA Books.

Mkandawire, T. and C. Soludo. (1999) *Our Continent, Our Future: African Perspectives on Structural Adjustment.* Dakar, Senegal: Council for the Development of Social Science Research in Africa.

Mkandawire, T. and C. Soludo, eds. (2003) *African Voices on Structural Adjustment. A Companion to: Our Continent, Our Future.* Trenton, NJ: CODESRIA, Africa World Press, IDRC.

Molyneux, M. (2006) Mothers at the Service of the New Poverty Agenda: Progresa/Oportunidades, Mexico's Conditional Transfer Program. *Social Policy and Administration*, 40(4), pp. 425–449.

Murphy, S. (2006) Concentrated Market Power and Agricultural Trade, EcoFair Trade Dialogue Discussion Paper. No. 1, August 2006.

Mutua, M. (2008) Human Rights and Powerlessness: Pathologies of Choice and Substance. *Buffalo Law Review*, 56, pp. 1027–1034.

Napon, Abdoul Razac. (2008) On a marché contre la faim, L'Evénement. (Online) 27 May 2008. Available at: www.naturavox.fr/conso/On-a-marche-contre-la-faim [accessed 2 November 2011].

Nelson, J., ed. (1989) *Fragile Coalitions: The Politics of Economic Adjustment.* New Brunswick: Transaction Books.

New Partnership for Africa's Development (NEPAD). (2003) *Comprehensive Africa Agriculture Development Program (CAADP).* (Online) July 2003. Available at: www.nepad.org/system/files/caadp.pdf [accessed 1 November 2011].

Nussbaum, M. C. (2000) *Women and Human Development: The Capabilities Approach.* Cambridge: Cambridge University Press.

O'Connor, A. (2001) *Poverty Knowledge: Social Science, Social Policy, and the Poor in Twentieth Century US History.* Princeton and Oxford: Princeton University Press.

Olukoshi, A. (2001) Towards Developmental Democracy: A Note. Draft paper prepared for the discussion at the UNRISD meeting on "The Need to Rethink Development Economics," Cape Town, South Africa, 7–8 September 2001.

Phillips, A. (2001) Feminism and Liberalism Revisited: Has Martha Nussbaum Got it Right? *Constellations*, 8(2), pp. 249–266.

Randriamaro, Z. (2001) Financing For the Poor and Women: A Policy Critique. In: Barry Herman, Federica Pietracci and Krishnan Sharma, eds. *Financing for Development: Proposals from Business and Civil Society*. New York: United Nations University Press, pp. 25–33.

Randriamaro, Z. (2002) The NEPAD, Gender and the Poverty Trap: The NEPAD and the Challenges of Financing for Development in Africa from a Gender Perspective. Paper presented at joint TWN-Africa/CODESRIA International Conference on Africa and the Development Challenges of the New Millennium, Accra, 23–26 April 2002.

Randriamaro, Z. (2003) African Women Challenging Neo-liberal Economic Orthodoxy: The Conception and Mission of the GERA Program. *Gender and Development*, 11(1), pp. 44–51.

Randriamaro, Z. (2005) Making the Missing Link: MDGs, Gender and Macroeconomic Policy. Presentation at the UNDAW Expert Group Meeting on "Achievements, Gaps and Challenges in Linking the Implementation of the Beijing Platform for Action and the Millennium Declaration and Millennium Development Goals," Baku, Azerbaijan, 7–10 February 2005.

Randriamaro, Z. (2006) Gender and Trade: Overview Report. BRIDGE Cutting Edge Pack, Brighton: Institute of Development Studies (IDS), University of Sussex.

Randriamaro, Z. (2009) The Impact of the Systemic Crisis on Women in Eastern Africa. In: Association for Women's Rights in Development (AWID). The crisis' impact on women's rights: sub-regional perspectives, Brief 10.

Randriamaro, Z. (2010) *The Impact of the Global Systemic Crisis on Women in Eastern and Southern Africa: Responses and Prospects*. Toronto: AWID.

Rankin, K. N. (2001) Governing Development: Neoliberalism, Microcredit and Rational Economic Woman. *Economy and Society*, 30(1), pp. 18–37.

Reardon, T. (1997) Using Evidence of Household Income Diversification to Inform Study of the Rural Non Farm Labor Market in Africa. *World Development*, 25(5), pp. 735–747.

Robbins, R. H. (1999) *Global Problems and the Culture of Capitalism*. Boston: Allyn and Bacon.

Schoepf, B.G., C. Schoepf and J.V. Millen (2000) Theoretical Therapies, Remote Remedies: SAPs and the Political Ecology of Poverty and Health in Africa. In: J. Y. Kim, J. V. Millen, A. Irwin and J. Gershman, eds. *Dying for Growth: Global Inequality and the Health of the Poor*. Monroe, ME: Common Courage Press, pp. 91–126.

Seguino, S. (2009) Emerging Issue: The Gender Perspectives of the Financial Crisis. Written statement at the Interactive Expert Panel, Commission on the Status of Women, Fifty-third session, New York, 2–13 March 2009.

Social Watch. (2010) Social Watch Report 2010: After the Fall. (Online) Available at: www.socialwatch.org/book/export/html/11571 [accessed 7 October 2010].

Taylor, V. (2000) *Marketization of Governance: Critical Feminist Perspectives from the South*. Cape Town: A DAWN publication.

Tsikata, D. and J. Kerr, eds. (2000) *Demanding Dignity: Women Confronting Economic Reforms in Africa*. Ottawa, Ontario: North-South Institute.

United Nations Development Fund for Women (UNIFEM). (2006) Strengthening Responses to Create Wealth and Reduce Poverty for Women in Informal Cross-border Trade in Africa. Program Document, New York.

United Nations Development Fund for Women (UNIFEM). (2008) Regional Cross-Country

Report on UNIFEM Baseline Studies of Women in Informal Cross-Border Trade in Africa. Prepared by Z. Randriamaro and D. Budlender.

United Nations Development Program (UNDP). (1994) *Human Development Report,* New York: Oxford University Press.

United Nations Division for the Advancement of Women (UNDAW). (2009) World Survey on the Role of Women in Development: Women's Control over Economic Resources and Access to Financial Resources, including Microfinance. United Nations, New York. (Online) Available at: www.un.org/womenwatch/daw/public/WorldSurvey2009.pdf [accessed 2 November 2011].

Vorley, B. (2003) Food Inc. Corporate Concentration from Farm to Consumer. UK Food Group, London. (Online) Available at: www.ukfg.org.uk/docs/UKFG-Foodinc-Nov03.pdf [accessed 1 November 2011].

Whitehead, A. (n.d.) The Gendered Impacts of Liberalisation Policies on African Agricultural Economies and Rural Livelihoods. Background Paper for the UNRISD report *Gender Equality: Striving for Justice in an Unequal World.*

Williams, M. (2003) Engendering African Governments' Participation in the Reform of PRSPS—How Effective and How Can this be in the Service of Gender Equality? (Draft).

Williamson, J. (1990) What Washington Means by Policy Reform. In: John Williamson, ed. *Latin American Adjustment: How Much Has Happened?* Washington, DC: Institute for International Economics, ch. 2.

World Bank. (2006) Gender Equality as Smart Economics: A World Bank Group Gender Action Plan (Fiscal Years 2007–2010). (Online) (September 2006) Available at: http://siteresources.worldbank.org/INTGENDER/Resources/GAPNov2.pdf [accessed 2 November 2011].

World Bank. (2008) Double Jeopardy: Responding to High Food and Fuel Prices. Paper for the G8 Hokkaido-Toyako Summit. (Online) (2 July 2008) Available at: http://web.worldbank.org/WBSITE/EXTERNAL/NEWS/0,,contentMDK:21827681~pagePK:64257043~piPK:437376~theSitePK:4607,00.html [accessed 1 November 2011].

World Bank. (2009) Impact of the Financial Crisis on Women and Families, Presentation by PREM Gender and Development, n.d.

World Bank. (2011) News & Broadcast: Poverty. (Online) (July 2011) Available at: http://web.worldbank.org/WBSITE/EXTERNAL/NEWS/0,,contentMDK:20040961~menuPK:34480~pagePK:64257043~piPK:437376~theSitePK:4607,00.html [accessed 1 November 2011].

4 African poverty, gender and insecurity

John Weeks and Howard Stein

Introduction

Almost without exception, the countries of Africa south of the Sahara have extremely high rates of poverty and deprivation, which are manifested concretely in low life expectancies and health indicators. Substantial progress in reducing poverty requires long-term sustained growth which is equitably distributed at rates considerably higher than those experienced since the early 1980s. These three necessary characteristics of long-term growth—that growth is sustained, equitably distributed and more rapid—require purposeful government intervention. This has not been the case over the 1980s, 1990s and 2000s, in no small part due to the ideologically driven policies of multilateral and many bilateral aid donors and lenders (Weeks and Stein, 2006).

This chapter presents a macroeconomic framework for sustained, equitable and rapid growth that is feasible for the low-income countries of the sub-Saharan region. The second section considers the character of poverty in the region and mechanisms to alleviate this poverty in the short term. The flaws in all varieties of means testing are discussed, leading to a proposal for gender-focused universal benefits. Poverty elimination is a long-term process that requires poverty alleviation in the short term. In other words, the immediate suffering of the poor should be addressed, be it hunger, ill-health or insecurity from conflict. However, poverty alleviation does not usually result in poverty elimination or even reduction, both of which are central to improving human security and require a process of pro-poor growth, the combination of poverty-reducing investment and redistribution. Moreover, the failure of gender-based poverty interventions has been particularly pronounced and, as we will argue, largely due to conceptual problems in orthodox approaches to understanding the causes of poverty. The third section of this chapter develops guidelines for poverty reduction that seek to balance breadth of application with the fiscal constraints of governments, a gender-inclusive poverty reduction strategy that is countercyclical and growth enhancing.

Poverty alleviation

Means testing and anti-social protection

Most work on poverty addresses measurement on the one hand and the incidence of social expenditure on the other. Explicitly or implicitly, both of these issues are based on the concepts of the nature and the causes of poverty. Essential to the design of a successful anti-poverty strategy is distinguishing between poverty reduction and poverty alleviation and specifying the particular strategy for each, while guaranteeing that these strategies encompass gender differentiation.

The implicit view of orthodox economics, manifested in policies of the World Bank and the IMF, is that market economies automatically provide the opportunity for people to move out of poverty. It follows from this analysis that poverty results from the level of development and is reduced through growth. Growth itself is enhanced by increasing the efficiency of markets. Because markets are intrinsically efficient, the important measures to improve market efficiency are negative in nature: elimination of government regulations, a balanced budget, a monetary authority independent of political influence and a minimal role for public provision of services. The limited role of public policy allows people to make choices based on market prices, which will result in a balance between consumption and investment. In turn, this balance will lead to a rate of growth that optimizes individual welfare.

Along these lines, in gender terms, the orthodox view arising out the World Bank in the late 1980s was that the most cost-effective route to deal with poverty was through investing in women to expand their choice in economic activity.[1] The issue is couched in terms comparable to international trade, such that poverty is a product of women being unable to pursue their comparative advantage. In this case focusing on women is both efficient and also instrumental, aimed at meeting other development objectives rather than viewing women's welfare as an end goal (Jackson, 1996).

Three types of public provision for the poor are consistent with the orthodox focus: (1) protection of those who cannot take advantage of the opportunities provided by markets ("safety nets"); (2) in low-income countries those at the bottom of the distribution may require transitory support until their own efforts to bring themselves out of deprivation are successful (temporary transfers); and (3) in all countries natural disasters and severe economic "shocks," such as the international financial crisis, may require temporary public provision beyond the "safety nets" (disaster relief). To this can be added both the provision of education, particularly focused on girls and young women, and the provision of health services, with the former providing a person with the skills and the latter with the vigor to work out of poverty.

This general approach, which maintains that markets reduce poverty and some limited amount of public provision is appropriate under certain conditions, is the basis of almost all the anti-poverty support to sub-Saharan countries provided by multilateral and bilateral development agencies. The approach explicitly or implicitly incorporates the concept of the "deserving poor," a category that includes all those who seek to improve their circumstances but suffer from constraints that prevent them from doing so.

This analysis and approach to poverty and its reduction is especially appealing for the sub-Saharan countries, where the majority of the poor appear superficially to be independent producers, with the vast majority engaged in agriculture. This appearance is often interpreted as implying that the poor have the potential to move out of poverty through hard work if provided with the help to take better advantage of market opportunities. The inference that most rural households are independent, potentially self-sufficient farmers is incorrect. It ignores the complex hierarchies and employment patterns that characterize rural communities in sub-Saharan countries, as well as the subordinated relationships of women in market and non-market settings. A large amount of evidence demonstrates inequality of land distribution that requires households at the bottom of the distribution to seek work from households with larger holdings.[2]

The stereotype of poor households as self-sufficient farmers is also consistent with an argument to minimize government intervention. For decades supporters of this argument produced the following stylized narrative about poverty in sub-Saharan countries. Poverty is an overwhelmingly rural phenomenon. Urban households are, by contrast, relatively privileged, with better access to health and education. The urban unemployment that exists is "voluntary," so-called school leavers that are inappropriately educated for manual work, and employment opportunities are limited by minimum wages and trade unions. This "urban bias" is compounded by excessive taxation of an undifferentiated class of farmers and depression of prices by public sector market boards. Such stylized characterization of "the African farmer" yields the policy conclusion that rural poverty would be reduced through a deregulation of agricultural markets, thereby freeing farmers to take advantage of market opportunities.

This description of rural households was never accurate[3] and rendered completely absurd by the two decades of economic stagnation and decline during the 1980s and 1990s. In no small part the result of the elimination of public interventions required by the IMF and World Bank as conditionalities to their lending programs, this decline should have demonstrated the analytical, empirical and practical fallacies of the "market-opportunities-eliminate-poverty" argument.[4] The 1980s and 1990s showed what heterodox economists had argued since the early nineteenth century: in the absence of public intervention, market competition punishes the weak and rewards the strong.[5]

Moreover, the treatment of the rural household as a unit of analysis by orthodox economists in the World Bank and elsewhere ignored the gendered distribution of resources within households where male adults and children were disproportionately allocated a larger share of pecuniary and non-pecuniary income. Instead incidence of female poverty focused on female-headed households when frequently women were worse off in male-headed households due to the male bias in resource distribution (Jackson, 1996; Baruah, 2009).

Not withstanding the fall in urban incomes in the sub-Saharan region during the 1980s and 1990s, the decline in use of modern inputs on small-scale farms, and the declines in per capita income in the majority of the countries of the region, the market opportunities view of poverty reduction continued to be the implicit basis of the development assistance provided by almost all donors and lenders. The principal change, to an emphasis on political intervention by donors and lenders under the rubric of "governance," had no impact on the anti-poverty strategy: the long-term process of poverty reduction follows from improving the operation of markets, including the reduction of public sector corruption. The growth rate will rise to lift most households out of poverty, and poverty is alleviated by "safety nets" for those not lifted by growth.

The benefits associated with these "safety nets" would be limited to poor households by "targeting" the poor. What the World Bank calls the "gold standard" of targeting is the estimation of the income of a household.[6] This method of targeting sets an income level which by some standard is judged to be the poverty level, and those households whose incomes fall below the "poverty line" receive benefits and those above do not. For means testing on the basis of income to be effective, it must be possible to (a) establish the relevant income level below which the special measures, such as free benefits and reduced charges, will begin; (b) measure individual or household income with appropriate accuracy; and (c) achieve the measurement at an acceptable administrative cost.

The identification of a non-arbitrary income for a benefit or service is itself problematic, though the wide practice of doing so lends it a superficial credibility. The most prominent example of spurious credibility heavily promoted by the World Bank is the international standard measures of one and two US dollars per day. While useful for specific analytical purposes, such as inspecting the relationship between poverty and income distribution, it provides only the roughest guide to the level of income at which basic needs would be met.

The measurement of household living standards is extremely difficult in any low-income country, in part because of differences in both household compositions and prices among regions and rural and urban areas, to name but two difficulties. The particular circumstances of sub-Saharan countries make the measurement task difficult to the point of futile. The first of these problems, common to almost all low-income countries, is that the structure of employment does not lend itself to administrative verification of income levels of households. In developed countries, this verification is made by inspecting the applicant's employment records or registration with unemployment centers. This approach is of little use in sub-Saharan countries where less than 10 percent of the economically active population is employed in the so-called formal sector (see Table 4.1).

Second, remittances from abroad, about 2–3 percent of GDP for the region as a whole, are a substantial supplement to household income in several countries.[7] Were it the case that the overwhelming proportion of remittances entered the

Table 4.1 Paid employment shares in sub-Saharan countries

Country	Year	% labor force
South Africa	2007	48
Cape Verde	2000	33
Botswana	2006	31
Swaziland	2000	27
Congo Republic	1990	16
Zimbabwe	2002	16
Equatorial Guinea	1983	15
Gabon	1996	15
Madagascar	2005	15
Kenya	2000	14
Malawi	1995	13
Zambia	1990	12
Cameroon	1985	11
Angola	1992	10
Côte d'Ivoire	1990	10
Ghana	1991	9
Guinea-Bissau	1983	8
Gambia	1990	7
Tanzania	2001	7
Senegal	1991	6
Eritrea	1998	5
Sierra Leone	2004	5
Benin	1992	4
Sudan	1992	4
Togo	1997	4
Ethiopia	2004	3
Mozambique	1988	3
Burundi	1991	2
Central African Republic	1992	1
Chad	1997	1
Niger	1991	1
Nigeria	1980	1

Source: http://laborsta.ilo.org/.

Notes
No data: Comoros, Congo DR, Djibouti, Guinea, Lesotho, Liberia, Libya, Mali, Mayotte, Maurita-nia, Namibia, Rwanda, and Sao Tome and Principe.

country through formal channels, these could be traced to specific households, but the great proportion is not recorded. Even more serious for measurement, non-marketed activities such as consumption of food grown by the household itself make a substantial contribution to the standard of living.

Third, poverty measured by household level income also says nothing about the individual accesses to income within the household. Men and women have joint and separate earning streams and consumption. Women have generally lower wages and less employment, different kin and conjugal access to transfers and other income sources, and differentiated obligations and responsibilities (for example, to children), all of which delimits any household income level as a measure of poverty among women (Jackson, 1996).

Fourth, it should be emphasized that the dollar a day measure is quite flawed and has been arguably manipulated by the Bank to understate poverty over time. Until 1999, the World Bank used $1/day in the US in 1985.[8] In 1999 the level was raised to $1.08/day in the US in 1993. Since inflation was 34.3 percent in the US between 1985 and 1993 this dramatically lowered what a dollar could purchase in 1993 and diminished the benchmark poverty level by 19.5 percent (1.08/1.34). This had the effect of instantaneously lowering poverty levels in the same countries in the same years.

The dollar a day measure was converted using purchasing power parity (PPP) tables of the World Bank (an exchange rate measure reflecting price differentials between countries). In 2008, new World Bank efforts to measure price differences between countries through the International Comparison Program (ICP) led to an update in its poverty measure to $1.25 per day at 2005 prices. The new level greatly understated poverty since inflation in the US between 1985 and 2005 rose by 80.61 percent thereby reducing the benchmark poverty rate compared to 1985 by 44.5 percent. Based on a proper reflection of inflation, the number of poor in 2005 goes from 51 percent of the population of SSA (or 390.6 million people) when using the $1.25 measure, to 68 percent of the population (or roughly 518 million people) when using the $1.80 measure.[9]

The measure is very low to begin with. By US Dept. of Agricultural standards, the expenditure needed to purchase a minimum base of calories (1,600–2,800 depending on age and gender) for a family of four would be $5,134 in 1999. But the $1/day would only provide $1,812, only around a third of the cost of food alone! This is a ridiculously low standard that understates the number of poor.

There are also problems associated with using the PPP for global poverty comparisons. The PPP relies on price levels between the US and developing countries that reflect an average bundle of goods. This bundle includes both tradable and non-tradable items, like services. However the poor actually consume fewer non-tradables since they focus their budgets mostly on basic tradable food commodities. Since non-tradables are much more expensive in the US relative to developing countries compared to tradables, this tends to overstate the purchasing power of the currency relative to the actual exchange rate (which is more closely aligned to tradables).

The characteristics of households imply that estimating income either has to rely on the reporting of the household itself, or on direct investigation of households, an intrusive policing function subject to corruption at the local level. Even more intrusive is the alternative proposed to income measures, so-called proxy targeting, which the World Bank defines as follows:

> Proxy means tests generate a score for applicant households based on fairly easy to observe characteristics of the household such as the location and quality of its dwelling, its ownership of durable goods, demographic

structure of the household, and the education and, possibly, the occupations of adult members.[10]

(World Bank, 2011c)

Not withstanding the substantial administrative capacity required for proxy testing,[11] this method has been applied, at least in name, in several sub-Saharan countries.[12] Even if incomes or proxies for incomes could be measured quickly, cheaply and with accuracy, all means testing still suffers from two fundamental flaws. First, the purpose of the exercise is to divide a population into two groups, the "poor" that receive benefits and the "non-poor" that do not. If those defined as poor are disproportionately concentrated geographically or ethnically, or if it is so perceived, the division is invidious and contains the potential to exacerbate the conflicts that have afflicted many sub-Saharan countries. Equally serious is the police function implied by means testing, all forms of which require the state to verify the poverty status claimed by a household. The invasion of privacy result-ing from verification is inconsistent with the principles of a democratic society and a dangerous extension of state authority in non-democratic countries. A third variant of means testing, "community-based targeting," is the most pernicious of all, replying on a "group of community members or a community leader ... to decide who in the community should benefit" (World Bank, 2011d).[13] It would be difficult to design a targeting mechanism more prone to abuse of power. Both approaches could exacerbate human insecurity in multiple ways.

From a purely technical point of view, the fatal flaw in the use of means testing in sub-Saharan countries is the implicit assumption that incomes remain stable over time. If a large portion of the population is clustered close to the poverty line, as must be the case for most African countries,[14] there will be a tendency for many households to move above and below the line over the eco-nomic cycle. This creates two problems. First, even if technically feasible, the administrative task of identifying the poor becomes so expensive as to be unmanageable, because households that are defined as poor in one period are not in another.

Second, as a result of the first problem, the entire purpose of the means testing exercise is rendered invalid if the "poor" are not a stable administrative or prac-tical category. Attempts to deliver benefits by income testing will result in an arbitrary delivery system with "leakages" to the non-poor. In such circum-stances, means testing fails its purpose of avoiding such leakages. The identifica-tion of the poor may be administratively possible at a particular point in time, but the identification is not valid over time. This represents an extreme example of the "borderline problem," in which benefit delivery on the basis of means testing systematically fails.

Income volatility in sub-Saharan countries

Empirical evidence on family incomes over time in sub-Saharan countries is extremely limited, because it requires identifying and following specific households over two or more surveys. A recently published study of Ethiopia does this and indicates that the population near the poverty line was quite unstable during the 1990s and early 2000s (Geda *et al.*, 2009).[15] Many households, both in rural and urban areas, dropped below the poverty line even as aggregate incomes grew rapidly. This implies that had benefits in the second half of the 1990s been distributed on the basis of poverty status from the survey of 1994, up to 20 percent of the "non-poor" would have been below the line in at least one year, and a greater proportion of the "poor" would have moved out of poverty.

This instability in the distribution of households near the poverty line indicates that poverty status is a static phenomenon even in the short run. "Poor" households fall into four conceptual groups: (1) those well above the poverty line that fall below it during an economic crisis (as at the end of the 2000s); (2) those close to the poverty line that move in and out of it depending on the phase of the economic cycle;[16] (3) those persistently in poverty that move out only when economic growth is strong and sustained; and (4) those households permanently trapped in poverty due to their structural circumstances, such as landlessness or few able-bodied adults.

Were it the case that in the sub-Saharan countries economic growth had been consistently above population increase for the 1990s and 2000s, the proportion of households in the first three categories would have substantially declined, as occurred in East and Southeast Asia. However, after declines in per capita income for most of the countries during the 1980s, growth rates during 1990–2008 were unimpressive, as Table 4.2 shows. Of the 44 countries in the table, 13 suffered declines and nine more had rates of less than 1 percent.

As important as slow growth is for reducing poverty, the variability of growth is just as significant. The growth rate across the 44 countries was 1.3 percent per annum, with an average standard deviation of 5.4, over four times the average for GDP growth. The importance of growth variation can be appreciated by first noting that the standard deviation is smaller than the average growth rate for only seven of the 44 countries; i.e., for 37 countries growth is less than a standard deviation from being negative. Such large annual variations in growth imply that even in a country with a relatively strong growth performance, in any year there is a high probability of per capita income falling. For example, Namibia, a mineral-rich middle-income country, enjoyed a rate of growth for two decades well above the regional average with substantially less than average variability. Nonetheless, in any year there was a 40 percent probability of growth being negative.

The great variability of growth rates in the sub-Saharan region implies that attempting to identify the poor is a futile task. Even in countries with a steady growth performance a substantial proportion of households move in or out of poverty every year. The one US dollar a day poverty rates in the final column show that in addition to futile, the identification process is pointless. Poverty rates in the sub-Saharan countries are so high that when the rates are combined with the volatility of incomes, the majority, even vast majority, of households should be part of poverty alleviation programs.

Table 4.2 Per capita income growth in sub-Saharan countries, 1990–2008

	Country	PCY US$ 1990	Index 2008 (1990 =100)	Growth rate (%)	Standard deviation	Headcount poverty
1	Equatorial Guinea	547	1,589	15.4	19.9	na
2	Sudan	261	204	4.0	3.7	na
3	Mozambique	185	198	3.8	4.1	75
4	Mauritius	2,535	194	3.7	1.0	na
5	Uganda	181	192	3.6	2.1	52
6	Cape Verde	854	191	3.6	2.8	21
7	Botswana	2,463	179	3.2	2.8	na
8	Angola	794	171	3.0	10.6	54
9	Lesotho	338	155	2.4	2.1	43
10	Burkina Faso	175	150	2.3	3.0	57
11	Ghana	281	150	2.3	1.0	30
12	Ethiopia	129	147	2.1	6.9	na
13	Namibia	1,828	147	2.1	3.0	na
14	Mali	213	139	1.8	3.5	61
15	Chad	181	139	1.8	9.7	62
16	Tanzania	267	136	1.7	2.3	89
17	Rwanda	234	134	1.6	15.9	77
18	Nigeria	370	131	1.5	3.0	64
19	Swaziland	1,196	130	1.5	2.4	63
20	Malawi	132	125	1.2	6.7	74
21	Guinea	340	123	1.2	1.6	70
22	Benin	294	122	1.1	0.9	47
23	South Africa	3,152	118	0.9	2.1	26
24	Senegal	460	115	0.8	2.3	44
25	Mauritania	419	115	0.8	4.1	21
26	Gambia	340	110	0.5	2.7	34
27	Eritrea	135	109	0.5	7.6	na
28	Congo, Republic	1,143	106	0.3	3.5	54
29	Sierra Leone	248	105	0.3	10.8	53
30	Kenya	450	103	0.2	2.2	20
31	Zambia	383	101	0.1	4.2	64
32	Cameroon	718	99	−0.1	3.6	33
33	Niger	193	93	−0.4	4.1	66
34	Madagascar	290	93	−0.4	5.0	68
35	Togo	273	90	−0.6	6.6	39
36	Gabon	4,640	89	−0.6	3.7	5
37	Comoros	416	89	−0.6	3.3	46
38	Central African Republic	271	85	−0.9	4.0	62
39	Côte d'Ivoire	658	80	−1.2	3.0	23
40	Liberia	200	74	−1.7	3.0	na
41	Burundi	152	73	−1.7	4.1	81
42	Zimbabwe	643	70	−2.2	6.4	na
43	Guinea-Bissau	182	70	−2.0	8.4	49
44	Liberia	200	74	−1.7	33.6	na
	Average	667	157	1.3	5.4	51
	Without oil exporters	595	122	0.9	4.2	52

Source: *World Development Indicators 2009*. Headcount poverty is the share of population with income less than one US dollar per day. Liberia excluded from averages for standard deviations.

Poverty alleviation with universality

The practical difficulties with means testing in sub-Saharan countries do not negate the fiscal resource constraints that limit the extent to which governments in the region can finance poverty alleviation and poverty reduction. Some mechanism is required to establish expenditure priorities, especially for current expenditure on poverty alleviation. An alternative to means testing for poverty alleviation programs is universal provisional with categorical targeting. This directs benefits to groups of the population that can be administratively identified (categorical targeting), without dividing the group between beneficiaries and non-beneficiaries (universal provision).[17] Examples are programs for mothers with young children, old age pensions and child allowances. The great advantage of this approach is its administrative feasibility, and the population categories can be chosen to maximize the poverty-reducing effect thereby enhancing human security. An argument against this approach is that occasional benefits accrue to those who by some definition "do not need them," so-called leakages, and as a result of making payments to the non-poor, the level of benefits to the poor is reduced.

The use of the term "leakages" reflects either analytical confusion or an ideological view of poverty. It was demonstrated above both analytically and empirically that no clear division between the poor and the non-poor is possible in the sub-Saharan countries. "Leakages" presupposes this division. Given the insurmountable difficulties of making the division, its application is a political vehicle to limit expenditures and maintain the ideological view that poverty is a marginal phenomenon in market economies.

Markets are part of the institutional framework of society that generates economic growth and development and therefore part of the long-term poverty reduction process. Markets also foster processes that create the conditions for poverty in the process of development. The most obvious mechanism in sub-Saharan countries by which markets are poverty creating is through the modernization of agriculture, as mechanization and land consolidation raise productivity and lead to landlessness. Of course, this process in which the labor is expelled from agriculture and then employed in secondary and tertiary sectors is the essence of the development process. However, it is a process that simultaneously causes poverty while generating the means by which that poverty can be reduced.

The transfer of labor from agriculture to urban employment, so famously described by W. A. Lewis,[18] is a process that creates landlessness, which can contribute to human insecurity. If the growth of urban employment is sufficiently rapid, the effect of landlessness on poverty can be minor. However, even in the East and Southeast Asian countries with their rapid employment growth, this labor transfer process generated landlessness and unemployment along with development.[19]

In addition to this fundamental objection to the concept of "leakages," the advantages of avoiding them are open to question. Considering the trade-off in level of benefits, for any level of benefit, the universal program is likely to have lower unit costs than the means tested program. This is for the obvious reason that the universal program would not need a bureaucracy to verify and to police qualification for benefits. Under a universal program each benefit unit accruing to the "non-poor" does not represent a full unit that would accrue to the "poor" if there were a shift to means testing.

Further, it appears from the experience of developed countries that means testing can undermine the political sustainability of social programs because those excluded from benefits have no direct material incentive to support increased funding for such programs. This prevents the development of a political coalition that would favor a pro-poor growth strategy. In an important sense, means testing is a barrier to poverty reduction because it fosters the belief that markets have no poverty-creating effect and perpetuates a growth strategy that excludes much of the population.

The alternative to means testing, targeting easily identifiable groups with universal programs, has the political advantage of giving the non-poor an incentive to support poverty-reducing programs. It also avoids the social stigma of dividing the population between the poor and the non-poor. Given the characteristics of sub-Saharan countries an effective and feasible poverty alleviation strategy would provide access to benefits by targeting clearly identifiable groups with programs of universal access, "universal access within categorical targeting."

Simple to administer and effective for poverty alleviation in sub-Saharan countries are those programs directed toward women. Such programs operate in the region, often associated with what are called conditional transfers, in which receiving the specified benefit requires some action on the part of the recipient. An example would be cash payments to mothers on the condition that their children attend school (Lund *et al.*, 2008). There is little or no evidence to assess the impact of setting behavioral conditions on benefits,[20] and as for means testing they suffer from the need for verification. The imposing of behavioral conditions for poverty alleviation is a continuation of the "deserving poor" view of poverty, in which benefits are not exclusively motivated by the purpose of aiding the poor, but aiding the poor to behave in a deserving manner.

An additional dimension is the gendered constraints on both targeted and universal programs. For example men and women may not be able to equally access food for work programs, either because of gender norms and pressures that constrain female participation or because of the high opportunity cost of time (Jackson, 1996). In fact, the issue of time is essential to a structural understanding of the gendered consequences of poverty interventions—an area badly neglected in orthodox approaches.

Central to the task is the recognition that it is typical for women to supply their labor to the household for socially vital and obligatory reproductive-related work without receiving direct payment in money or kind. A gendered analysis of human security should focus on time poverty dimensions of these relational responsibilities and with them the associated reigning care regimes which are balanced between the market, the state and the household level. Poor women spend great parts of their day collecting water and fuel, providing care for members of the family, managing household maintenance-related activities like cooking, cleaning, transporting, purchasing food, etc., along with income-generating or subsistent economic activities. Increasing public investment in the infrastructure and services aimed at addressing time poverty can enhance women's participation in education, governance and wage employment, which can enhance their human security. Poverty-reducing interventions need to take into account the socially defined temporal barriers that restrict equality of opportunity (Akram-Lodhi, 2009).

We can summarize the practical guidelines for poverty alleviation programs as follows: they should be made administratively and fiscally feasible by categorical targeting, universal within the category, equitable, directed to girls and women with particular consideration for related interventions that allow them to better participate, and consistent with the government's long-term poverty reduction strategy. The design of the associated poverty reduction strategy is considered next.

Poverty reduction

The neoliberal macroeconomic policy that prevailed in the sub-Saharan region before the crisis of the 2000s expected market forces to drive development. Fiscal policies were constrained to keep deficits low, monetary policies fixated on low inflation targets and exchange rate policies committed to full flexibility. This combination was unlikely to foster growth and, as shown in Table 4.2, it did not.

The pro-growth poverty-reducing alternative has the following elements, each a break with neoliberal policy:

1   Fiscal policy should be expansionary and include short-term poverty alleviation expenditure from the current budget and poverty-focused public investment in the capital budget.
2   The exchange rate should be managed in order to promote export competitiveness and currency stability.
3   Monetary policy should accommodate fiscal expansion and export promotion, with low real rates of interest that promote private investment and moderate public-sector debt.
4   Time and its implications to gender need to be included in macroeconomic analysis.

The conditionalities imposed by stabilization and structural adjustment programs that compelled governments to seek very low fiscal deficits, as well as low inflation rates, constrained growth (Stein, 2006). The obsession with low deficits prevented a growth-focused fiscal policy in sub-Saharan African countries. Evidence for 30 countries for which the IMF reports relevant statistics shows that deficits over 5 percent of GDP have not been common. During 1985–2005 never more than one quarter of these countries had a larger deficit in any year.

For all years during this period at least half the countries had a deficit below 3 percent (Weeks and Patel, 2007).

In a poverty reduction growth strategy deficits would be used as a policy instrument, not treated as a problem to be minimized.[21] The movements of both revenues and expenditures are linked to the economic cycle: revenues fall when private income falls but social expenditures need to rise in order to compensate for income losses. Insisting on low deficit targets renders fiscal policy "pro-cyclical"; it aggravates downturns rather than moderating them. Deficits also should be used as part of a long-term strategy through borrowing to finance public investment in essential economic and social infrastructure. Without exten-sive public investment in part financed by public borrowing, poverty reduction would not be possible.

While stabilization and structural adjustment programs were decommission-ing fiscal policies with deficit limits, they converted previously active manage-ment of exchange rates into so-called floating or "free market" regimes. Contrary to expectations, non-intervention led to increased volatility of nominal exchange rates, often precipitated by transitory external "shocks," such as international price changes or manipulation by large traders in narrow currency markets (see Weeks *et al.*, 2006). In the small open economies of the region, exchange rate volatility gravely jeopardized macroeconomic stability. As the prices of some primary products, especially petroleum and minerals, rose in the 2000s, exchange rates briefly appreciated before the crisis at the end of the decade. Under such conditions of global instability, exchange rate management is an essential policy instrument to reduce the volatility of economies. Exchange rate management is central for maintaining short-term stability of the nominal exchange rate and achieving a real exchange rate that can foster broad-based export competitiveness and structural diversification of the economy.[22]

Orthodox macroeconomics assumes that there is a free supply of caring labor. Women's unpaid responsibilities are social assets that both markets and states fail to provide but are taken for granted by conventional measures of efficiency. Once care is seen as an important relational service that can be substituted by public or private sources, then macroeconomic frameworks should incorporate strategies to lower the burden of household maintenance services aimed at redu-cing women's time constraints (Akram-Lodhi, 2009).

However, in practice neoliberal policies have often done the opposite by con-tributing to time poverty. Conventional macroeconomics says nothing about gender distributional parameters, yet time has a significant effect on the division of labor. An increase in the burden of household expenditures can have a dra-matic impact on intra-familial equity. For example, introducing user fees in health care and other public goods not only has a well-documented dispropor-tionate effect on the poor in general, user fees also put pressure on poor women who must absorb the increased home care sometimes at the expense of income earning activities (Stein, 2008; Akram-Lodhi, 2009).

A macroeconomic framework oriented towards poverty reduction does not have to be discovered: it is known and it is feasible (Weeks, 2009b). Fiscal policy should be expansionary and focused on poverty alleviation programs in the short term and public investment in the medium and long term. Exchange rates should be managed in order to maintain short-run price and currency stability and foster long-term competitiveness and diversification of the economy. Monetary policy should accommodate fiscal expansion instead of restricting it through the targeting of unreasonably low inflation rates with correspondingly high real rates of interest. Over the long term, this framework implies a greater reliance on domestic finance and less on official development assistance, which often is unpredictable (UNCTAD, 2000).

Public investment, key to long-term poverty-reducing growth, requires careful design. The principal guidelines should be that the investments contribute directly to improving the lives of the poor, are implemented with methods that are labor using, and have an explicit impact on the welfare of girls and women. The type of investments that would directly help the poor will vary among countries. Projects that provide safe water to villages and urban slum areas would meet all three guidelines. Another type of project is the provision of electricity to rural and urban areas, as in Sierra Leone. The repair of power lines requires considerable labor, and the electricity would reduce the work load of poor women through the pumping of water and cooking.[23]

A much neglected mechanism for directly generating income for poor women is to assign gender quotas to public projects. Despite resistance to such quotas by many national and local governments, there are very few projects that could justifiably exclude women on health grounds. In what one hopes could be a precedent setting measure, in 2008 the government of Sierra Leone set a quota for women participants at 40 percent in a cash-for-work program funded by the World Bank (Weeks, 2009a). Quotas for women are of great practical importance for poverty reduction in countries recovering from conflict and those characterized by substantial labor migration, but as discussed above, associated policies to take advantage of these opportunities must also be in place. For both types of countries the proportion of households is high in which women are the only sources of income.

Summary and conclusions

Central to the neoliberal macroeconomic framework that came to dominate policy in the sub-Saharan region was the faith that markets that were "freed" from public regulation would generate widespread growth with only a few left behind, which could be supported by "safety nets." This policy framework did not generate much growth, much less was that growth pro-poor. To achieve poverty reduction purposeful government action is required, which integrates poverty alleviation and poverty reduction in a long-term strategy.

That long-term strategy should be based on the principle of universality. Short-term measures to alleviate poverty should not divide the population arbitrarily between the "poor" and the "non-poor." Nor should the poverty reduction strategy be based on market processes that reward the "winners" while consoling the "losers" with "safety nets." Due to the nature of the economies and societies of sub-Saharan countries, the poor/non-poor dichotomy is invalid. It is a false dichotomy both technically with regard to measurements and administratively with respect to identification of households. The mistakes and lack of fairness inherent in that false dichotomy can be avoided by categorical targeting of poverty alleviation benefits to girls and women without means testing and providing them with social goods that will allow them to take advantage of the opportunities.

Making the long-term poverty reduction strategy effective requires a fundamental shift in the macroeconomic framework. This shift abandons the procyclical neoliberal obsession with low fiscal deficits and low inflation and adopts a strategy that both employs current expenditure to counter external shocks in a countercyclical manner and uses capital expenditure to foster poverty-reducing expansion of productive capacity.

Notes

1 The view has not changed. To quote from the World Bank website on education: "Girls' education yields some of the highest returns of all development investments, yielding both private and social benefits that accrue to individuals, families, and society at large" (World Bank, 2011a).

2 A study of five sub-Saharan countries found high degrees of inequality of arable land distribution, with Gini coefficients for land per adult of over .50 for four of the countries (Ethiopia, Kenya, Malawi and Rwanda) and just below for the fifth (Mozambique). The average land worked by the lowest quartile in all five countries was less than a tenth of an acre (Jayne *et al.*, 2002).

3 "Under existing conditions, the ability of households in the bottom per capita land quartile to escape from poverty directly through agricultural productivity growth is limited by their constrained access to land and other resources" (Jayne *et al.*, 2002: p. 5).

4 See Stein (2010) for a study of the impact of World Bank agricultural policies on poverty and income inequality in Africa.

5 Bhorat (2005) provides a survey of poverty and labor markets demonstrating this conclusion.

6 From the relevant World Bank web page: "A verified means test is usually regarded as the gold standard of targeting. It seeks to collect (nearly) complete information on households' income and/or wealth and verifies the information collected against independent sources" (World Bank, 2011b).

7 Based on balance of payments data, the IMF study estimated remittances to the sub-Saharan region to be seven billion US dollars per year in the early 2000s. This is certainly an under-estimate, as the authors acknowledge (Gupta *et al.*, 2007).

8 It should be noted that the levels were very low to begin with. In 1985 the poverty line was set at around $3,663 per person in a family of four. The poverty measure was based on the controversial Orshansky formula where the poverty threshold was considered to be three times the cost of a minimum diet. Even based on this formulation of a dollar a day the $365 is only 33 percent of the cost of food alone for the poor in the US and a mere 10 percent of the US poverty line prior to any cost of living adjustments through the usage of the PPP (US Census Bureau, 2011). See Fisher (1992) for a history of the development of the US poverty line.

9 The figures for $1.25 per day are from Chen and Ravallion (2008) and calculated from World Bank (2009).

10 These proxy elements must be combined into a single indicator:

> The indicators used in calculating this score and their weights are derived from statistical analysis (usually regression analysis or principal components) of data from detailed household surveys of a sort too costly to be carried out for all applicants to large programs.

By whatever statistic method they are weighted, the resulting weights are arbitrary because the units in which the separate elements are measured are not unique (World Bank, 2011c).

11 The World Bank web page on proxy testing states, "Proxy means tests are most appropriately used where there is reasonably high administrative capacity" (2011c).

12 The World Bank described the food subsidy program in Mozambique as follows:

> The program provides a monthly cash transfer to recipient households. The value of the transfer is low and depends on the size of the household, starting at Mt70,000 (US$3) per month for a one-person household and rising to a maximum of Mt140,000 (US$6) for households with five or more members. Despite its name, the program is not a subsidy, but a cash transfer for the poor to buy food. Target groups include people who are temporarily or permanently unable to work or satisfy their subsistence needs. Eligibility is determined by a combination of proxy indicators (age, disability), means testing (per capita monthly income below Mt70,000), and health status (chronically sick or malnourished).
>
> (World Bank, 2011e)

13 In what must be considered an understatement, the World Bank web page states, "It would not be surprising if such a system continued or exacerbated any existing patterns of social exclusion" (2011d).

14 Consider the case of a country with a per capita income of US$365. If income were normally distributed, half the population lies below the one US dollar a day poverty line. If most people are above the level of starvation (though suffering from malnutrition), their incomes cannot be far below the poverty line. Since the income distribution is skewed, the clustering under the poverty line is all the greater.

15 A similar conclusion, that households move in and out of poverty, is implied by the statistics presented in a case study of Zambia, though the data did not allow a strict comparison across surveys for the same set of families (Weeks *et al.*, 2006, Chapter 3, Annex 2).

16 Variations can be over the course of the year. Dostie *et al.* (2002) point to the seasonal variations in food consumption in Madagascar that add roughly 1 million people to the ranks of the normally counted poor during the rainy season.

17 On the World Bank website this is called "demographic targeting," where the discussion is almost entirely on programs based on age (2011f).

18 In his famous article Lewis makes only passing reference to unemployment (Lewis, 1954).

19 For a discussion of development in Asian countries and the relevance for the sub-Saharan region, see Stein (1995).

20 "[T]here have been no rigorous analyses there of the respective costs and benefits of conditional versus unconditional transfers, so that the impact of conditionality itself is unknown" (Schubert and Slater, 2006: p. 571).

21 In 2009 the chief economist for Africa of the World Bank, Shanta Devarajan, in his blog argued against a fiscal stimulus "for Africa" on the grounds that increasing a fiscal deficit would result in inflation or a reduction in private investment ("crowding out") or both.

22 The necessary complementarity between a poverty reduction strategy and exchange rate management is discussed analytically and applied empirically to the case of Sierra Leone in Weeks, 2009a and 2009b.

23 Increasing the provision of electricity was one of the most important projects in the government's Poverty Reduction Strategy Paper (Sierra Leone, 2008).

Bibliography

Akram-Lodhi, A. (2009) The Macroeconomics of Human Insecurity: Why Gender Matters. In: J. Leckie, ed. *Development in an Insecure and Gendered World*. London: Ashgate, pp. 71–90.

Baruah, Bipasha. (2009) Monitoring Progress Toward Gender-Equitable Poverty Alleviation: The Tools of the Trade. *Progress in Development Studies*, 9(3), pp. 171–186.

Bhorat, Haroon. (2005) Poverty, Inequality and Labour Markets in Africa: A Descriptive Overview, Working Paper 9631, Development Policy Research Unit, University of Cape Town.

Chen, S. and M. Ravallion. (2008) The Developing World is Poorer Than We Thought, But no Less Successful in the Fight Against Poverty. World Bank Policy Research Working Paper No. 4703, September.

Devarajan, Shanta. (2009) A Fiscal Stimulus for Africa? Africa Can … End Poverty, [blog] 9 March. Available at: http://blogs.worldbank.org/africacan/a-fiscal-stimulus-for-africa [accessed 3 November 2011].

Dostie, B. A., S. Haggblade and J. Randriamamonjy. (2002) Seasonal Poverty in Madagascar: Magnitude and Solution. *Food Policy*, 27, pp. 493–518.

Fisher, Gordon. (1992) The Development and History of the Poverty Thresholds. *Social Security Bulletin*, Winter; 55(4), pp. 3–14.

Geda, Alemayehu, Abebe Shimeles and John Weeks. (2009) Growth, Poverty and Inequality in Ethiopia: Which Way for Pro-poor Growth? *Journal of International Development*, 27(7), pp. 947–970.

Gupta, Sanjeev, Catherine Pattillo and Smita Wagh. (2007) Impact of Remittances on Poverty and Financial Development in Sub-Saharan Africa. IMF Working Paper, 07/38, International Monetary Fund, Washington, DC.

Jackson, Cecile. (1996) Rescuing Gender From the Poverty Trap. *World Development*, 24(3), pp. 489–504.

Jamal, Vali and John Weeks. (1989)   *A Critique of Neoclassical Macroeconomics*. London and New York: Macmillan and St. Martin's.

Jayne, T. S., Takashi Yamano, Michael T. Weber, David Tschirley, Rui Benfica, Antony Chapoto, Ballard Zulu and David Neven. (2002) Smallholder Income and Land Distribution in Africa: Implications for Poverty Reduction Strategies. Policy Synthesis, USAID, No. 59.

Lewis, W. A. (1954) Economic Development with Unlimited Supplies of Labor. *The Manchester School*, 22(2), pp. 139–191.

Lund, Frances, Michael Noble, Helen Barnes and Gemma Wright. (2008) Is There a Rationale for Conditional Cash Transfers for Children in South Africa? Working Paper No. 53, Centre for the Analysis of South African Social Policy, Department of Social Policy and Social Work, University of Oxford.

McKinley, Terry. (2007) Raising Domestic Revenue for the MDGs: Why Wait until 2015?. One Pager, Number 39, International Poverty Centre, Brasilia.

Schubert, Bernd and Rachel Slater. (2006) Social Cash Transfers in Low Income African Countries: Conditional or Unconditional? *Development Policy Review*, 24(5), pp. 571–578.

Sierra Leone, Republic of. (2008) An Agenda for Change: Second Poverty Reduction

Strategy. (Online) Available at: http://unipsil.unmissions.org/portals/unipsil/media/publications/agenda_for_change.pdf [accessed 5 November 2011].

Stein, Howard. (1995) *Asian Industrialization and Africa: Studies in Policy Alternatives to Structural Adjustment*. New York: Palgrave Macmillan.

Stein, Howard. (2006) Structural Adjustment. In: David Alexander Clark, ed. *The Elgar Companion to Development Studies*. Northampton, MA: Edward Elgar, pp. 596–600.

Stein, Howard. (2008) *Beyond the World Bank Agenda: An Institutional Approach to Development*. Chicago: University of Chicago Press.

Stein, Howard. (2010) World Bank Agricultural Policies, Poverty and Income Inequality in Sub-Saharan Africa. *Cambridge Journal of Regions, Economy and Society*, March; 4(1), pp. 79–90.

United Nations Conference on Trade and Development (UNCTAD). (2000) *The Least Developed Countries Report 2000*. Geneva: UNCTAD.

United States Census Bureau. (2011) Poverty Thresholds, 1985. (Online) Available at: www.census.gov/hhes/www/poverty/data/threshld/thresh85.html [accessed 2 November2011].

Van Domelen, Julie. (2006) Issues and Design Options in Reaching the Poor through Social Funds and other Community-Driven Programs. Paper commissioned by the Social Protection Team, Human Development Network, World Bank.

Weeks, John. (1993a) *Fallacies of Competition*. London: SOAS. Available at: http://jweeks.org.

Weeks, John. (1993b) *Africa Misunderstood: Whatever Happened to the Urban-rural Income Gap*. London: Macmillan.

Weeks, John. (2009a) *The Impact of the Global Financial Crisis on the Economy of Sierra Leone: A Report for UNDP Freetown and the Ministry of Finance and Economic Development, Republic of Sierra Leone*. Freetown: UNDP.

Weeks, John. (2009b) The Global Financial Crisis and Countercyclical Policy. Key Presentation at the 2009 African Caucus "Global Crisis and Africa-Responses, Lessons Learnt and the Way Forward," Freetown, Sierra Leone, 12–13 August 2009. (Online) Available at: www.soas.ac.uk/cdpr/publications/papers/file53491.pdf [accessed 3 November 2011].

Weeks, John and Shruti Patel. (2007) Fiscal Policy, Training Module #1, International Poverty Centre, Brasilia. (Online) Available at: www.undp-povertycentre.org/pub/IPC-TrainingModule1.pdf [accessed 5 November 2011].

Weeks, John and Howard Stein. (2006) Washington Consensus. In: David Alexander Clark, ed. *The Elgar Companion to Development Studies*. Northampton, MA: Edward Elgar, pp. 676–679.

Weeks, John, Victoria Chisala, Alemayehu Geda, Hulya Dagdeviren, Terry McKinley, Alfredo Saad-Filho and Carlos Oya. (2006) *Economic Policies for Growth, Employment and Poverty Reduction: Case Study of Zambia*. United Nations Development Program, Ndola, Zambia: Mission Press.

World Bank. (2009) PovcalNet. (Online) Available at: http://iresearch.worldbank.org/PovcalNet/povDuplic.html [accessed 2 November 2011].

World Bank. (2011a) Girls' Education. (Online) 18 August 2011. Available at: http://web.worldbank.org/WBSITE/EXTERNAL/TOPICS/EXTEDUCatION/0,,contentMDK:20298916~menuPK:617572~pagePK:148956~piPK:216618~theSitePK:282386,00.html#Top [accessed 3 November 2011].

World Bank. (2011b) Means Testing. (Online) Available at: http://web.worldbank.org/WBSITE/EXTERNAL/TOPICS/EXTSOCIALPROTECTION/EXTSAFETYNETSAN

DTRANSFERS/0,,contentMDK:20795779~isCURL:Y~menuPK:1552914~pagePK:21 0058~piPK:210062~theSitePK:282761,00.html [accessed 2 November 2011].

World Bank. (2011c) Proxy Means Testing. (Online) Available at: http://web.worldbank. org/WBSITE/EXTERNAL/TOPICS/EXTSOCIALPROTECTION/EXTSAFETYNET SANDTRANSFERS/0,,contentMDK:20795790~isCURL:Y~menuPK:1552914~pageP K:210058~piPK:210062~theSitePK:282761~isCURL:Y~isCURL:Y~isCURL:Y,00. html [accessed 3 November 2011].

World Bank. (2011d) Community-based Targeting. (Online) Available at: http://web. worldbank.org/WBSITE/EXTERNAL/TOPICS/EXTSOCIALPROTECTION/EXTSA FETYNETSANDTRANSFERS/0,,contentMDK:20795813~isCURL:Y~menuPK:1552 914~pagePK:210058~piPK:210062~theSitePK:282761~isCURL:Y~isCURL:Y,00. html [accessed 3 November 2011].

World Bank. (2011e) Mozambique: Food Subsidy Program. (Online) Available at: http:// web.worldbank.org/WBSITE/EXTERNAL/TOPICS/EXTSOCIALPROTECTION/EX TSAFETYNETSANDTRANSFERS/0,,contentMDK:22202397~pagePK:210058~piP K:210062~theSitePK:282761,00.html [accessed 3 November 2011].

World Bank. (2011f) Demographic Targeting. (Online) Available at: http://web.world-bank.org/WBSITE/EXTERNAL/TOPICS/EXTSOCIALPROTECTION/EXTSAFETY NETSANDTRANSFERS/0,,contentMDK:20834872~isCURL:Y~menuPK:1552914~p agePK:210058~piPK:210062~theSitePK:282761~isCURL:Y~isCURL:Y,00.html [accessed 3 November 2011].

5 Food crises

The impact on African women and children

Meredeth Turshen

I stopped a 27-year-old woman called Marie-Jean Bisimwa, who had four little children toddling along beside her. She told me she was lucky. Yes, her village had been burned out. Yes, she had lost her husband somewhere in the chaos. Yes, her sister had been raped and gone insane. But she and her kids were alive. I gave her a lift, and it was only after a few hours of chat along on cratered roads that I noticed there was something strange about Marie-Jean's children. They were slumped forward, their gazes fixed in front of them. They didn't look around, or speak, or smile. "I haven't ever been able to feed them," she said. "Because of the war." Their brains hadn't developed; they never would now. "Will they get better?" she asked.

(Hari, 2008)

The long trajectory of Africa's food crises begins with a mother's daily struggle to feed her family and ends in the financial centers in London and New York. Along the way food is transformed into a commodity and commodities lose their physical reality as traders gamble on their future value. The ability of a woman to prepare a simple bowl of porridge for her child each day is constrained by decisions she cannot affect, decisions taken by financiers who control international markets and trade.

In agriculture-based countries in Africa, agriculture makes up about a third of overall economic growth. Sub-Saharan African countries account for 89 percent of the global total of rural populations in agriculture-based countries, and more than half of sub-Saharan Africans are poor people living in rural areas. The World Bank estimates that agricultural development is twice as effective at reducing poverty as other sources of growth (World Bank, 2008). The hope is that agricultural development will lift African countries out of poverty as it did for some Asian countries.

Women produce 80 percent of the food in sub-Saharan Africa and constitute 75 percent of the labor force in agriculture, yet they own just 1 percent of the land, receive only 7 percent of agricultural extension services and are beneficiaries of less than 10 percent of the credit given to small-scale farmers. Women have no representation in policy formulation, program development or budgetary planning; in other words they have no say when decisions are made about their work and their life.

Women's access to land has been eroding for more than a century. Local land tenure systems, which claim to draw their legitimacy from "tradition" and are commonly referred to as "customary," were profoundly changed by a century of colonial and post-colonial governmental and intergovernmental (mainly World Bank) policy making (Cotula, 2007). Social, political and cultural changes appear to drive the continual adaptation and reinterpretation of land tenure, but in reality, economic demands of colonial powers, post-colonial corporate forces and weak (or corrupt) governments have determined those changes.

Hunger challenges the resources of farmers coping with crop failures caused by drought or floods possibly accelerated by climate change, and with the pressures of debts that tempt them to sell up and move on. Off the land, women and men confront rising prices for corn, wheat or rice (paradoxically, higher prices might have helped them remain on their farms if they had received them[1]); the disappearance of subsidies that enabled them to buy these staples; and new expenses for water and fuel for cooking, heating or lighting their homes, services that have been privatized in many countries.

National agricultural policy makers view as intertwined the variables of population growth, rural to urban migration, environmental sustainability and the capacity of the agricultural sector to meet the needs of domestic consumers and export markets. Government budgeters juggle income from the sales of export commodities, foreign aid and investment from public and private sources with demands for services—everything from the building and maintenance of roads on which commodities move to the administration of thousands of contracts with small private voluntary organizations promising to train farmers and herders as well as with major multinational agribusiness corporations.

All of these issues surround food security in Africa. Food security is but one aspect of human security, redefined by the United Nations Development Program (UNDP) to include job security, income security, health security, environmental security and personal security (from criminal attack) (UNDP, 1994). Because insecurity is associated with vulnerability and women are thought to be more vulnerable and at higher risk of poverty, the new interpretations of human security are of special importance to women. All of the issues of food security touch the lives of women and children and affect, or are affected by, women's land rights. Women's greater responsibility for food crop production in Africa and for securing food for the family in times of crisis magnifies the importance of food security for women. At all times, women are charged with food preparation, which governs their own and their children's nutritional regimes, the determinants of health and resistance to infection. Because women are responsible for supplying their families with food and care, they often have special knowledge of the value and diverse use of plants for nutrition, health and income. Consequently, they are frequently the preservers of traditional knowledge of indigenous plants, in effect preserving biodiversity and plant genetic resources (FAO, 1998).

This chapter considers the causes of food crises, current debates around land rights policies and feminist critiques of those policies. It ends with a discussion of land grabs in Africa.

Is there a food crisis today?

The latest headlines confirm the current crisis: "More than 13 million people in East Africa are facing desperate food shortages following the worst drought in 60 years." "Rains have failed for successive seasons, and families across Somalia, Ethiopia and Kenya are struggling to find anything to eat or drink. Hundreds of thousands of livestock have already died. Food prices have rock-eted" (Oxfam, 2011).

In April 2008, IRIN (the United Nations news agency) reported soaring food and fuel prices and quoted the UN Economic Commission for Africa as saying that rising food and energy prices could hurt Africa's growth in the twenty-first century (IRIN, 2008a). In June 2008, the United Nations Food and Agriculture Organization (FAO) convened the High-Level Conference on World Food Security at its Rome headquarters; speaking at the conference, the United Nations International Research and Training Institute for the Advancement of Women (INSTRAW) called for the protection of women in the global food crisis (INSTRAW, 2008). In July 2008, ActionAid reported that food prices were up 82 percent since 2006, putting 760 million people at risk of hunger, pushing 100 million below the $1-a-day poverty line and making 850 million more people chronically hungry (ActionAid, 2008). Also in July, the International Monetary Fund (IMF) announced that it would augment an existing facility and reshape a second to help the countries worst hit by the food and fuel price crises, especially in sub-Saharan Africa (IRIN, 2008b). In August 2008, the Norwegian Council on Africa reported that poor families now spend up to 80 percent of their budget on food; that 30 million people face hunger or even death by starvation in sub-Saharan Africa; and that 21 out of 36 countries in food security crisis are in sub-Saharan Africa (Norwegian Council for Africa, 2008).

But by April of 2009, the UN reported that the previous year's food crisis had eased, although prices remain very high in developing countries (United Nations, 2009); worldwide food prices fell about 30 percent. Presumably the relief relates to the fall in fuel prices, which dropped 70 percent. The IMF noted that com-modity prices had collapsed in the second half of 2008 after a spectacular run-up from early 2002 (IMF, 2009); but the food price index continues to fluctuate (157 in 2008, 134 in 2009, back up to 149 in 2010 and at 213 in the first quarter of 2011) (IMF, 2011). Other conditions, particularly climate change, threaten to worsen food production. Some scientists predict that half the world's population could face a climate-induced food crisis by 2100 (Morgan, 2009).

Causes of the food crisis

Climate change is one of the most often mentioned causes of the food crisis. Yash Tandon suggests several sources of the food crisis of 2008: the first is global warming, which has produced both droughts and floods, and in drought-stricken parts of Africa this means that yields from rain-fed agriculture could drop 50 percent by 2020. Second is the volatile price of hydrocarbons (oil prices peaked in July 2008 at $140 per barrel). Third is the rising cost of fertilizers and transport, both related to volatile fuel prices. Finally, he and others mention rising food consumption (especially of meat, making fodder and pastureland more profitable than grain) with implications for land use and conversion of food crops to animal feed and agrofuels (Tandon, 2008).[2]

The demand for agrofuels comes in for heavy commentary (Lynas, 2008; Martin, 2008). Ashworth notes the conversion of land use from food crops to export crops and agrofuels and comments that biofuel subsidies to US and EU farmers are worth $16–18 billion a year, four times as much as all agricultural aid to the developing world (Ashworth, 2008). According to ActionAid, around 260 million people are either hungry or at risk of hunger because of agrofuels (ActionAid, 2008), and the Norwegian Council on Africa estimates that 100 million tonnes of grain per year are being redirected from food to fuel globally. Filling the tank of an average car with agrofuel consumes the same amount of maize an average African eats in a year (Norwegian Council for Africa, 2008); US government subsidies for maize-based ethanol, which has very little net energy benefit, have a terrible impact on the welfare of the poor. There is also a water dimension to the demand for agrofuels: maize is a thirsty crop, pitting fuel consumption against water consumption.

Other causes of the 2008 rise in food prices include the agricultural policies of the international financial institutions, which led to the dismantling of agricul-tural infrastructure (for example, marketing boards and parastatals, which helped farmers sell their produce); the failure to resolve North/South disputes on food product tariffs at the last round of World Trade Organization (WTO) negotia-tions; US farm policy generally and the subsidies, in particular, that the US and EU pay to their farmers; and continued population growth in Africa, but more especially accelerated rural to urban migration, with predictions that more than half of all Africans will be living in urban areas by 2020.[3]

Jeffrey Sachs, Director of the Earth Institute at Columbia University, and Stephen Lewis, former UN Special Envoy for AIDS in Africa, blame hunger on inadequate food supplies for growing populations, invoking the specter of Malthusian overpopulation.[4] Famine and overpopulation are old tropes, as famil-iar as the technological fix that is their answer. Sachs, Lewis and others are calling for an African green revolution (the use of genetically modified organ-isms [GMOS], high-yield seed varieties [HYVs], fertilizers and irrigation). Although it is true that productivity is low and that women farmers have few options for obtaining the inputs that would improve productivity (for example, access to credit and a larger share of family income to purchase inputs), the call by AGRA (Alliance for a Green Revolution in Africa) ignores both the human and the political dimensions of the technology. Especially problematic is the insistence by the Gates Foundation and others on the introduction of GMOs—a still untested technology with possibly major health ramifications (Wolfenbarger and Phifer, 2000; Sharife, 2009)—and the negative outcomes of the green revolution in India that recent research has uncovered,[5] as well as the political implications of a strategy designed to gain and keep control over the global South's food systems firmly in the hands of northern corporations and institutions. The green revolution is not a single entity or even a group of trans-national corporations: it includes public and private research institutions, supported by both tax dollars and investments from a handful of powerful seed, chemical and fertilizer companies. It entails industrial modernization of agricultural production, as well as a campaign for penetrating agricultural markets in the global South (Patel and Holt-Giménez, 2008).

So although productivity is low and in some cases stagnating in parts of Africa, greatly harming food security, it does not necessarily follow that the answer lies in a technological fix. Some observers (Yash Tandon) maintain that policy changes like encouraging food self-sufficiency and promoting food crop over export crop production would accomplish as much if not more to raise productivity at less cost to the environment and to personal health.

One cause of the food crisis that has received too little attention outside of economic circles is financial speculation in food as tradable commodities (Collins, 2008). L. Randall Wray explains the role of hedge funds in bidding up commodity prices this way: the three main participants in commodity futures markets are hedgers (who have a direct interest in the commodities), traditional speculators (who take on price risks) and index speculators (hedge funds, pension funds, university endowments, life insurance companies, sovereign wealth funds and banks—generally thought of as prudent investors) (Wray, 2008). Index speculators (so called because they typically buy commodity futures index funds) bought just over half of all futures contracts. The size of these managed money funds is "gargantuan" relative to the size of commodity futures markets. Wray's argument is that the huge volumes of money flowing into the commodity futures markets have driven the price of commodity futures ever higher. In other words, notions of supply and demand bear no relation to money manager capitalism.[6] Oil constitutes the largest share of total commodity production and is also subject to the most volatility in price; when combined with agricultural commodities in index funds, oil pushes up food prices (UNCTAD, 2011).

Writing for *The Economist* in October 2008, Ashworth dissented from this picture of Africa in crisis and saw instead opportunity knocking at Africa's doors (Ashworth, 2008). Far from facing crisis, 48 sub-Saharan countries enjoyed unparalleled economic success with GDP growth averages up 5 percent since 1995, annual GDP per person up 4 percent in the period 2004–2006, the percentage of Africans living in poverty dropping to 41 percent in 2004 from 47 percent in 1990, and inflation down (except in Zimbabwe). But when one reads the fine print, it turns out that oil producing countries—Angola, Nigeria, Sudan—account for most of the growth and that most foreign investment has gone to extractive industries (copper, iron, cobalt). Ashworth published his article in *The Economist* just as oil prices were falling, and lower prices had a negative effect on the economies of African oil producers, as they had on most oil exporters. In addition, following the banking crisis of 2008, foreign direct investment and foreign aid both decreased (Afrol News, 2012).

Other commentators are questioning the usual descriptions of the causes of the food crisis from a different perspective.[7] Accounts that focus on the particularities of Africa do not explain a crisis that is world-wide. Nor do the common explanations (rising food prices, growing populations, environmental degradation) clarify why the crisis is happening now. The same conditions were said to account for the 1970s food crisis, when world population was only 4 billion and pressures on the environment were fewer. Do we know whether this is a short-term crisis, a long-term structural crisis or a cyclical phenomenon?

Among the long-term structural problems is the gutting of government investment in the countryside that some say brought prosperity to African farmers in the decades following independence (Bello, 2008). Structural adjustment programs, coupled with the massive influx of subsidized US and EU agricultural imports that followed the WTO Agreement on Agriculture, resulted in the destabilization of peasant producers, turning food exporting countries into food importers.[8] Sub-Saharan Africa imported 45 percent of its wheat and 84 percent of its rice in 2008, causing wheat prices to rise 120 percent and rice prices to rise 75 percent (Norwegian Council for Africa, 2008).

Agriculture for development: continuities, inconsistencies and contradictions at the World Bank

The *World Development Report 2008* continues the World Bank's policies for rural sub-Saharan Africa of the past 25 years (Havnevik *et al.*, 2008). World Bank funding for sub-Saharan African agriculture dropped from 32 percent of total lending in 1976/78 to 11.7 percent in 1997/99; in the period of 1991–2006, Bank lending for agriculture has been about $4.5 billion or 11.2 percent (World Bank, 2007). Yet in *World Development Report 2008* the World Bank argues that agriculture is key to poverty alleviation in sub-Saharan Africa. Once again the World Bank stresses liberalized national markets as the primary force for higher productivity; in other words the World Bank is still promoting agricultural exports over food self-sufficiency.

A new focus of the World Bank's rural development policy is help for smallholders and for diversifying livelihoods, but this concern amounts to lip service. Humanitarian concerns are new to the World Bank, but these interests clash with market fundamentalism. The World Bank now questions privatization policies that gave land titles to male heads of households, but its suggested correction—a return to local control and customary land laws (congruent with a long-standing World Bank policy of decentralization)—may still not help women's access to land, an issue discussed in more detail below (Cevallos, 2008).

Principles for food security and the part women play

A global food crisis does indeed exist, as more than two billion people around the world struggle daily to meet basic food needs (Shattuck and Holt-Giménez, 2008; Food First, 2009). As an answer to the crisis, Tandon proposes five principles for food security: food sovereignty to ensure domestic production and supply of food; priority (in national and international policy) to food crops over export crops; self reliance and national ownership and control over main food production resources; the maintenance of food safety reserves; and fair and equitable distribution of reserves (Tandon, 2008). Governments, intergovernmental organizations and multinational corporations regularly violate these principles by distorting state policies on production and trade; when they enable rich commercial farmers to grab the land of smallholders; when people lose effective control of food production resources, including land; by generating dependence on donor aid, including bad advice given by those donors; and through the disruption of the food production infrastructure (as happened under structural adjustment programs).

Women play a critical role in achieving food sovereignty, a fact the World Bank acknowledged after feminists critiqued structural adjustment programs (Razavi, 2003). In revising its policies, the Bank shifted its focus from women's role in reproduction to their role in production, a reality that Ester Boserup explained as early as 1970.[9] In its *World Development Report 2008* the Bank concludes that resource allocation is unequal, and the focus shifts once more, this time to women's inadequate access to land. In effect the Bank is recognizing that women's access to or ownership of land enhances family food security.

There are two aspects of women's land rights to consider in this context: women's customary access to land—which is an old issue—and land sales and leases to foreign countries and corporations—which is a new issue. The common thread is this: as land gains in commercial value, power shifts from women to men. Note that there were and still are two legal systems—customary (so-called "traditional" law) and statutory (or formal law)—both legacies of colonialism.

Women's land rights are entangled in customary and statutory law.[10] In much of sub-Saharan Africa, women access land mainly through marriage. But a husband's family will grab the land of a divorced or widowed woman, using customary law to justify their actions. For years the World Bank has pushed for land titles, but these are usually awarded to male household heads. When land becomes a commodity women lose out because they rarely have the cash to buy land.

Enforcing women's rights, then, is complicated: statutory law, even when reformed in women's favor, is hard to enforce, and traditional patriarchal systems (many invented under colonialism) resist change and continue to influence customary law (Palmer, 2002). Family law, if reformed, might protect divorced and widowed women, but the legal world perceives family law as "soft." The World Bank may advocate return to customary land laws, but women don't trust customary law or local control. Women have too little political voice at all decision-making levels—formal law and government, local management, civil society—to be able to protect their rights. Any revival of traditional authorities will disempower rural women (Whitehead and Tsikata, 2003).

Feminist critiques of land rights policies center on the multiple uses and multiple users of land in sub-Saharan Africa. Historically embedded in social relations, claims to land in indigenous tenure systems vary from strong claims to discriminatory inheritance laws (Razavi, 2003). In addition, the exclusive focus on land access disregards worse constraints: women have a weak command of labor, suffer under severe capital limitations, find markets all but inaccessible and are limited by what women are now calling "time famine." Current debates in feminist circles highlight "bundles of rights," that is, multiple claims in land that are both hierarchical and gendered; for example, women have use rights while men own or control land. Tenure relations and land claims tend to be fluid, negotiated and dynamic. They do not tend to be divided into hierarchies of primary and secondary rights, as some would have it.

Feminists conclude that governments must manage and direct change to produce greater justice, as well as ensure better resource allocation for rural women. The World Bank may advocate return to customary land laws, but there is little evidence of this in practice. Privatization and land grabs proceed apace.

A new threat?

Land grabs are not just an internal problem, with rich commercial farmers coveting the land of smallholders. In the past few years, a new international land grab has emerged, as land-hungry wealthy countries, many in the Persian Gulf and in Asia, eye the vast lands of sub-Saharan Africa. According to the Food and Agricultural Organization, only about 14 percent of the land suited to agriculture on the continent is presently cultivated (Godoy, 2009). In terms of land available to small local cultivators, most remaining suitable land is already under use or claim, but existing land uses and claims go unrecognized because the law and institutions marginalize land users from formal land rights and access. Meanwhile pressure is growing on higher value lands, like those with irrigation potential or closer to markets.

South Korea's Daewoo Logistics announced in November 2008 that it had negotiated a 99-year lease[11] on some 3.2 million acres of farmland in Madagascar, nearly half of the island's arable land (Walt, 2008). Daewoo planned to put about three quarters of it under corn and use the remainder to produce palm oil—a key commodity for the global agrofuels market. This deal fell through, but a 452,500 hectare agrofuel project has been approved (Cotula *et al.*, 2009).

Between 2004 and early 2009, at least 2.5 million hectares were transferred from local users to foreign investors in five African countries alone. These were Ethiopia, Ghana, Madagascar, Mali and Sudan, involving an estimated $1 billion (Cotula *et al.*, 2009). The study confirms the dominance of foreign private investors in land deals in sub-Saharan Africa, "though often with strong financial and other support from government, and significant levels of government-owned investments." The study also finds that where foreign governments are acquiring equity stakes in land, the most common arrangements happen via state-owned enterprises and minority shares in private companies. Most African countries do not have legal or procedural mechanisms in place to protect local rights and take account of local interests, livelihoods and welfare (Von Braun and Meinzen-Dick, 2009). Other approved projects (as of May 2009) are a 150,000 hectare livestock project in Ethiopia and a 100,000 hectare irrigation project in Mali.

The private sector dominates these land deals, though often with strong financial and other support from foreign government, and significant levels of government-owned investments. The Chinese government announced in April 2008 a commitment of US$5 billion for Chinese corporations to invest in African agriculture over the next 50 years through the new China–Africa Development Fund. The CADF is a private equity fund whose shareholder is the China Development Bank (Johnny, 2008). Some 30 agricultural cooperation deals have been sealed in recent years to give Chinese firms access to "friendly country" farmland in exchange for Chinese technologies, training and infrastructure development funds in Asia and all over Africa. Since 2006 China has sought large land leases in Mozambique, particularly in the fertile Zambezi valley in the north and the Limpopo valley in the south (Horta, 2008). Chinese farmers have already been successful in Uganda which has leased an area of about 10,000 acres to around 300–400 Chinese who grow corn and other crops and employ hundreds of local workers (Patton, 2008).

Saudi Arabia and United Arab Emirates have made land deals in Sudan and Senegal.[12] Qatar cut a land lease deal with Kenya, in return for a new port on the island of Lamu.[13] There has been some fightback: Kenyan critics ask how the government can do this, with drought threatening 10 million people and a national food emergency looming.

One may well ask whose food security is being served by these land leases (Razavi, 2003). To many it looks like predation: land grabs by overseas interests for agricultural development, tourism, dams and industrial production (Clavreul, 2008; Petras, 2008). Even the World Bank finds that the current "land rush" does not benefit communities and that the conditions under which most of these deals are being pursued reduce countries' ability to regulate investments and protect local property rights (Deininger and Byerlee, 2011).[14] Considerable land scarcity is developing in some sub-Saharan African countries. Land titling and registration promoted by the World Bank help land alienation, not productivity. Three trends are emerging: land grabs, which represent investors seeking to profit from high food prices; land leases, which reflect fear of future food insecurity; and Chinese and Indian farmers and workers, laid off in the global crisis or pushed out by climatic changes such as prolonged drought, seeking opportunities in African agriculture (Huggler, 2004; Patton, 2008).

Reflections

Four factors distinguish the present food crisis from the one Africans experienced in the 1970s. First, the structural adjustment programs imposed by the World Bank, the International Monetary Fund and most donors in the 1980s destabilized agriculture (and much else besides). Second, foreign direct investment by agribusiness is occurring on a new, much grander, scale, and it is happening in combination with new purchases or leases of vast tracts of land leading to land shortages in some areas. Third, a demand for agrofuels from newly carbon conscious consumers has converted acreage from food crops to non-nutritive exports. Fourth, and perhaps most important, speculators are responsible for the financialization of commodities, which has caused the prices of staple foods to soar. Two new aspects of older problems add to Africans' woes: accelerating climate change is aggravating older problems of environmental degradation; and two decades of setbacks for Africans, beginning in the 1980s, have left them worse prepared, less resilient and more vulnerable to the current crisis.

Women and children will suffer most from this crisis because women are physically more in need of good nutrition and health care in their childbearing years than adult men and because children—with their immature immune systems and greater growth needs for protein-rich foods—will succumb more readily to the common illnesses (pneumonia, diarrhea) for which there are no vaccines or immunizations and for which curative care is expensive and inaccessible.

War and armed conflict compound all of these problems. Even as some conflicts are resolved, Africa will be saddled by a generation of survivors like the children of Marie-Jean Bisimwa.

Notes

1 Higher prices don't always funnel down to poorer farmers who are subject to poor marketing and storage options and who frequently sell at harvest because they are cash poor and buy at peak season (I thank Howard Stein for pointing this out).
2 Agrofuels is the term critics adopted for industrial-scale biofuels based on agricultural crops as feedstocks.
3 On US farm policy see IRIN (2008c); on African urbanization see UN Habitat (2008).
4 Interventions made at the Third International Policy Conference on the African Child, United Nations Conference Centre, Addis Ababa, Ethiopia, 12–13 May 2008. See also Turshen (2008).
5 As soils die and the water table falls, India's green revolution is facing collapse (Zwerdling, 2009).
6 Wray claims that speculation, market manipulation by commodities producers and traders as well as higher demand for food are all plausible explanations for higher food prices and are mutually reinforcing; but the rise of investments in commodities indexes (index speculation) is the most important cause (Wray, 2009; Jones, 2010).
7 Dharam Ghai, former Executive Director of UNRISD, intervening at the Third International Policy Conference on the African Child. See also Turshen (2008).
8 WTO's Agriculture Agreement was negotiated in the 1986–94 Uruguay Round.
9 Ester Boserup (1970) *Woman's Role in Economic Development*. London: Allen & Unwin.
10 Best source of information on women's land rights: Oxfam (n.d.), www.oxfam.org.uk/resources/learning/landrights/index.html.
11 Land leases, rather than purchases, are predominant in Africa, and host country governments tend to play a key role in allocating them (Cotula *et al.*, 2009).
12 Best source of information on international land grabs: www.grain.org; see also Global Information Network (2009a).
13 Global Information Network, 2009b; "Qatar and Kenya are in negotiations that would see the Gulf state lease 100,000 acres of land and fund a new £2.4 billion port on the Indian Ocean island of Lamu to help the east African country cope with increasing trade volumes" (*The Telegraph*, 2008); see also "Clashes at Nairobi food protest."

(BBC News, 2008); and "In the wheat fields of Kenya, a budding epidemic of stem rust, vanquished by science five decades ago, has returned in a destructive new form" (Schmickle, 2009).

14 World Bank concludes, however, that the potentials and opportunities outweigh unsustainability and inequality.

Bibliography

ActionAid. (2008) Three Nails in the Coffin: The G8's Contribution to the Global Food Crisis. (Online) 3 July. Available at: www.actionaid.org.uk/101377/press_release.html [accessed 7 November 2011].

Afrol News. (2012) Financial crisis to cost Africa over $200 billion, ECA. Afrol News, (Online) 30 April. Available at: www.afrol.com/articles/33122 [accessed 30 April 2012].

Ashworth, John. (2008) Africa's Prospects: Opportunity Knocks. *The Economist*, 9 October 2008.

BBC News. (2008) Clashes at Nairobi Food Protest. BBC News, (Online) 31 May. Available at: news.bbc.co.uk/2/hi/africa/7429303.stm [accessed 7 November 2011].

Bello, Walden. (2008) The Destruction of African Agriculture. *Pambazuka News*, No. 392, 5 August.

Boserup, Ester. (1970) *Woman's Role in Economic Development*. London: Allen & Unwin.

Cevallos, Diego. (2008) Decentralization, a Double-Edged Sword for Women. Inter Press Service. (Online) 24 November. Available at: www.ips.org.

Clavreul, Laetitia. (2008) Agrarian Neocolonialism Gains Ground. *Le Monde*, 23 September.

Collins, Ben. (2008) Hot Commodities, Stuffed Markets, and Empty Bellies; What's Behind Higher Food Prices? *Dollars & Sense*. (Online) July/August, Available at: www.dollarsandsense.org/archives/2008/0708collins.html [accessed 7 November 2011].

Cotula, Lorenzo, ed. (2007) *Changes in "Customary" Land Tenure Systems in Africa*. London: International Institute for Environment and Development.

Cotula, Lorenzo, Sonja Vermeulen, Rebeca Leonard and James Keeley. (2009) *Land Grab or Development Opportunity? Agricultural Investment and International Land Deals in Africa*. London/Rome: IIED/FAO/IFAD.

Deininger, Klaus and Derek Byerlee. (2011) *Rising Global Interest in Farmland: Can it Yield Sustainable and Equitable Benefits?* Washington, DC: World Bank.

FAO. (1998) *Gender Food Security*. Food and Agriculture Organization of the United Nations.

Food First. (2009) "Business as Usual" Will Not Solve Global Hunger Crisis. Online. 16 April. Available at: www.foodfirst.org/en/node/2419 [accessed 7 November 2011].

Global Information Network. (2009a) Ex-Wall St. Banker Scores Major Land Deal in Sudan. (Online) 27 January. Available at: www.globalinfo.org.

Global Information Network. (2009b) Kenyan Land Giveaway Under Scrutiny. (Online) 13 January. Available at: www.globalinfo.org.

Godoy, Julio. (2009) Africa: The Second Scramble for Africa Starts. allAfrica.com. (Online) 20 April. Available at http://allafrica.com/stories/200904201447.html [accessed 7 November 2011].

Hari, Johann. (2008) How We Fuel Africa's Bloodiest War. *Independent* (UK), (Online) 30 October. Available at: www.independent.co.uk/opinion/commentators/johann-hari/

johann-hari-how-we-fuel-africas-bloodiest-war-978461.html [accessed 7 November 2011].

Havnevik, K. *et al.* (2008) African Agriculture and the World Bank. *Pambazuka News*, No. 353, 11 March.

Horta, Loro. (2008) The Zambezi Valley: China's First Agricultural Colony? Africa Policy Forum, Center for Strategic and International Studies.

Huggler, Justin. (2004) India Exports Farmers to Amin's Homeland. *Independent* (UK), (Online) 6 November. Available at: www.independent.co.uk.

International Monetary Fund (IMF). (2009) Roller Coaster: The Latest Sharp Rise and Fall in Commodity Prices Is Not the First Nor the Last. *Finance & Development*, 46(2), p. 56.

International Monetary Fund (IMF). (2011) IMF Primary Commodity Prices. (Online) Available at: www.imf.org/external/np/res/commod/index.asp.

INSTRAW. (2008) UN-INSTRAW Calls for Protection of Women in the Global Food Crisis. Press release, 25 July. Online. Available at: www.un-instraw.org.

Integrated Regional Information Networks (IRIN). (2008a) Africa: Soaring Food and Fuel Prices May Hurt Growth. Addis Ababa, 7 April. Online. Available at: www.irinnews.org.

Integrated Regional Information Networks (IRIN). (2008b) Africa: IMF Steps into Food Crisis. New York, 7 July. Online. Available at: www.irinnews.org.

Integrated Regional Information Networks (IRIN). (2008c) Global: US Farm Bill "Too Little, Too Late" for Developing World. New York. (Online) 1 July. Available at: www.irinnews.org.

Johnny, T. Michael. (2008) China Earmarks US$5 Billion for Food Production on Continent. *The News* (Monrovia) 23 April.

Jones, Tim. (2010) The Great Hunger Lottery: How Banking Speculation Causes Food Crises. *World Development Movement*, July.

Lynas, Mark. (2008) How the Rich Starved the World. *New Statesman.* (Online) 17 April. Available at: www.newstatesman.com/world-affairs/2008/04/food-prices-lynas-biofuels [accessed 7 November 2011].

Martin, Andrew. (2008) Food Report Criticizes Biofuel Policies. *New York Times*, 30 May.

Morgan, James. (2009) Heat May Spark World Food Crisis. BBC News. (Online) 9 January. Available at: http://news.bbc.co.uk/2/hi/science/nature/7817684.stm [accessed 7 November 2011].

Norwegian Council for Africa. (2008) The Food Crisis: Fuel or Food? Must Some People Starve to Produce Bio Fuel for the West? 7 August. Online. Available at: www.afrika. no.

Oxfam. (n.d.) Land Rights in Africa. (Online) 2011. Available at: www.oxfam.org.uk/resources/learning/landrights/index.html [accessed 7 November 2011].

Oxfam. (2011) East Africa Appeal. Online. Available at: www.oxfam.org.uk/oxfam_in_action/emergencies/east-africa-drought-2011.html [accessed 7 November 2011].

Palmer, Robin. (2002) Gendered Land Rights—Process, Struggle, or Lost C(l)ause? Oxfam GB. Online. Available at: www.oxfam.org.uk/resources/learning/landrights/downloads/genderedrtf.rtf 28 November [accessed 7 November 2011].

Patel, Raj and Eric Holt-Giménez. (2008) New Green Revolution and World Food Prices. *Pambazuka News*, No. 367, 1 May.

Patton, Dominique. (2008) China Eyes Idle Farmland in Country. *Business Daily* (Nairobi) 6 April.

Petras, James. (2008) The Great Land Giveaway: Neo-Colonialism by Invitation; Colonial Style Empire-building Is Making a Huge Comeback. Global Research, (Online) 1 December. Available at: www.globalresearch.ca/index.php?context=viewArticle&code =PET20081201&articleId=11231 [accessed 7 November 2011].

Razavi, Sharha. (2003) Introduction: Agrarian Change, Gender and Land Rights. *Journal of Agrarian Change*, 3(1&2), pp. 2–32.

Schmickle, Sharon. (2009) In the Wheat Fields of Kenya, a Budding Epidemic. *Washington Post*, (Online) 18 February. Available at: www.washingtonpost.com/wp-dyn/ content/article/2009/02/17/AR2009021703174.html?wpisrc=newsletter [accessed 7 November 2011].

Sharife, Khadija. (2009) GM: The Food of the Future? *Pambazuka News*. Issue 459. (Online) 26 November. Available at: http://pambazuka.org/en/category/features/60523 [accessed 7 November 2011].

Shattuck, Annie and Eric Holt-Giménez. (2008) The Wall Street Mega Bailout: Bad News for the World's Hungry. CommonDreams. (Online) 3 October. Available at: www.commondreams.org/view/2008/10/03-4 [accessed 7 November 2011].

Tandon, Yash. (2008) The Principles of Food Sovereignty. *Pambazuka News*. (Online) No. 383, 24 June. Available at: www.pambazuka.org.

The Telegraph. (2008) Qatar to Lease 100,000 Acres in Kenya in Return for Port Loan. *The Telegraph* (UK), (Online) 3 December. Available at: www.telegraph.co.uk/news/ worldnews/middleeast/qatar/3543887/Qatar-to-lease-100000-acres-in-Kenya-in-return-for-port-loan.html [accessed 7 November 2011].

Turshen, Meredeth. (2008) Child Poverty in Africa. *Review of African Political Economy*, 35(3), pp. 494–500.

United Nations. (2009) Interactive Thematic Dialogue of the UN General Assembly on the Global Food Crisis and the Right to Food. (Online) 6 April. Available at: www. un.org/ga/president/63/interactive/globalfoodcrisis.shtml [accessed 7 November 2011].

UNCTAD. (2011) *Price Formation in Financialized Commodity Markets: The Role of Information*. New York and Geneva, June.

United Nations Development Program (UNDP). (1994) *An Agenda for the Social Summit. Human Development Report*. Oxford: Oxford University Press.

UN-Habitat. (2008) *State of the World's Cities 2010/2011*. London: Earthscan.

Von Braun, Joachim and Ruth Meinzen-Dick. (2009) "Land Grabbing" by Foreign Investors in Developing Countries: Risks and Opportunities. IFPRI Policy Brief 13. International Food Policy Research Institute (IFPRI). Washington, DC. Available at: www. ifpri.org/sites/default/files/publications/bp013all.pdf.

Walt, Vivienne. (2008) The Breadbasket of South Korea: Madagascar. *Time Magazine*, 23 November.

Whitehead, Ann and Dzodzi Tsikata. (2003) Policy Discourses on Women's Land Rights in Sub-Saharan Africa: The Implications of the Return to the Customary. *Journal of Agrarian Change*, January & April; 3(1&2); pp. 67–112.

Wolfenbarger, L. L. and P. R. Phifer. (2000) The Ecological Risks and Benefits of Genetically Engineered Plants. *Science, New Series*, 290(5499), pp. 2088–2093.

World Bank. (2007) *World Bank Assistance to Agriculture in Sub-Saharan Africa*. Washington, DC: World Bank.

World Bank. (2008) *World Development Report 2008: The Agenda for Agriculture-based Countries of Sub-Saharan Africa Agriculture for Development*. Washington, DC: The World Bank.

Wray, L. Randall. (2008) The Commodities Market Bubble: Money Manager Capitalism and the Financialization of Commodities. The Levy Economics Institute of Bard College, Public Policy Brief No. 96.

Wray, L. Randall. (2009) Money Manager Capitalism and the Global Financial Crisis. *Real-World Economics Review*, 51, pp. 55–69.

Zwerdling, Daniel. (2009) India's Farming "Revolution" Heading For Collapse. National Public Radio, All Things Considered. 13 April. Available at: www.npr.org/templates/story/story.php?storyId=102893816&ft=1&f=1001.

6 Gender, environment and human security in the Greater Accra Metropolitan Area (GAMA), Ghana[1]

Jacob Songsore

> In societies the world over, women are both producers and carers; they care for children, for old people, the sick, the handicapped, and others who cannot look after themselves. They serve the household with food, cleanliness, clothing, and in many cases water and fuel.
>
> (Vickers, 1993: p. 15)

Since women play a pre-eminent role in the care and management of the home and its environs, the household environment can be said to be engendered. Moreover, the home and neighborhood environments are especially critical to the health, human security and well-being of children, the elderly and, among active adults, women. Adult men tend to spend more time away from home and thus face fewer of the household environmental hazards. For many women, especially those categorized as housewives or homemakers, the place where they live is also the place where they work (Muller and Plantenga, 1990: p. 14). Included in this group are the many women and men engaged in home-based production, which is very prevalent in GAMA's largely informal economy.

It is therefore of special relevance to women, children and the elderly that in many cities in low-income developing countries, such as GAMA, the most significant environmental health hazards tend to be encountered within people's houses and neighborhoods (see also Benneh et al., 1993; Songsore and McGranahan, 1993; McGranahan and Songsore, 1994):

> The immediate environmental threats for the residents of these cities are not long-term global warming, cumulative exposure to carcinogens, or even decade-long desertification but rather the life and death immediacy of malaria, respiratory illness, and diarrhea. Their threats are derived in part from household environments characterized by indoor air pollution, a bug-filled outdoors, near-the-door feces, and far-from-the-door water. There are also the dangers connected with the use of insect sprays, uncontrolled sewage, and ambient air pollution.
>
> (Kates, 1994: p. 1)

In Ghana the few readily available statistics on housekeeping activities indicate that females of all ages contribute to household chores more than males, but the gender differential in the domestic workload is especially large among adults (Ghana Statistical Service, 1995). This confirms the general perception that women bear an inordinate share of the labor burden of household environmental management (ROG/UNICEF, 1990; Ardayfio-Schandorf, 1993; Oppong, 1994).

Far from being egalitarian and harmonious units, households have a hierarchy mediated by gender, age and kinship. Both the state and all social groups in Ghana recognize the man as the head of household. The patriarchal construct of the household underpins power relations between the sexes. Determining who has control over assets and who retains decision-making powers forms the basis of both cooperation and conflict within the household (Friedmann, 1992: p. 108). As home managers and housewives, women are in a subordinate relationship with their husbands within the subsistence production of the household. There is an economic element to this subordination: to the extent that men can retain preferential access to liquid financial resources, men both reinforce their own power within the household and can often cushion themselves against the worst deprivations of poverty. As a result, "Poor men in the developing world have even poorer wives and children" (Vickers, 1993: p. 15). But the reasons why women are the most exposed to household environmental hazards go beyond women's relative poverty.

Although such a study may yield different results in other cities, several features of the situation in GAMA undoubtedly represent broader tendencies. We have argued elsewhere that the environmental problems of the poor tend to be more local and more directly threatening to health than the environmental problems of the wealthy (McGranahan and Songsore, 1994; Songsore and McGranahan, 2007). It would also seem from this chapter's more gender-sensitive analysis that the environmental problems of poverty are more likely to be a burden for women and to affect the health of children and the collective security of households. Recognizing the inadequacy and pitfalls of both gender-blind approaches to environmental problems and those approaches which merely provide a narrative of women's roles, the analysis here relies on a micro political-economy perspective.

This chapter examines the micro-politics of power that surround household environmental management in GAMA in general (Songsore and McGranahan, 1996, 1998) and utilizes an illustrative example from the low-income community of La (Songsore and Denkabe, 1998).

It also indicates some of the housing and environmental health risks that women and children are exposed to on account of their environmental caring role for the collective security of their households and their communities (see Songsore and McGranahan, 1996, 1998, 2000). The chapter therefore concludes by making a case for gender mainstreaming in GAMA and the country at large.

This analysis draws on the results of a much broader study of the household environmental problems in the Greater Accra Metropolitan Area, whose main findings and detailed methodologies have already been presented elsewhere

(Benneh *et al.*, 1993). The quantitative data is from 1991/92 and is based on a sample survey of 1,000 representative households, as well as physical tests of water quality and exposure to air pollution from a subset of 200 of these households. In order to capture intra-household struggles and politics of environmental management, follow-up research was conducted in five low-income neighborhoods using in-depth interviews and focus group discussions with selected women's and men's groups. The five selected areas cover the different socio-ecological zones where low-income households predominate in the metropolis and where environmental management challenges were most acute for women.

A gender sensitization workshop undertaken in 1997 in La, a low-income community, shows that these gendered structural inequalities are especially prevalent among poor households in GAMA and are only being slightly mitigated from year to year in the context of structural adjustment and globalization (Songsore and Denkabe, 1998).

Gender and human security issues within the home

As a result of the unequal power relations within the home and in the context of economic crisis and structural adjustment, human security becomes an important concern both at the national and the household levels and within the household of particular concern to women. In its protective role, human security recognizes that people, especially women, are fatally threatened by events well beyond their control, such as during the period of economic decline from the mid 1970s to 1982 and about two decades of adjustment from 1983 to 2002 in Ghana (Alkire, 2003). This refers to both the environmental and economic threats to the survival of families and survival within the family unit, particularly for women and children who happen to be the most vulnerable on account of their relative poverty and powerlessness.

There are several mechanisms by which structural adjustment threatened the human security of poor urban households, specifically women in Ghana and the disadvantaged communities within GAMA. These included labor retrenchment, which particularly affected the less-skilled labor dominated by women; escalating prices of goods and services, which worsened the vulnerability of the poor and created burdens for women in their home-keeping activities; and cost recovery with regard to the use of public services including water, sanitation and garbage collection, which imposed further burdens on women in terms of their environmental management responsibilities within the home (Schoepf *et al.*, 2000; Songsore and McGranahan, 2000; Stein, 2008). The comprehensive programs of adjustment under the tutelage of the IMF and the World Bank often leave no sector of the economy untouched. These interventions are generally aimed at maintaining macroeconomic balances rather than ensuring human security (Escobar, 1986).

As the 1994 Human Development Report puts it,

> In the final analysis, human security is a child who did not die, a disease that did not spread, a job that was not cut, an ethnic tension that did not explode

into violence, a dissident who was not silenced. Human security is not a concern with weapons—it is a concern with human life and dignity.

(UNDP, 1994: p. 22; see also Alkire, 2003: p. 13)

Human security extends downwards from the security of nations to the security of people and individual men and women. As we seek to demonstrate, there is a sense in which unequal power relations within the home may endanger the human security of women, particularly with regards to women's health. This is because of the pattern of intra-household gender division of labor, which places disproportionate burdens on women. As a result there are unequal human capabilities between men and women on account of the unequal social and political circumstances between them. "Women in much of the world lack support for fundamental functions of human life. They are less well nourished than men, less healthy, more vulnerable to physical violence and sexual abuse" (Nussbaum, 2000: p. 1).

But what is the nature of gender relations within the home which exacerbates women's vulnerability to ill-health and excessive work burdens?

Gender relations within the household

Gender issues within the home

The secondary or subordinate status of women in the Greater Accra Metropolitan Area appears to be universally considered the norm, despite considerable cultural diversity and some recent erosion of men's relative power (see following section). Both women's groups and men's groups acknowledge the man as the head of the household, whether in the nuclear household consisting of man, wife and children or in the multi-generational extended family. As stated in one of the women's focus group discussion, "since it was the man who married the woman and takes care of all members of the household, he is the head." Women generally seemed to feel that this man ought to provide guidance, protection, support and care to all members of the household.

This view was reiterated by the men, who put it only slightly differently: "it is the man who has married the woman, so it is his responsibility to provide for the house, and hence he is the head." Men also emphasized the decision-making aspects of male leadership. As one male respondent crudely put it, "the man gives orders; and the orders he gives must be obeyed by the woman first and foremost, then the children will follow suit. Then everything will go on well in the home." In Ghanaian society generally, and among men in particular, the assertive female is abhorred and labelled a "he-woman." "There are many instances where a wealthy woman owns the 'marital' house and supports the family—husband included—yet the authority figure in the house remains the man" (Aidoo, 1985: p. 25).

It is therefore not surprising that a number of writers have drawn attention to the hierarchical and patriarchal structure of most households, with the household and family as the arena of women's subordination and the architecture of dis-criminatory gender roles. "The feminist appraisal opened for public view the privacy of family life and exposed not only affection and protection but also ine-quality and misogyny" (O'Connell, 1994, p. x).

This unequal power between men and women is manifested in spheres such as access to and control of resources, decision-making powers in the allocation of resources, control of decisions on reproduction, selection of the economic activities wives can undertake, and the allocation of tasks at the household level. The notion of the male "breadwinner" is common, but most men keep the size of their earnings secret, and the woman is often expected to manage with whatever "chop money" she is given, making up for deficits from her own resources. Auntie Vic represented this common problem well. She said her husband, a fish-erman, rarely discloses his income, especially during the fishing season in August. She claims that he spends a lot on girls, drinks and friends. These days, she has learnt a few tricks to enable her to keep a bit of what she gets from selling his fish. She says that for most of the year she uses money from baking bread and frying doughnuts to take care of the family. Her husband is therefore not the sole provider for the home; she actually contributes almost all her earn-ings to feed, clothe and educate the children.

Men do not necessarily see this type of arrangement as reflecting the deprivation of women. As one male respondent in the indigenous Ga settlement of Jamestown puts it: "In this community, the women generally earn higher incomes than the men. This is largely due to their trading activities. So if the men should pool financial resources with the women, the latter will not respect them." Another took the view that many women have developed the tendency of exploiting their male partners and want to use the man's money without controls.

> The woman hides her money in such places that it would take a thief to locate it. The only time you, the man, will know that your wife has money is when she puts on a new cloth. She can even tell you that she bought it on credit and so get you to pay for it. So if you make a mistake of keeping a joint account with your wife, you are just about a few steps from your grave.

By contrast, women respondents (both individually and in group discussions) held that men, especially when men and women pool resources together in joint economic ventures, tend to monopolize income to the exclusion of women. There is, however, considerable intra-urban variation between and within resi-dential areas depending on the cultural setting, level of education of household members, and the economic status of the household and of the particular woman.

In the old, typically low-income, indigenous Ga neighborhoods of central Accra, such as Jamestown and Mamprobi, and in the Ga villages found in the rural fringe, women tend to exhibit considerable autonomy in decision making and control of resources. This is partially due to the duolocal pattern of residence of husband and wife; the cultural norm is for each to reside in a house compound of their pre-marital family. However, once they have moved out of these communities, most upwardly mobile Ga men and women live neolocally, i.e., co-residentially, in newly developed mixed neighborhoods. There is also a long tradition of independent commercial activity among the women.

> Many women appreciated the freedom associated with living apart from their husbands. One woman who was divorced by her first husband because of her (assumed) infidelity said, "If you live together with your husband you feel ill at ease; it is better when you go and see him occasionally."
>
> (Robertson, 1993: p. 66)

By contrast, in low-income migrant communities such as Nima and Ashaiman the control of decision making by men tended to be more complete. Most migrant women did not have an equally strong footing in commerce and lived co-residentially with husbands who in most cases earned higher incomes. Polygamous marriages also tend to be both unstable and very undemocratic in their internal organisation.

Economic crisis and adjustment, women's empowerment and changing gender relations

Though the degree to which women control household resources and decision-making processes within the home may vary among different communities, clearly the subordination of women in GAMA society is widespread and perpetuated systemically. However, more recently the power of men within the household has come under threat from two processes: economic crisis and the growing unemployment of men on the one hand, and the reverberations of the global movement for the empowerment of women on the other.

Although the economic conditions of households in general have deteriorated in recent decades, women as a group have experienced some measure of progress in education, income-earning abilities and their overall status in society. In general, it was the men who most clearly articulated this looming threat to their hegemony over women. As the men's group in Mamprobi put it:

> One can say that in the past men's control over their wives was somehow absolute. But this control is diminishing. One can attribute this to the general trends of economic hardships which have made some men exist only in name.

This view was reiterated by other men's groups in the low-income neighborhoods surveyed because of labor retrenchment in the initial period of structural adjustment and more recently as a result of jobless growth.

The industrial workers of Ashaiman who were most negatively affected by the industrial decline of the adjacent industrial township of Tema carried the same message:

We are in a community where we count much on industrial work and other wage employment. In recent times many men have been laid off in an attempt to restructure the economy. So the women have taken over the head-ship of many households because they provide the money.

In support of this view the poor fishermen and working class elements in the blighted inner city residential district of Jamestown argued that: "Often when the man is unemployed the woman takes control. She is the one who has the money and so if you dare display your authority the cash flow will stop. So she becomes the head."

Although in group discussions and in-depth interviews women also stressed their growing role in generating household income, most women saw it more in terms of an increase in the pressure on their labor time than an increase in their power over men. This "reproductive squeeze" has led many women to disrespect their male partners and disapprove of their discretionary consumption.

According to Auntie Stella of Mamprobi:

In the olden days the men worked and took good care of their families. These days a lot of them have no proper work to do—just bits of fishing work, carpentry, construction labor and other menial jobs—so they do not have enough money for the home. The bits of extra money they make go into drinking and girl friends.

As another woman put it: "Nowadays the men can no longer cope with the burden of looking after us well, so most of us are on our own with our children." As has been shown elsewhere, women's income provides them with a psycho-logical and practical leverage in their gender relations. Women, however, may use their often low earnings not so much to increase their power in gender rela-tions but to diminish conflict by asking their husbands for money less often (Kanji, 1995: pp. 51–52; Kanji and Jazdowska, 1995). Quite a large proportion of women, though recognizing positive changes in the status of women, felt that they were not part of this process.

To the extent that the economic crisis and the increasing role of women in informal economic activities have enhanced women's influence in the house-hold, these processes are being augmented by the growing power of women's movements and associations which are creating a consciousness for the need for greater gender equality. Some men see this growing women's movement as a real threat to their social power at the household level. The following statements by two men interviewed articulate these fears well:

With educated women who have been enlightened by the campaign on the empowerment of women, they think that men have been having the upper hand for far too long and that this is the time to rub shoulders with the men. To me this whole question of empowerment of women is likely to lead us to a situation where women will become men and men become women.

These days there are many educational programs on radio and television telling women what their rights are and what they too can do. So there is some change in their attitude in the home. I can say that these educational programs are doing more harm than good.

Both statements implicitly blame strategic gender conflict on feminism rather than on the men who seek to keep the upper hand. The first statement makes a point upon which radical feminists and conservative anti-feminists actually agree: that existing male and female roles are fundamentally patriarchal. The second statement suggests that challenging these roles does more harm than good. The question is, whose interests are being harmed?

Women saw their increasing power principally as the result of changing economic realities at the household level, even though these might have been enhanced by the growing women in development (WID) activities. In general, as Sister Gloria indicated:

Because women do not depend solely on their husbands for money for food, clothing and health care, they are a bit more vocal and can also take part in decision making in the family. In fact, in a lot of homes, the men are heads only in name.

Such women have often overruled decisions taken by the men without their prior consultation. Other studies have shown that women with independent incomes have a long, slow struggle to increase their power in relation to men, whereas a loss in income often implies a rapid decline in influence because of the loss of "bargaining power" with men over a range of issues affecting themselves and their households (Kanji, 1995: p. 53).

As a consequence of these developments and the growing pressures for survival at the household level, one institution which has come under threat is the family itself, as the incidence of divorce grows (Fayorsey, 1992/93; Fayorsey, 1994).

Having analyzed to some extent the power relations within the household, the next section discusses the gender division of labor in the management of the home environment arising from these socially constructed power relations.

Layers of engendered environmental niches

Although the internal relations and systems of mutual support are rather complex and unique to individual households, neighborhoods and subcultures in the Greater Accra Metropolitan Area, there is obvious asymmetry in the roles and responsibilities men and women play within the home. Extending beyond the household, networks of solidarity and other social and economic exchanges also exist between household members, as well as other extended family members, neighbors and community residents, and various community and state institutions. It is important to recognize "that the household is not a closed, autonomous unit or separate sphere" (Varley, 1994: p. 120). Nevertheless, it is necessary to acknowledge the importance of the household and other local-spatial constructs when discussing both environmental management and disease transmission (Cairncross *et al.*, 1995).

One important aspect of women's subordination is the gender division of labor that gives women overall responsibility for household environmental care, the principal subject of the present analysis. In order to unravel the gender relations in this and neighboring spheres, it is important to identify the environmental niches at the household and community levels, as well as how the responsibilities for the management of these niches are ordered.

The environmental niches and their management can be conceptualized in terms of a series of overlays of hierarchically arranged layers of engendered environments (Figure 6.1).

Each niche can be defined in terms of the principal social interactions through which environmental management must emerge. The most basic sphere is within the homes of individual households where women encounter some of the most

Figure 6.1 Layers of engendered environmental niches: household, community and the state in GAMA (source: Songsore and McGranahan, 1996, p. 9).

bitter conflicts and struggles over their subordination and work burdens. Much of the discussion of the previous sections focused on this niche.

At the next level, especially within house compounds where the internal architecture is designed for the use of several households (either as extended family members or as a collection of unrelated households in tenement housing units), are the communal areas shared by members of the various households. This niche can include the courtyard, shared kitchen, toilet, bathroom, gate leading out of the house compound, and the immediate surroundings of the house compound, including especially its frontage.

On the peripheries of this niche are the shared and intervening commons between neighboring house compounds in closely built-up areas, which need to be managed as a different sphere. This includes areas where formal responsibilities are often very poorly defined, but effective management typically will require arrangements between adjoining compounds. These areas may be in need of weeding and cleaning by the residents in the adjoining house compounds, and yet no arrangements exist for this activity in low-income areas.

The fourth tier consists of community sanitary sites, such as public toilets and waste collection points, where an overlay of the wider community environment and community regulations impinge on specific household members with specific responsibilities for managing specific niches. These sites are managed by individuals connected with neighborhood organizations or hired by the metropolitan assembly, and households have to pay user fees for the public toilets and the skips located for garbage collection. Women's roles at this point begin to wane, as these activities now become income earning and dominated by men, as opposed to the free services performed by women in the other spheres.

The next overlay, which at least formally superordinates all the other tiers mentioned, is where the environmental management decisions emerge through the executive and regulatory framework of state environmental management institutions on city-wide and national levels. These refer to regulations issued by the metropolitan authorities concerning overall environmental management of the metropolis and at the national level. At the executive level, very few women are represented at the metropolitan assemblies and in government, where key decisions affecting women's managerial roles at the household levels are made.

Finally, there is a wider environment which refers to external influences and processes that are largely beyond the control of the state or any of the other relevant actors. These relate to issues such as global warming, international conventions to which the state is legally bound, or other externalities arising from environmental abuse due to the over-consumption of industrialized countries.

It is the particular combination of elements from all these layers that gives communities and neighborhoods their character. The evidence presented below suggests a waning influence of women as one moves from the inner to the outer layers of decision making and environmental management within the city. But how are environmental caring roles carried out in reality within these niches and by whom?

The case of La

Introduction of gender awareness in CEMIS implementation

Women from the above analysis are clearly the main stakeholders in urban environmental management in Ghana, especially in low-income areas such as La. Yet they are often ignored in development planning related to shelter and environment. In designing policies and projects to increase access to shelter, it is important to consider the different needs of men and women. It therefore became necessary to undertake a gender disaggregation of environmental management tasks and use a community-training workshop as a tool for creating gender awareness in the La community. This was incorporated as part of the pilot testing in La of a Community-based Environmental Management Information System (CEMIS) developed by UNCHS (Habitat). The CEMIS project presents an alternative means of providing environmental infrastructure facilities with communities playing a central role, assisted by governments, local authorities and NGOs, among others. The workshop was to begin capacity building in the La community to recognize structural causes of gender disparity, identify the actions needed to redress these disparities, and institutionalise a dialogue on gender issues in the community with regard to environmental management (Songsore and Denkabe, 1998).

Gender, housing and environmental management in La

In their focus group discussions, both women and men suggested that a widespread disparity exists in gender division of labor at the household, house compound and community levels. The same applied to other caring roles, such as child care and care for the sick and the elderly within the household.

At the level of the household, women did all the physically demanding domestic chores, such as cooking, cleaning and washing. They acquired the water from the tap and the fuel and food from the market. They also controlled pests and managed living areas, as well as contributed to the payment of bills, especially those for health, clothing and education for children. By contrast, men dominated the decision-making arena within the home. Men were supposed to provide money for household sustenance, take major decisions on production, reproduction and maintenance, and exercise final authority on household relations within La. They were recognized as being responsible for physically exerting jobs, such as digging and de-silting drains, undertaking home repairs and defense of the household.

At the level of the house compound, women do the cleaning of the compound facilities shared with other households, such as toilets, baths, kitchens and open spaces within the compound. In addition, women attended meetings on the sharing of bills for joint facilities, such as electricity. By contrast, men de-silt drains, construct houses and attend meetings on regulations, governing rights and responsibilities within the house compound.

Moving to the next layer, which is the community-wide level, men and women join together to provide communal labor during some community-wide activities. In general, men dominate this space where it matters most by taking control of the management of public toilets and communal dump sites with skips and collecting the appropriate tolls and fees.

Gender and child care and care for the sick and elderly

With respect to the gender division of labor on the caring roles listed above, a similar asymmetry is noted. In the sphere of child care both men's and women's groups in La thought that women are responsible for 90 percent of the responsibilities of feeding and bathing children, about 70 percent of the responsibility of meeting the clothing needs of children, and almost entirely for taking care of sick children. Men only occasionally performed these roles, in addition to disciplining the children and sometimes women as well.

Both within the home and the hospital, women undertake over 90 percent of the care for the elderly and the sick. This includes feeding, washing, bathing and administering of drugs. Conversely, men occasionally care for the sick and the elderly. Most herbal preparations are administered by the men. Boys may also take the elderly for walks.

Participants indicated that at the household and community levels, the functions women performed remained unchanged both in nature and degree. Participants referenced women's dominance in teaching, nursing and day care services and noted that women's contributions to child care and care for the sick and elderly were likely to be higher at the wider community level than at the household level.

As a whole, the rigid rules concerning what men and women do in the La community are fastly evolving due to the changing economic situation. Depending on incomes and education of spouses, many of these tasks are done by all members of the household.

Causes of gender disparities and interventions to redress the gender gaps

The general consensus during the workshop was that women shoulder a disproportionate share of household chores, including child care. This therefore puts women at a disadvantage. On the other hand, men are seen as bread winners and spend time looking for funds for household sustenance. It was agreed that on the whole, since men controlled economic power, men make decisions and lord it over the women.

Some of the causes of gender disparities include:

• Societal norms—Ga society and indeed Ghanaian society in general have definite notions of what men and women should do in the community. Men are said to have married women, and so women are obliged to be obedient.

Therefore women are supposed to comply with whatever men say. Furthermore, it is conceived that maintaining gender disparities is easier than changing them.

- There is a communication gap in many homes. As a result, family members do not share decisions and chores.
- Most women are illiterate and are confined to the home. Hence, they do not earn much income and are also not aware of their rights.

It is lamentable that while many people in society are aware of the extent of the inequalities and disparities between men and women, many community members adopt an indifferent attitude towards these disparities. Culture, tradition, poverty and ignorance have often been the interlocking reasons for perpetuating gender imbalances. Many men defend the subordination of women by saying it is tradition.

Some of the actions that various groups suggested for redressing gender disparities in the La community included providing equal access to education and equal opportunities to learn vocations and skills for both girls and boys. It was also thought that men and women should communicate more effectively to create the understanding needed for cooperating with each other. According to the gender expert who facilitated the program, other measures include "affirmative action" through government legislation and the adoption of gender policy approaches in development projects that promote women's welfare, are anti-poverty, advocate equity, and provide income generation activities and other empowerment programs for women. If social justice, human security and economic development are to be achieved, an understanding of existing disparities will enable the creation of new gender relations for the benefit of all in La and GAMA in general.

Health implications for women and children in GAMA

Gender, class and exposure to indoor air pollution hazards

The above case study of La corroborates findings of the broader study in GAMA as most respondents in GAMA's communities stressed that women, as the principal homemakers, do practically every household task, very much like the proverbial "hewers of wood and drawers of water," to satisfy men's needs and the needs of the household. In most low-income communities, female children are normally by their mothers' sides, assisting in the household work from about age seven onwards. Depending on a child's age, her assignments may include washing utensils, participating in meal preparation, sweeping and washing clothes. Female children may also go on short trips to the market to buy any necessary items, while others do petty selling to help generate additional income for the family's sustenance. Child labor, especially for girls, was very common in most low-income areas, as children were involved in petty trade before and after school hours. The mother's burden can easily become a young daughter's—

a sacrifice rarely demanded of boys. School dropout rates tended to be high in these low-income communities, again, especially for the girls. Boys were considered a second-best choice among the interviewed households and rarely did such work, except in households with no female children. As such, the gender division of labor can be seen to form an important basis for understanding urban environmental health problems at the household level.

About 73 percent of the one thousand representative households surveyed in the larger study of GAMA were male-headed, with the remaining 27 percent being headed by women. Other studies have shown that households formally headed by women have been on the increase in Ghana and now constitute about 29 percent of all households (Lloyd and Brandon, 1991: p. 7). Over half (i.e., 54 percent) of all female-headed households had no adult men in the household. The intra-urban distribution of such female-headed households in GAMA shows a marked cluster in the indigenous Ga enclaves, such as La where women exhibit a much greater autonomy and often live separately from their husbands (Aidoo, 1985: p. 22). These indigenous areas include the High Density Indigenous Sector (HDIS), Medium Density Indigenous Sector (MDIS) and Rural Fringe (RF) where 45, 43 and 32 percent respectively of all households were female-headed. All other residential sectors had percentage scores well below the average for the city.

Overall, female-headed households tended to be appreciably poorer than the male-headed households, as shown in Table 6.1. This tendency has been noted in discussions of the feminization of poverty (Vickers, 1993) and is not at all peculiar to Accra. The summary data showed that the average household size of the male-headed households was 6.2, while for female households it was 5.4. The difference in size is very slightly less than the "missing" male household head.

Consistent with the findings from the La case study, data from this larger study also suggests that irrespective of the gender of the head of household, women played the dominant role in environmental management within households in GAMA. Overall, 95 percent of all households had women as the principal homemaker, with a mere 5 percent of all surveyed households having a male as the principal homemaker. These men were either bachelors living alone or hired male domestic servants and cooks, often within very wealthy

Table 6.1 Relationship between gender of household head and class location of household (%)

Class	Male-headed (%)	Female-headed (%)
Low	77	84
Medium	17	13
High	6	3
Total	100	100
(N)	(730)	(270)

Source: Songsore and McGranahan (1996, p. 17).

households. Most middle-income households tend to employ other females as homemakers. To put it differently, the data revealed that only 4 percent of the 730 households that were male-headed had the household head also playing the role of principal homemaker. By contrast, about 90 percent of the 270 households that were female-headed also had the head of household playing the role of principal homemaker.

Women as a group therefore bear the primary responsibility of managing the household environment. However, based on their class location, women can be confronted with an entirely different array of environmental hazards, and rich women may be in a position to transfer these burdens to poor working class women and men hired by the household.

The results of the study in GAMA also suggested a fuel transition as one moves from poor to wealthy households, with woodfuels being replaced by LPG and electricity in wealthy households. This shift from woodfuels to LPG and electricity, often described as the "energy ladder," is a noticeable feature of urban households (Benneh *et al.*, 1993: p. 62; McGranahan and Kaijser, 1993; Songsore and McGranahan, 1996, 1998). As a result of the initial expenses for investment in electric and gas cooking equipment and because of the cost of electricity and gas, most poor households cannot take advantage of the benefits of using these cleaner fuels, especially as subsidies are proscribed under structural adjustment.

The predominant source of in-house air pollution is fuel combustion.

> As such, many of the relevant pollutants are the same as those outdoors: sulphur dioxide, carbon monoxide, nitric oxide, nitrogen dioxide, polycyclic organic matter, and particulates generally. Predominantly indoor pollutants include formaldehyde, radon and aerosols associated with tobacco smoke. In some in-house environments, the level of particulates and polycyclic organic matter can be orders of magnitude higher than outdoor levels, and other pollutant concentrations can also be considerably higher than outdoors.
>
> (McGranahan, 1991: p. 22)

In addition to the composition of the pollutants, the degree of health damage is related to the exposure situation, concentration, time extent of exposure, and the physiological and psychological status of the individual. Many of the emitted compounds also have chronic long-term effects on health (Ellegård and Egnéus, 1992: p. 4). The exposure of women in GAMA to respirable particulates and carbon monoxide shows a wide variation in relative risk depending on the cooking fuel used (Songsore and McGranahan, 1996, 1998).

A subset of 199 women were monitored for respirable particulates (RSP) and carbon monoxide (CO). These women were made to wear portable pumps with filters for about three hours, spanning the time spent cooking a meal. The particulates collected for this period were measured, and the results were used to calculate average concentration of respirable particulates in the vicinity of the woman's face during this time span (Benneh *et al.*, 1993). Men were not part of the sub-sample, as the focus of the research was on the principal homemakers who were often female.

Table 6.2 shows the average concentrations of RSP ($\mu g/m^3$) in three groups of fuel users. Wood users were subject to the highest average concentrations, followed by charcoal users, with kerosene, LPG and electricity users (who were lumped together because of small sample size) experiencing far lower average concentrations. Analysis of variance indicates statistically significant differences in exposure to RSP among the three fuel-user groups ($p=0.002$), though as indicated by the standard errors there was considerable variation within each fuel user group. According to WHO guidelines for outdoor air, the mean daily concentration of total suspended particulates (TSP) should not exceed 150–230 $\mu g/ m^3$ more than seven days per year. In light of this, these levels appear to be disturbingly high, especially for wood and charcoal users.

Since women in poor households are more likely to use wood (especially those in the rural fringe who engage in subsistence fuelwood foraging) together with charcoal as their principal fuel, one can safely conclude that poor women face the highest exposure to these respirable particulates, with possible short- and long-term health damage. Part of the difference in exposure may come from fuel combustion by neighboring households.

Carbon monoxide (CO) emitted from cooking fires can also be injurious to health depending on the concentration of the gas in the inhaled air, duration of exposure, respiratory volume, cardiac output, oxygen demand of the tissues and the concentration of haemoglobin in the blood. Table 6.3 shows the average exposures and the time-weighted average concentrations for the three groups of fuel users. Charcoal users were most exposed to CO, followed by wood users, and finally the group of fuel users consisting of kerosene, LPG and electricity. About 6 percent of the charcoal users were exposed to an average CO concentration greater than 25 ppm, the UNEP-WHO guideline for one hour of exposure (Songsore and McGranahan, 1996, 1998).

There are a number of other pollutants, whose exposure levels can be expected to be correlated to exposure to CO or particulates. Overall, the exposure monitoring suggests that smoke from cooking fires is a matter of some concern.

The analysis of the female principal homemakers presented below suggests that many of the more critical risks these women face, at least in relation to respiratory problems, are closely tied to their gender role. Without looking at the

Table 6.2 Average concentrations of RSP ($\mu g/m^3$) in three groups of fuel users

Wood			Charcoal			Kerosene, LPG, electricity		
Mean	*SE*	n	*Mean*	*SE*	n	*Mean*	*SE*	n
587	94.0	21	341	34.4	122	195	55.0	24

Source: Songsore and McGranahan (1996, 1998).

Table 6.3 Average concentration of CO measured as dose units (ppmh) and calculated time-weighted averages (ppm) in three fuel-user groups

Wood exposure (ppmh)			Charcoal			Kero/LPG/electric		
Mean	*SE*	n	*Mean*	*SE*	n	*Mean*	*SE*	n
24.1	9.1	24	33.1	2.9	137	3.8	1.1	32
Concentration (ppm)								
Mean	*SE*	n	*Mean*	*SE*	n	*Mean*	*SE*	n
7.5	3.0	24	11.0	1.0	137	1.2	0.4	32

Source: Songsore and McGranahan (1996, 1998).

environmental health problems away from home, it is not possible to make any general statements about the overall environmental health risks men and women encounter. It is evident, however, that women, in terms of practical gender needs, have a special interest in a good local environment, not only for the sake of their children, but to protect their own health working within the home.

Respiratory problems of women homemakers

A large number of environmental factors and predisposing conditions influence the prevalence and severity of respiratory infections and common respiratory problem symptoms, such as sore throats and coughs. Although the survey was not designed for epidemiological analysis, many of the relevant factors and conditions were covered. These include indicators of smoke exposure (e.g., smoking patterns, cooking practices, cooking fuels, cooking location and ventilation, and use of mosquito coils), crowding, damp and poor hygiene, as well as the age and socio-economic status of the woman.

Table 6.4 summarizes the results of three logistic regression models of respiratory problem symptoms reported by the principal woman of the household. The environmental risk factors included in the basic model, which has already been presented in an earlier report (Benneh *et al.*, 1993; Songsore and McGranahan, 1996), are those with coefficients found to be statistically significant with at least 95 percent confidence. Environmental variables not included because of a lack of significance were use of a cooking hut, principal cooking fuel, observed evidence of dampness, and selected water and sanitation variables also included in the analysis of diarrhea (see below). The wealth quintile of the household and the age of the woman entered as control variables, but were not statistically significant and are not presented. Respiratory problems were identified through two-week recall of tracer symptoms including sore throat, persistent cough and hoarseness, which could reflect a broad range of respiratory problems including chronic conditions. The summary results of the logistic regressions are odds ratios, which are estimates of the approximate relative risk associated with the factor in question

(Armitage and Berry, 1994). Thus, for example, the basic model estimates that always cooking indoors is associated with a 40 percent increase in the likelihood (or more precisely the odds) of having had respiratory problem symptoms in the last two weeks (Songsore and McGranahan, 1996, 1998).

Most of the environmental variables in the basic model could be interpreted as indicators of suspected risk factors for respiratory problems, such as smoke exposure, dampness, poor hygiene and pesticide exposure. It is important not to over-interpret individual coefficients. Environmental risk factors are closely interrelated, and the variables may be acting as indicators for a variety of more difficult to measure factors.

What is particularly interesting from a gendered perspective is that two of the four environmental risk factors, the use of pump spray insecticides and cooking indoors, are not only features of the home environment, but probably specific to the women's role as principal homemaker. Even dampness and poor hygiene are more relevant to women than to men, because of the greater time they spend in the home. Smoking is relatively uncommon among women (only 35 women smoked at all), but is both the only significant factor that is not an environmental risk encountered in and around the home, and the only one that is likely to be higher among men (Songsore and McGranahan, 1996).

It is also notable that while most of the environmental burdens discussed above clearly fall more heavily on poor women because of the deprived home and neighborhood environment within which they work, those that are indicated as risk factors in respiratory problems are more mixed. The use of pump spray insecticides is somewhat more common in wealthier households, and smoking has not become a poor person's habit as is increasingly the case in wealthy countries (Benzeval *et al.*, 1995). Leaky roofs and water supply problems are clearly associated with poverty. Overall, the relationship between risk factors and wealth is somewhat ambiguous, while women in wealthy and poor households alike tend to face environmental hazards on account of their gender role.

The second model includes a variable identifying female-headed households. This variable is not significant, and its inclusion does not alter the other coefficients appreciably. While being a household head undoubtedly influences the activities of women, it does not add significantly to the explanatory power of the basic model. It is worth noting, however, that the use of pump spray insecticides in the home is only 6 percent in female-headed households as opposed to 13 percent in male-headed households, which is itself a statistically significant difference. A possible explanation is that women dislike spraying in part because of the respiratory irritation, but that it is the men that purchase the insecticide (since spraying is sometimes done by men, however, this finding must be interpreted with care).

The third model includes a variable which identifies households with small children under six who have had symptoms of acute respiratory infection within the past two weeks. The estimated odds ratio for this variable implies that having a sick child is associated with a 3.5 fold increase in the likelihood that the women will report that she herself had a respiratory problem symptom. Somewhat surprisingly, the other coefficients are not greatly affected. While there are

Table 6.4 Logistic models of approximate relative risk of respiratory problem symptoms among principal women of household

Factor	Basic model		Model identifying female-headed households		Model identifying households with sick children	
	Odds ratio	95% confidence interval	Odds ratio	95% confidence interval	Odds ratio	95% confidence interval
Use pump spray insecticides	3.5	2.2–5.6	3.4	2.2–5.5	3.4	2.1–5.5
Water interruptions are common	1.6	1.1–2.3	1.6	1.1–2.3	1.4	1.0–2.1
Roof leaks during rains	1.5	1.1–2.2	1.5	1.1–2.2	1.5	1.0–2.1
Always cooks indoors or on veranda	1.4	1.0–2.0	1.4	1.0–2.0	1.5	1.0–2.1
Number of cigarettes smoked per day	1.1	1.0–1.2	1.1	1.0–1.2	1.1	1.0–1.2
Household is female-headed			0.9	0.6–1.3		
Child in house has respiratory symptoms					3.5	2.0–6.2

Source: Songsore and McGranahan (1996, 1998).

Notes
Number of observations=939.

different interpretations that could be given to this high odds ratio, one obvious possibility is that the women contract a significant share of their respiratory illnesses from their children. As indicated above, caring for sick children is one of the traditional female tasks. These results are similar to those found in Jakarta on the basis of a companion survey (Surjadi, 1993, p. 82).

Health implications for children and the collective security of citizens

The overall poor neighborhood quality for about 70 percent of the residents of GAMA means that urban children in these communities are exposed to problems of diarrhea arising out of poor water supply and sanitation conditions and poor hygiene. The same problem applies for respiratory conditions, which were also monitored, and these afflictions were more related to the poverty of the household or neighborhood rather than the sex of the child. The problem of diarrhea for the young and vulnerable members obviously will have implications for their growth and nutritional status.

For the GAMA population as a whole, cholera and typhoid have become endemic, especially in these environmentally deprived communities, and there is a yearly cholera epidemic in some communities. These everyday risks and their accumulation in communities tend to exacerbate and amplify disaster events, such as during floods in low-income communities that lie along flood-prone areas of GAMA.

Conclusions

Household and neighborhood level environmental problems do not receive the attention they deserve in environmental debates, and this probably reflects, at least in part, a form of gender discrimination: once the water has left the tap, the fuels have been purchased, and more generally the environmental problems have entered the home, these problems are considered less-important "women's" problems. From the perspective of the practical gender needs of women, and especially low-income women, improvements in environmental services almost certainly deserve more support to reduce the burdens and hazards women are exposed to on a daily basis.

The analysis thus far suggests that the future of environmental management in the homes and neighborhoods in GAMA will be determined in part by external developments which include:

*   changes in formal government policies on environmental services and regulation;
*   economic changes which affect the circumstances of the poor majority; and
*   changes in relations between the genders.

All of these processes have global as well as local dimensions and are closely interrelated. Many of the recent shifts in government policy affecting local environmental management reflect adherence to a structural adjustment program (SAP) promoted internationally in support of global capitalism (Songsore and McGranahan, 2000). As a result, the economic prospects for the poor majority also depend critically upon the global political economy.

The economic setbacks which have affected large parts of Africa in recent decades have had repercussions on household relations in the Greater Accra Metropolitan Area, as have the structural adjustment policies Ghana has had to adopt. Indirectly, international economic processes and economic ideologies have played an important role in shaping the development of gender relations locally. More directly, the international women's movement has changed the meaning of women's daily struggles to improve their position.

While many men are feeling threatened by women's empowerment, the actual gains women have made have been minimal. There still exists a critical disjuncture between those who manage the household environment and those who take strategic decisions that can help make environmental improvements possible. The key decision makers in terms of allocation of resources to support environmental improvement are principally male household heads and male policy makers within the state bureaucracy and not women. Those who bear the burden of environmental management within the home are almost exclusively women. Compounding the difficulties that may arise due to the dominance of men and male perspectives within government is the related problem that formal state regulations are ill suited to many of the local environmental management problems that women face. These are however critical matters affecting our collective security.

Improvements should come with better economic conditions and improved services, but also through changes in gender relations to the advantage of women. In some cases this may involve increasing the status of or easing the burden of traditional women's roles, while in others it may involve challenging existing roles, but in all cases, it will involve significant changes in relations of power.

Note

1 This paper draws heavily on Songsore and McGranahan (1996, 1998) and Songsore and Denkabe (1998) as indicated in the Bibliography.

Bibliography

Aidoo, A. A. (1985) Women in the History and Culture of Ghana. *Institute of African Studies: Research Review*, 1(1), pp. 14–51.

Alkire, Sabina. (2003) A Conceptual Framework for Human Security, Center for Research on Inequality, Human Security and Ethnicity (CRISE) Working Paper Series, No. 2. (Online) Available at: www.crise.ox.ac.uk/pubs/workingpaper2.pdf [accessed 5 November 2011].

Ardayfio-Schandorf, E. (1993) Women's Health Status in Africa: Environmental Perspectives from Rural Communities. *Journal of Health Care for Women International*, 14(4), pp. 375–386.

Armitage, P. and G. Berry. (1994) *Statistical Methods in Medical Research.* Oxford, Blackwell Scientific Publications.

Benneh, G., J. Songsore, J. S. Nabila, A. T. Amuzu, K. A. Tutu, Y. Yangyuoru and G. McGranahan. (1993) *Environmental Problems and the Urban Household in the Greater Accra Metropolitan Area (GAMA)—Ghana.* Stockholm: Stockholm Environment Institute.

Benzeval, M., K. Judge and M. Whitehead, eds. (1995) *Tackling Inequalities in Health: An Agenda for Action.* London: King's Fund.

Cairncross, S., U. Blumenthal, P. Kolsky, L. Moraes and A. Tayeh. (1995) The Public and Domestic Domains in the Transmission of Disease. *Tropical Medicine and International Health*, 39, pp. 173–176.

Ellegård, A. and H. Egnéus. (1992) Health Effects of Charcoal and Woodfuel Use in Low-Income Households in Lusaka, Zambia. Energy, Environment and Development Reports, No. 14. Stockholm: Stockholm Environment Institute.

Escobar, A. (1986) Power and Visibility: Development and the Invention and Management of the Third World. *Cultural Anthropology*, 3(4), pp. 428–443.

Fayorsey, C. K. (1992/1993) Commoditization of Childbirth: Female Strategies Towards Autonomy Among the Ga of Southern Ghana. *Cambridge Anthropology*, 16(3), pp. 19–45.

Fayorsey, C. K. (1994) Poverty and the Commoditization of the Life Cycle, accepted for University of Ghana Research and Conferences Committee Seminar on Poverty. Legon 19 September 1994.

Friedmann, J. (1992) *Empowerment: The Politics of Alternative Development.* Cambridge, MA: Blackwell.

GSS (Ghana Statistical Service). (1995) *Ghana Living Standards Survey: Report on the Third Round: GLSS3 September 1991—September 1992.* Accra: Ghana Statistical Service.

Kanji, N. (1995) Gender, Poverty and Economic Adjustment in Harare, Zimbabwe. *Environment and Urbanization*, 7(1), pp. 37–55.

Kanji, N. and N. Jazdowska. (1995) Gender, Structural Adjustment and Employment in Urban Zimbabwe. *Third World Planning Review*, 17(2), pp. 133–154.

Kates, R. W. (1994) A Tale of Three Cities (Editorial). *Environment*, 36(6), p. 1.

Lloyd, C. B. and A. J. Brandon. (1991) Women's Role in Maintaining Households: Poverty and Gender Inequality in Ghana. The Population Council Working Papers, No. 25.

McGranahan, G. (1991) *Environmental Problems and the Urban Household in Third World Countries.* Stockholm: Stockholm Environment Institute.

McGranahan, G. and A. Kaijser. (1993) Household Energy: Problems, Policies and Prospects. Energy, Environment and Development Reports, No. 19. Stockholm: Stockholm Environment Institute.

McGranahan, G. and J. Songsore. (1994) Wealth, Health, and the Urban Household: Weighing Environmental Burdens in Accra, Jakarta, and São Paulo. *Environment*, 36(6), pp. 4–11, 40–45.

Muller, M. S. and D. Plantenga. (1990) Women and Habitat: Urban Management, Empowerment and Women's Strategies. Bulletins of the Royal Tropical Institute, No. 321. Amsterdam: Royal Tropical Institute.

Nussbaum, M. C. (2000) *Women and Human Development: The Capability Approach.* New York: Cambridge University Press.

O'Connell, H. (1994) *Women and the Family.* London: Zed Books.

Oppong, C. (1994) Some Roles of Women: What Do we Know? In: E. Ardayfio-Schandorf, ed. *Family and Development in Ghana*. Accra: Ghana Universities Press.

Robertson, C. C. (1993) *Sharing the Same Bowl*. Michigan: The University of Michigan Press.

ROG/UNICEF. (1990) *Children and Women of Ghana: A Situation Analysis*. Accra: Government of the Republic of Ghana.

Schoepf, B. G., C. Schoepf and J. V. Millen. (2000) Theoretical Therapies, Remote Remedies: SAPs and the Political Ecology of Poverty and Health in Africa. In: J. Y. Kim, J. V. Millen, A. Irwin and J. Gershman, eds. *Dying for Growth: Global Inequality and the Health of the Poor*. Monroe, ME: Common Courage Press, pp. 91–125.

Songsore, J. (1992) Review of Household Environmental Problems in the Accra Metropolitan Area, Ghana, Working Paper. Stockholm: Stockholm Environment Institute.

Songsore, J. and A. Denkabe. (1998) Final Report on Field Trial of CEMIS in La, Ghana, Report prepared for Ministry of Environment, Science and Technology (MEST) and UNCHS (Habitat), Accra.

Songsore, J. and G. McGranahan. (1993) Environment, Wealth and Health: Towards an Analysis of Intra-urban Differentials within the Greater Accra Metropolitan Area, Ghana. *Environment and Urbanization*, 5(2), pp. 10–34.

Songsore, J. and G. McGranahan. (1996) Women and Household Environmental Care in the Greater Accra Metropolitan Area (GAMA), Ghana, Urban Environment Series, No. 2. Stockholm: Stockholm Environment Institute.

Songsore, J. and G. McGranahan. (1998) The Political Economy of Household Environmental Management: Gender, Environment and Epidemiology in the Greater Accra Metropolitan. *World Development*, 26(3), pp. 395–412.

Songsore, J. and G. McGranahan. (2000) Structural Adjustment, the Urban Poor and Environmental Management in the Greater Accra Metropolitan Area (GAMA), Ghana. *Bulletin of the Ghana Geographical Association*, 22, pp. 1–14.

Songsore, J. and G. McGranahan. (2007) Poverty and the Environmental Health Agenda in a Low-income City: The Case of the Greater Accra Metropolitan Area (GAMA), Ghana. In: P. J. Marcotullio and Gordon McGranahan, eds. *Scaling Urban Environmental Challenges: From Local to Global and Back*. London: Earthscan, pp. 132–155.

Stein, H. (2008) *Beyond the World Bank Agenda: An Institutional Approach to Development*. Chicago: University of Chicago Press.

Stephens, C., I. Timaeus, M. Akerman, S. Avle, P. B. Maia, P. Campanario, B. Doe, L. Lush, D. Tetteh and T. Harpham. (1994) *Environment and Health in Developing Countries: An Analysis of Intra-Urban Differentials Using Existing Data*. London: London School of Hygiene & Tropical Medicine.

Surjadi, C. (1993) Respiratory Diseases of Mothers and Children and Environmental Factors Among Households in Jakarta. *Environment and Urbanization*, 5(2), pp. 78–86.

UNDP (United Nations Development Program). (1994) *Human Development Report*. New York: Oxford Press.

Varley, A. (1994) Housing the Household, Holding the House. In: G. Jones and P. M. Ward, eds. *Methodology for Land and Housing Market Analysis*. London: University College London Press, pp. 120–134.

Vickers, J. (1993) *Women and the World Economic Crisis*. London: Zed Books.

7 Negotiating security

Gender, violence and the rule of law in post-war South Sudan

Jok Madut Jok

Introduction

The end of the two-decade-long north-south civil war in Sudan in 2005 brought expressions of hope from soldiers and civilians that stability and security both at individual and community levels would prevail. South Sudan responded to the creation of a neoliberal state with euphoria and a sense of triumph. The post-war government, with its national and state legislative assemblies, the passing of the interim national constitution and the interim constitution of South Sudan, the establishment of the judiciary and the training of the police force are all a symbol of a new security, legal and political order. In particular, women and other marginalized groups who had been most affected by the war received this new order with elation. Security was the peace dividend most expected to accrue immediately. However, five years into the peace agreement, the emerging system of government and the legal framework that undergirds it fell disastrously short of providing protection to all citizens. The entire justice system, the deeply rooted cultural practices in many South Sudanese communities and the legacy of the war itself all compounded to limit women's access to security and to the protection of the law.

In the post-war era, the new government promised to pursue a form of the security agenda that Sudanese civil society groups, such as the Sudanese Women's Voice for Peace, international human rights agencies and non-governmental organizations (NGOs) had advocated during the course of the war. Such security agenda focused on strengthening institutions of law in order to ensure a transparent justice system and to develop a culture of respect for human and civil rights. The Government of Southern Sudan (GOSS) and the Government of National Unity (GoNU) established a presidential advisor position on gender and human rights, created a ministry for family and social welfare, and above all, instituted affirmative action policy to guarantee at least 25 percent of government positions and parliamentary seats to women. These changes, endorsed in the 2005 interim constitution, represented strong signals to a commitment to end women's exclusion from political decision making. Such steps also indicated that violence against women, in the form of physical abuse or the failure of the justice system to protect women's rights, would no longer be tolerated. The constitution clearly spells out the equality of the Sudanese people regardless of race, ethnicity, religious orientation and gender. Optimistic commentators stated that some of the greatest impediments to building a viable neoliberal state had been removed: war was replaced by peace, gender inequity was being redressed and the new justice system had replaced the near lawlessness of wartime. Government officials were quick to announce these developments as the peace dividends long awaited to promote the protection of basic human and civil rights and to make peace and stability the "foundations of a New Sudan" (Garang, 1989).[1]

In this article, I argue that as a matter of policy, these were the right steps, but the policies did not translate into practice. Evidence presented in this article suggests that the notion of a simple transition from war and conflict to peace, security and equitable implementation of the law does not easily lend itself to the realities of ordinary people, especially women. The formal end of conflict is not a shift of violence from war to domestic spheres and other forms of institutional and structural violence.[2] The experiences of women's groups and other marginalized sectors of Sudanese society, however, suggest that the cessation of armed conflict between warring parties in the north and south may not mean the end of socially rooted violence and other forms of insecurities. Although the government and other interested agencies maintain that the idea of universal security is an achievable goal after the end of the war, ethnographic evidence from various sources suggests that the deeply rooted gender-based violence is the norm rather than the exception. Such insecurities militate against equity in access to legal protection, and exacerbate the impact of war on women (Jok, 1998; Fitzgerald, 2002).[3] Thus the state pronouncement of commitment to equitable provision of security, which does not address sociocultural roots of gendered violence, has not granted women security in practice. I argue that the official discourse on security does not appear to translate into legal practices of safety and protection for Sudanese women. Although elite women may benefit more from such legislation, poor women on the peripheries in the south, the northeast and Darfur are caught in between the claims of progress made through affirmative action policies on the one hand, and deeply rooted ideas about women's subordinate status in society on the other. This environment reveals how the women's movement, the government and other marginalized groups negotiate the process of equal protection and security to ensure their safety and inclusion. In this chapter I show that despite the myriad odds against women's access to protection, various women's associations and women-led civil society groups are dedicated to hold government accountable and to ensure women's full participation in governance and decision-making processes. There is no question that many women will continue to live with violence, whether it is state violence, domestic violence or exclusion from government institutions, but it can no longer be said that these women are helpless victims.

In this chapter, I look at the nature of inequitable application of the legal system in post-war South Sudan. I will contextualize this inequitable use of the justice system within a broad history of the war, highlighting the role of gendered socialization, the role of the state in the persistence of violence against women, the reproduction of that violence within the communities long affected by the conflict and the failure of the state to provide equal protection according to the new laws stipulated in the immediate post-war period. Using interviews, participant-observation and other material collected since 1993 from various locations in South Sudan, mainly in Lakes, Western Bahr el-Ghazal, Northern Bahr el-Ghazla and Warrap states, I argue that some gendered insecurities and injustices, though magnified by the protracted north-south conflict, actually pre-dated the war. They are built upon deeply rooted socialization practices that differentiate between men and women. Such gendered insecurities are also related to the way that the peace agreement was reached—a process that excluded women's voices. The end of the armed conflict itself actually intensified certain forms of insecurity, especially domestic violence, which increased with the return of the combatants from war fronts. But blaming the conflict for every social ill glosses over the cultural injustices and inequities rooted in gendered social relations and the construction of femininity and masculinity. It is important to assert that unless such gender disparities are challenged at the level of cultural practices in the process of establishing equitable justice systems, violence against women will remain pervasive in Sudanese societies. In other words, violence against women is fueled by inherent gendered "traditions," whether there is war or not. While it is important to point out that the war has had detrimental effects on the social order that traditionally offered security, it is not entirely unproblematic to single out the war as the only cause of insecurity and lack of protection for women. Doing so obfuscates a long pre-war social history of violence, and undermines a legitimate question about where the line lies between wartime and peacetime gendered violence.

Gendered violence during the north-south war

Since independence, Sudan has suffered from some of Africa's deadliest and most complex civil wars. The root causes, social and economic impacts, and regional implications of these wars have been widely documented (Keen, 1994; Burr and Collins, 1995; Hutchinson, 1996; Johnson, 1998, 2003; Jok, 1999a, 2007; Patterson, 1999). In regards to violence against women during the course of the most recent war, and as other studies of post-war environments have recognized, there are no clear boundaries between the violence of wartime and the violence of the post-war era (Enloe, 1998; Hutchinson and Jok, 2002). The popular discourse among people in the many communities where I did my field-work attributed both deliberate and indirect acts of violence by the state, opposition armies, other armed groups and individuals to a "culture" of war. But it is important to probe the social relations and cultural practices that may subtly promote gendered violence but may be unrelated to the war.

The popular perception that gender-based violence can be completely attributed to the war fails to explain the violence that remains long after the cessation of hostilities. In the heat of the war ordinary civilians were subject to gruesome and unspeakable violence because armies often considered the civilians a resource with which to fight the war. On the one hand, the Khartoum government was always suspicious that certain groups were a part of a "fifth column" in support of the opposition. On the other, the opposition armies expected that the civilians would pay the cost of the war, in both human and material terms. At times military personnel extracted this cost by force, and women shouldered much of this burden.[4] But when the war ended, these wartime abuses were never part of the peace-making processes, and no form of recompense for women was built into the peace agreement. Despite reference to human rights in the peace agreement, the provision of justice still lacks in practice.

The gruesome abuses against civilians and the destruction of communities' resources during the war attest to the failure of the state to meet its welfare responsibilities. In such a state vacuum, private humanitarian aid agencies and human rights groups championed the plight of civilians. Humanitarian agencies filled a gap left by the state, especially in rural areas and remote regions such as Darfur where humanitarian crises were exacerbated by the war. As humanitarian aid became the sole source of services in the peripheries and in displaced persons' camps around Khartoum, the state became more entrenched in the war. The atrocities committed against civilians during the war support the contention that neither the government nor the opposition can be considered to have exercised restraint in their use of violence against women and other non-combatants. I will draw attention to three important arguments: First, that violence against women stems from unequal socialization practices that subjugate women and render them politically invisible. Thus while war may exacerbate the level of violence, armed conflict is not the underlying cause of such violence. Second, the war tactics and the competition between warring parties to attract civilians to each other's side created a subculture of violence that discarded civilian protection as a primary concern, and allowed women to be treated as war trophies. Third, this disregard for law and justice emerged as an instrument of state control. This is a practice that remains pervasive in peace time, and creates a situation whereby women do not reap peace dividends in areas of purported security and the rule of law. I suggest that inequities emerging from gendered socialization practices provided a fertile ground for the war-related targeting of women.

While studies of gendered violence in South Sudan are scant, there are several key resources that should inform any attempt to understand the nature and scope of violence against Southern Sudanese women and girls. The first is a study conducted by Suzanne Jambo on behalf of the New Sudan Women Federation, in which she assiduously details a wide spectrum of gender-based inequities and abuse. She concludes that with regard to women's development, "besides civil war, there are a number of other obstacles and challenges to be overcome, the most challenging being negative customs and gender conflict" (Jambo, 2001). Another significant study based on Mundri and Yei Counties in 2004 found that 7 percent of female respondents in Mundri and 4 percent in Yei personally experienced rape, while 12 percent of female respondents in Mundri and 11 percent in Yei reported that a relative had been raped. This report also calculates a high prevalence of child sexual abuse among the study population and points out that the number of incidents is probably much higher than reported given the associated stigma and general reluctance to acknowledge exposure to sexual violence.[5] I note that victims of sexual violence rarely talk about their experiences of sexual violence, and particularly in cultural contexts where the victim is likely to be blamed for this violence. At times silence may be a way for these women to cope. Sexual assault is not an experience that is easy to report, and so the frontline responders to sexual violence (the police, medical personnel and the judiciary) have to be aware that what the woman does not report may be more important than what she says. This situation is enforced by both the stigma a woman is likely to live with and the fact that the justice system has been ineffective in providing restitution.

A report by the NGO World Vision International on customary law in South Sudan analyzes the varying customary traditions according to a categorization of 10 ethnic groups. Researchers on this study concluded that a number of individual and human rights violations are embedded within the application of some aspects of customary family law. Some of the issues that feature prominently in these reports relate to family attitudes and sexual behaviors. They involve various forms of gendered violence in the context of sexual and marriage relationships in South Sudan, such as domestic violence and rape during the war. For example, in the World Vision study many women's leaders and legal experts repeatedly identified women's property ownership, divorce rights, forced and early marriage, adultery, wife inheritance, child custody and domestic violence as issues needing urgent legal attention (WVI, 2004a and b). Another study conducted by The Civilian Protection Monitoring Team, a group instituted and supported by the United States government and other countries that mediated in the conflict, investigated, evaluated and reported incidents of attacks against civilians by armed force. They estimated that 30 percent of the cases they have investigated involved sexual violence against women, almost exclusively perpetrated by Sudan Armed Forces.[6] Although these studies illustrate the multiple vulnerabilities of women related to war and traditional practices and customary law,[7] they also show that NGOs and international humanitarian actors during the war have built a foundation of a post-war culture and language of human rights to foster a neoliberal post-war state. These reports also show how traditional practices and customary law are being rearticulated within a human rights, neoliberal framework.[8]

However, many of these studies, while documenting and showing that violence against women is heightened in war times, have neglected the structural violence embedded in the socio-economic and cultural structures which exacerbate the violence of wartime. During the war, three factors reproduced violence against Sudanese women: cultural norms that paint women as the pillars of a society at war, the violent actions of individual soldiers who themselves were embedded within long-term contexts of violence, and gendered ideologies that describe women as subordinate to men. These factors inform a subculture of violence embedded in both customary practices and gendered attitude towards women. As military authorities and other state actors highlight the chaos of the war as the reason for gendered violence, they manage to deflect attention away from the deliberate targeting of women and the military authorities' disregard for the law.

Such discourse naturalizes gender violence and undermines its socio-political contexts. Sudan's wars have strengthened the connection between wartime violence and long-established gendered hierarchies that view men as the protectors of women and women as supporters in the domestic sphere. The violence of wartime gave rise to a militarist culture that capitalized on deeply rooted constructions of gender that socialize men to be aggressive and women to be submissive in many aspects of their lives. It is undeniable that the war experience is gendered and that it affects women more gravely and in far more ways than it affects men. However, women struggle as individuals and as groups to fend off the impact of war in their lives. For instance, my work suggests that women's political activism has proven a serious antidote to the application of gendered socialization as a weapon of war. Such efforts are often more subtle than an outright opposition. Unfortunately, women's subtle political tools of resistance are often counteracted by the increasing targeting of women and by a stronger push for a militarized culture (Jok, 1999b; Enloe, 2000). As young men encounter prolonged periods of militarization, they view women's assertion of their rights as a direct challenge to the long-established gendered hierarchies. During my fieldwork in South Sudan one informant explained to me that a wife who questions a decision made by a husband returning from a war front is quickly viewed as a woman who has "developed horns," during the man's absence and needs to have "these horns trimmed." This means that violence against women is no longer confined to the actions of the military against the women of the opposing side, but protracted conflicts create situations where violence is often reproduced within families, domestic contexts and communities (Jok, 1999a).

It is important to emphasize that the generalization of war-time violence often provides authorities with the ability to carry out more selective gender-based actions as military tactics. Among many cultural groups in Sudan, women are situated at the center of social organizations as the bearer and reproducer of moral and cultural ideals. Warring parties often target women during conflict as a mechanism by which to destabilize the society's perceived moral core. The rationale that seems to have been followed in the north-south war, especially from 1989 to 2003 during the period when the Islamist regime in Khartoum had opted for a military solution to Sudan's protracted political woes, was that women had become intrinsic to the military tactics and were fair game. Raping women during the war became a strategy to dishonor and humiliate the enemy.

Furthermore, there are other subtle ways in which both parties to the war, the SPLM and the Khartoum government, contributed to gender violence during the war. The SPLM Nationalist position furthered the expectation that every southerner must contribute to the struggle. This developed a military ethos that pushed women to the "reproductive front," in order to replenish the society being deci-mated by war, and to "birth the nation" (Cody, 2005). This nationalizing of "women's wombs" foreground reproduction as a revolutionary act. While this was not an official policy of the SPLM, it was common to hear military men talking about how they were constantly at risk of getting killed and must, there-fore, have as many children as possible. My extensive interviews with combat-ants have revealed that this attitude developed over time into a license that gave men the belief that they should control reproductive decisions, including the demand that one's wife becomes sexually available anytime he wishes (Hutchin-son and Jok, 2002).

The government of Khartoum, on the other hand, committed violent atrocities against southern women. While they may have been random acts, such atrocities by government army and militias created a pattern that made violent actions useful as war tactics. Such tactics include the government and its allied militias' raid of civilian villages and the sexual abuse of women and children in targeted areas. Within garrison towns such as Wau, Juba or Malakal, it was common for officers of the Sudan Armed Forces to use the pretext of intelligence-gathering to round up women and to transport them into barracks where they were repeat-edly raped within the interrogation cells. Some women were often held and raped for days before they were released and threatened with more violence if they spoke to anyone about their experience. Interviews conducted with a number of women who went through these ordeals in Wau have revealed the regime's engagement in widespread and vicious persecution that was also ani-mated by racism and religious intolerance, as the language used in these "inter-rogations" suggests. A number of reports show that such actions did not just happen in the south, but also in the Nuba Mountains, and currently in Darfur (Ryle, 2004; de Waal, 2006).

There is no question that Sudanese women in the areas covered by this study were caught in this conflict and were deliberately targeted as the bedrock of the social order. But the prolonged conflict also conditioned large numbers of male youth to violence and they often reproduced this violence against members of their own communities and families (Jok, 2005; Ellis, 2006). Despite the impor-tance I give in this chapter to the targeting of women in South Sudan's war zones, it is significant to note that women's rights are both subtly and flagrantly violated in all parts of the country as a result of war-related attitudes and the emergence of a subculture of violence. This culture of violence increased women's subordination and gave the ruling elite legitimacy to govern the country.

Everyday life, gendered violence and the law

In this section I discuss how everyday cultural practices are gendered and how constructions of femininity and masculinity perpetuate women's subordination and justify violence against them in a variety of ways. I argue here that wartime violence, as described above, is intertwined with pre-existing gendered cultural biases. For example, due to women's socialization to normative subordinate feminine roles, the security sector, the legal system and other forms of law enforcement do not prioritize the protection of women in the same ways that they do for men who have access to security and protection.

While there are no statistics on the prevalence of domestic violence, it was often reported in the course of my fieldwork in the southern states that families differed in the ways they enforced gender subordination and the mechanisms by which they resolved gender conflict. While many men would defend their daughters and stood up against other men, gender-based violence pervades political and social arenas through humor and other cultural tactics that reproduce gendered ideas about men's and women's place in society. Southern Sudanese humor is full of references to women who misbehave and who can only be disciplined by their male guardians: fathers, brothers and husbands. There are also many jokes about domestic violence as a form of discipline that maintains social order. Among the Dinka, for instance, there are jokes about women who desire to be beaten by their husbands in order to be assured of their husbands' assertive personality and masculine dominance. Among men and some women these may be jokes but they are rooted in actual practices, and their impact on the lives of many women is quite real. They reflect a widely held perception that there is a psychological and developmental state of existence that ranks women below that of men. These jokes function as justification for women's subservient status in society, thus creating discourses and practices of gendered power inequality. The power of such cultural practices manifests in how women themselves employ such a language to socialize their daughters and maintain their subordinate position within domestic contexts. In other words, while the women appear to subtly perpetuate the tools of their own oppression, such jokes reveal the tension that pervades gender relations and the social construction of men's power through ideas of physical strength and violence.

Such gender ideologies and practices surrounding women's subordinate status in the family become the basis for exclusionary policies that relegate women to less visible political roles, jobs and decision-making positions in larger society. These ideologies transform women into objects whose bodies become sites for enacting masculine ideals. In other words, jokes of violence are not without detrimental consequences. Moreover, joking discourses help to create an environment where women's complaints and reports of violence are taken less seriously by the justice system. Reports of violence by women often become laughing matters among law enforcement agents. Cases of domestic violence in the judicial system are depoliticized and rendered private affairs to be resolved within the domestic domains. This is why legislation that prohibits wife beating, forced marriages, child marriage or restrictions on women's demand for divorce are rare, and even harder to enforce when they do exist. My ethnographic interviews in the towns of Wau, Rumbek and Kuajok show that in situations of domestic abuse, and particularly in rural areas and poor urban centers, the police are always reluctant to respond because violence against women is seen as the result of women's disobedience. It is not uncommon for police officers to refrain from intervention in cases of domestic abuse on the pretext that it is a man's right to discipline his wife, daughter or sister. The interviews also show how magistrate judges presiding over such cases are more hostile toward women in court. These judges at times blame women for their own role in provoking violence against themselves and for not adhering to their expected subordinate roles. Common phrases such as "It is just women's talk" reflect men's responses to a woman's cry about abuse.

Another cultural practice that can be disadvantageous to women is the payment of bride-wealth. Among the Southern Sudanese cultural groups I worked with, the payment of numerous cattle as bride-wealth is demanded. Although this is a system that has endured for generations and that is believed to cement strong marriages and social order among communities, the demands for bride-price payment can be disadvantageous to women. Bride-wealth depends upon the movement of large amounts of wealth, thus it allows women to be regarded as a family's main resource and property. Bride-wealth transactions are often at the root of child marriage, the young age at which women start having children, the amount of physical domestic labor that women are expected to perform during marriage and men's disciplinary techniques that may involve extreme physical violence. For example, it is not uncommon to hear a man say to his wife that, "I have purchased you and you must do as I say," or a father threatening his young daughter to marry her off because, "I paid very dearly for your mother and I must get my wealth back." A poor family might be pressured to give their young daughter in marriage to a powerful man not only because of what bride-price he might pay but also because he could be called upon by the family to provide political, legal and economic favors in times of great need. Bride-wealth payment is also used as a justification for why women should have as many children as their reproductive health allows them.

Social Science arguments surrounding the issue of gender and bride-wealth have focused on two rigid positions: those who blame bride-wealth payment for women's subjugation and those who praise it as a social norm that builds strong marriages and social bonds. The former argument is often held by humanists, local women's rights advocates, Western feminists and human rights groups (Mwamwenda and Monyooe, 1997). The latter involves cultural relativists who argue that bride-wealth is a practice too central to the social fabric to under-mine.[9] However, Southern Sudanese women are increasingly challenging the concept that the bride-wealth system is central in preserving cultural identities and the social order. These women oppose the bride-wealth system based on the fact that they perceive the practice as detrimental to their well-being because such practices justify violence against women. For example, in Western Dinka communities, there are strong and growing voices among urban women for equitable decision making regarding marriage, bride-wealth, age of marriage and girls' education. "It is not that we do not cherish our culture, but that there are some negatives that come with that system of marriage, which we are saying should be modified gradually in order to fit with our changed circumstance," remarked Miriam, a woman activist in Kuajok, the capital of Warrap state.

We now live in towns, we desire education, we see educated women taking political office, some of them flying planes, and others as doctors, but we still want to practice things that will hold them back from becoming these things? That does not sound right.

Although bride-wealth itself is not a form of violence against women, the practice informs repressive gender ideologies and inequalities in various domestic and legal socio-political arenas. Girls' lack of access to education, for example, especially in rural areas, results in early marriages and early pregnancies. Many and frequent pregnancies may result in a plethora of reproductive health problems that are related to a lack of autonomy regarding sex and sexual health issues. This often leads to difficult pregnancies and maternal mortality for women. The United Nations reports that in South Sudan a girl is more likely to die of childbirth-related causes than to graduate from primary school.[10]

This in turn means that women and girls are expected to have limited decision-making power over sex. A woman is expected to accommodate her husband's sexual demands in order to respect ideologies that emphasize procreation as the main reason for marital union and the man's "husbandly rights" that are supposedly guaranteed by his bride-wealth. His rights to "sexual services" are also protected by both his status as "the man of the house," and her status as a mere appendage to him. During my interviews many women were engaged in resistance strategies to these practices, amidst other struggles against poverty and lack of health services. Women's perspectives reveal that family pressure is a challenge that women would not have to respond to if families realize that these practices impede women's access to resources and equal reproductive decision making, and in turn, affect the well-being of entire families. The examples I presented in this section show that such violence against women, not just in the south, but also in Darfur and other parts of the country, continues to take place due to the failure of the justice system to implement rigorous security measures. Although civil society groups continue to advocate for gender-based reforms the institutional commitment to the implementation of such policies remains short of protecting women.

This is, however, not to typify women as passive victims. Feminist political analysis highlights the political nature of subjects and demonstrates women's agency, political subjectivity and their resistance and struggles against marginalization in war and post-war situations (Enloe, 2007). Women's political strategies and activism to combat violence in recent years have allowed the family, society and the state to recognize them as political subjects. Here is evidence that women in South Sudan and other regions of the country have often engaged and made claims on the emerging state and that they have always articulated a particularly gendered notion of rights to reform existing laws. Indeed there is a long history of Sudanese women's activism, and the political space for women's resistance has widened over the past two decades. Women have negotiated with social institutions, the state and other political movements to ensure equitable access to protection, security and basic rights that are endorsed by the national constitution (Ahfad University, 1995; Hale, 1997).

Conclusion: gendered violence in post-war South Sudan

Although the 2005 comprehensive peace agreement has brought a welcome end to hostilities between the government and SPLA/SPLM forces, and despite the establishment of security systems by the government, there remains a general feeling among Southern Sudanese that they are not safer in a post-war period than they were during war times. Southern Sudanese expected that security would become the most immediate peace dividend, and they expected security to be provided in all sectors of society in the form of adequate policing, a strong and equitable justice system, and the cooperation of all public institutions to uphold laws to protect citizens. Instead, general insecurity manifested itself in the form of gender-based violence, ethnic conflicts, police abuses in urban centers and a lack of judges in remote towns. This generalized sense of insecurity also relates to the circulation of weapons among citizens. Moreover, the gruesome fighting that continues to pit southern ethnic groups against one another often affects women more than other sectors of the population. Such feelings of insecurity related to the infancy of the state and the lack of protection are also exacerbated by rapidly increasing urbanization that creates an unhealthy concentration of poor unemployed youth in swelling slums and makes southern towns breeding places for crime and disease. The result is a higher incidence of rape and other kinds of assaults against women. According to news reports in both local and international media, thousands of women are raped each year, with nearly half of the cases occurring in the context of tribal conflicts and the other half in urban centers and many more rapes go unreported. The vast majority of rapes also go unpunished, and it is difficult to win justice for rape victims.

As I have shown in this chapter, the failure to bring perpetrators of violence against urban women to justice is rooted in social attitudes toward women. But this failure can also be attributed to the poor reporting of sexual violence and domestic abuse by police and by medical professionals. In Southern Sudan, the procedure is that any person who claims sexual assault has to obtain a police report before going to the emergency room. For this study, I examined hospital records, police records, and I interviewed hospital staff in Juba and Wau. It was difficult to obtain records of the doctor's assessment of the victim's conditions. However, I was granted access to a limited number of them after the names of the victims had been concealed. The cases I examined revealed the disturbing pattern that doctors performed medical examinations of rape victims horrendously. The descriptions of the women who reported rape, i.e., their heights, weights and other physical features, appear to be uniform and reflect the possibility that medical officers may have simply recorded the same features for all women who reported rape without actually examining them. The reports often contained puzzling comments such as "alleged rape," which is not a medical conclusion. In practice, such a comment in a medical report means that if the case were brought to court, the chances of the perpetrator getting convicted are limited because the doctor did not make a conclusive report.[11] Police work on this issue is also disastrously unprofessional. Aside from Juba and Wau, police officers often objected to my attempts to study police records of reported rape cases. The result is that everyone knows there is gruesome sexual violence committed in southern communities but there is very little anyone can do about it since the justice system is flawed and flagrantly complicit.

Just as the government, policy makers and NGO workers have held the war itself responsible for women's suffering, there is now a tendency to shift accountability for violence against women to the weakness of the post-war system of justice and its failure to provide restitution for women. While NGOs and human rights organizations were largely in charge of implementing or debating security policies during the war, the post-war state must reclaim responsibility for protection and welfare. Instead of blaming the legacy of the war for the lack of protection, actors of the neoliberal state have to take responsibilities for law enforcement and other welfare provision. For instance, a case that I witnessed in Wau town, the capital of Western Bahr el-Ghazal State, reveals the vulnerability of women in the context of the rampant misapplication of the law. On a visit to Wau town police detention center, I came upon a middle-aged woman who had been in jail for many days. When I inquired about the reason for her arrest, she told me she was arrested at the behest of her husband who accused her of facilitating their daughter's elopement. Because of her husband's connection with the police chief and the county magistrate, the woman languished in jail without being formally charged or afforded any legal counsel. Cases of this kind are very common, for men are invested in marrying off their daughters or sisters, and a girl's elopement means a material and financial loss for her family as well as a challenge to her family's authority.[12]

Different women's groups, human rights associations and transnational groups, however, began to contest such injustices. More and more anti-discrimination associations emerged on the political scene to demand political inclusion and protection of all citizens' basic rights granted by the constitution. Thus, the years of conflict have important implications for the changing roles of women and other marginalized groups. For example, the adverse circumstances that women have had to confront during war have forged a subculture of expanded collective action and self-reliance among women. This capacity for self-reliance is an important foundation for the reconstruction efforts that promoted women's full participation with the recent formation of the republic of South Sudan. Despite the obvious societal norms that work against women's well-being and despite the exclusionary policies practiced by the state, what cannot be denied is that women and other marginalized social groups view the establishment of the new state as an opportunity for women's political engagement in the reconstruction process, especially the strengthening of an equitable justice system. Women are now better situated than they have ever been to make claims upon the state to become more accountable and to institute plans for developing a more efficient law enforcement system.

Despite women's slow inclusion in key positions of military and political power and their marginalization within the formal structures of the SPLM, they found avenues to challenge the direction of the new state (Fitzgerald, 2002). For example, since the SPLM National Convention at Chukudum in 1994, women have begun to demand representation at all levels of government (Winter, 2000). The formation of women's activist movements, such as the SPLM Women's League, the Sudan Women's Voice for Peace and a variety of state-level women's associations, has succeeded in registering women's rightful demands and their inclusion within formal political structures. There is now a marked engagement of women within civil society groups and in government and the legislature. This will provide opportunities for women to promote gender equality, especially now that there is recognition of the equal rights of men and women in the documents that brought the peace agreement. Indeed, women are increasingly active in South Sudanese formal politics and a number now hold prominent offices within the government of Southern Sudan. But because much of this progress is achieved partly due to increasing pressure from international human rights groups, aid agencies and donor countries that emphasize nation-building efforts to ensure gender equality, it would be extremely important for elite Sudanese women to own such gains in order to achieve lasting gender equalities. There is no question that the women's movement in Southern Sudan has reached a point of no return and that it has become a stronger voice to reckon with. Despite this progress, however, challenges remain in regards to the concerns of poor women in both rural and urban settings.

As critical as it is that South Sudanese women join hands with women's groups around the world, it will be crucial to ensure that both the SPLM and GOSS are moving beyond discourse in their promotion of the safety, security and rights of women. Of the widespread reforms being demanded by South Sudanese women, the most important are the ones relating to greater participation of women in all levels of government, the provision of legal protection, reforms of customary practices, and above all, an affirmative action that ensures women's access to education. For example, the challenges of instituting legislative and judicial reforms are even more difficult to achieve considering that there are very few women lawyers in South Sudan. A post-war nation that needs speedy reconstruction can only achieve it through the full participation of all its citizens regardless of gender and ethnic affiliation.

Despite the end of military hostilities, the promise of post-war security and the persistence of gender inequality leave women and girls unprotected by new and seemingly progressive gender sensitive legislation. The new laws and the justice system continue to be influenced by customary practices that legitimize men's claim to authority. Although the war exacerbated violence against women, it is important to examine the socio-cultural history of wartime violence.

In this chapter I gave much attention to discourses and practices that reproduce violence against women, however, I also suggest that women wage resistance against the constraints they face in South Sudan. This resistance includes demands for basic rights and full participation in nation-building processes. As

South Sudanese women continue to demand basic rights and full participation, it is significant that the state prioritizes security issues related to women's protection against violence. While it is important to investigate war trauma, the growth of military culture or ideas of masculinity as causal factors in gendered-violence, it is equally crucial to probe community-level social and cultural structures that undergird men's attitudes towards women—and that often emerge more vividly in war times.

Notes

1 The term New Sudan was coined and popularized by John Garang, the chairman and commander-in-chief of Sudan Peoples' Liberation Movement/Army (SPLM/A), and it has been interpreted to mean the establishment of a democratic Sudan, free of discrimination based on creed, race, gender or ethnic origin.

2 Structural violence refers to the many types of violence that occur due to the failure of the structures of government to respond, but that are not committed by any specific individuals (Galtung, 1996; Gilligan, 1997).

3 My analysis of this paper is based on interviews I conducted in southern Sudan between 2007 and 2009.

4 It was common for rebel soldiers to order girls and women to function as porters to carry military supplies, or prepare meals, which was extremely labor-intensive, involving the pounding of grain, fetching of water from distant wells, collection of firewood, etc.

5 Status of Women in the New Sudan: Report for Mundri and Yei Counties (July 2004).

6 It is worth noting that the Civilian Protection and Monitoring Team publicized the incidents of abuse, which appears to have had positive impact in so far as the number and severity of incidents is reportedly decreasing. Moreover, they were the only group that made a commitment to assisting survivors—often in vain given the lack of services. They provided many women with the first and only form of support they will receive.

7 See for example the study by Save the Children "Southern Sudan Vulnerability Study." London and Nairobi: Save the Children UK (1998).

8 In some Sudanese subcultures where the wife receives part of the bride-wealth, this payment confers some responsibilities upon the husband and his family, while arming the woman with tools to use the transaction to her advantage.

9 The debate between the two positions is even more intense in reference to the Southern African system of "Lobola," as the bride-wealth system is well known there (Ansell, 2001).

10 In a lecture delivered at London School of Economics in 2009, the UN resident coordinator in South Sudan remarked, in what she called "scary statistics," that South Sudan is witnessing a "perfect storm," which was made of ethnic violence, maternal and child mortality, malnutrition and the impact of the global economic downturn on the government of South Sudan.

11 Medical personnel who make this type of conclusion cannot always be blamed for issuing such a report, however, as victims of rape are not so easy to work with. They are often traumatized and cannot be expected to trust anyone, and the result is that they may not even answer questions. Medical interview of victims of sexual violence is something that needs a special professional preparation on the part of health workers.

12 See also New Sudan Women Federation (2001), "Overcoming Gender Conflict and Bias: The Case of New Sudan Women and Girls," a report from a field-based search conducted by Suzanne Jambo on behalf of Federation.

Bibliography

Abdel Haleem, Asma M. (1995) Rituals and Angels: A Case Study of Female Circumcision in the Sudan. In: Margaret Schuler, ed. *From Basic Needs to Basic Rights*. Washington, DC: Institute of Women, Law, and Development.

Abdel Haleem, Asma M. (1999) Reconciling the Opposites: Equal but Subordinate. In: Courtney Howland, ed. *Religious Fundamentalisms and the Human Rights of Women*. New York: St. Martin's Press.

Ahfad University for Women. (1995) Warshat amal dor al- Malomat wa al-Tawtheeg fi Tanmyat al-Mara (Workshop on the Role of Information and Documentation in the Development of Sudanese Women). Omdurman: Ahfad University for Women.

Ansell, N. (2001) "Because it's our Culture!" (Re)negotiating the Meaning of Lobola in Southern African Secondary Schools. *Journal of Southern African Studies*, 27(4), pp. 697–716.

Burr, M. and R. Collins. (1995) *Requiem for the Sudan: War, Drought and Disaster Relief on the Nile*. Boulder, CO: Westview Press.

Cody, Lisa F. (2005) *Birthing the Nation: Sex, Science, and the Conception of Eighteenth Century Britain*. Oxford: Oxford University Press.

De Waal, Alex. (2006) *Averting Genocide in the Nuba Mountains, Sudan*. New York: Social Science Research Council.

Ellis, Stephen. (2006) *The Mask of Anarchy: The Destruction of Liberia and the Religious Dimension of an African Civil War*. Leiden: African Studies Center.

Enloe, Cynthia. (1998) "All the Men are in the Militias, All the Women are Victims…'"Gender, Militarism and Nationalism in Bosnia. In: Jennifer Turpin and Lois Lorentzen, eds. *The Women and War Reader*, New York: New York University Press.

Enloe, Cynthia. (2000) *Maneuvers: The International Politics of Militarizing Women's Lives*. Berkeley: University of California Press.

Enloe, Cynthia. (2007) *Globalization and Militarism: Feminists Make the Link*. Lanham, MD: Rowman and Littlefield.

Fitzgerald, Mary Anne. (2002) *Throwing the Stick Forward: The Impact of War on Southern Sudanese Women*. Nairobi: UNIFEM and UNICEF.

Galtung, Johan. (1996) *Peace by Peaceful Means: Peace and Conflict Development and Civilization*. London, UK: Sage Publications.

Garang, John. (1989) *John Garang Speaks*. Mansour Khalid, ed. London and New York: Kegan Paul International (KPI).

Gilligan, J. (1997) *Violence: Reflections on a National Epidemic*. New York: Vintage Books.

Hale, Sondra. (1997) *Gender Politics in Sudan: Islamism, Socialism, and the State*. Boulder, CO: Westview Press.

Hutchinson, Sharon E. (1996) *Nuer Dilemmas: Coping with Money, War, and the State*. Berkeley: University of California Press.

Hutchinson, Sharon E. and Jok Madut Jok. (2002) Gendered Violence and the Militarization of Ethnicity: A Case Study from South Sudan. In: R. Werbner, ed. *Post-Colonial Subjectivities in Africa*. London and New York: Zed Books.

International Rescue Committee. (2004) *Freedom from Fear: Promoting Human Security for the Return and Reintegration of Displaced Persons in South Sudan*. New York: IRC.

Jambo, Suzanne. (2001) *Overcoming Gender Conflict and Bias: The Case of New Sudan Women and Girls*. Nairobi: New Sudan Women Federation.

Johnson, Douglas. (1998) The Sudan Conflict: Historical and Political Background: Analysis and Evaluation Paper. Munich, Germany: Conflict Prevention Network.

Johnson, Douglas. (2003) *The Root Causes of Sudan's Civil Wars*. London: James Currey.

Jok, Jok Madut. (1996) Information Exchange in the Disaster Zone: Interaction between Aid Workers and Recipients in South Sudan. *Disasters*, 20(3), pp. 206–215.

Jok, Jok Madut. (1998). *Militarization, Gender, and Reproductive Health in South Sudan*. New York and London: Edwin Mellen Press.

Jok, Jok Madut. (1999a) Militarism and Gender Violence in South Sudan. *Journal of Asian and African Studies*, 34(4), pp. 427–442.

Jok, Jok Madut. (1999b) Militarism, Gender and Reproductive Suffering: The Case of Abortion in Western Dinka. *Africa: Journal of the International African Institute*, 69(2), pp. 194–212.

Jok, Jok Madut. (2005) War, Changing Ethics and the Position of Youth in South Sudan. In: Jon Abbink and I. van Kessel, eds. *Vanguard or Vandals: Youth, Politics and Conflict in Africa*. Leiden and Boston: Brill.

Jok, Jok Madut. (2007) *Sudan: Race, Religion and Violence*. Oxford: OneWorld Publications.

Keen, David. (1994) *The Benefits of Famine: A Political Economy of Famine and Relief and Southwestern Sudan*. Princeton, NJ: Princeton University Press.

Mwamwenda, T. S. and L. A. Monyooe. (1997) Status of Bridewealth in African Culture. *The Journal of Social Psychology*, 137(2, April), pp. 269–271.

Patterson, Donald. (1999) *Inside Sudan: Political Islam, Conflict and Catastrophe*. Boulder, CO: Westview Press.

Ryle, John. (2004) Disaster in Darfur. *The New York Review of Books*, 51(13), 12 August 2004.

Shweder, Richard, 1991, *Thinking Through Cultures: Expeditions in Cultural Psychology*. Cambridge, MA: Harvard University Press.

Winter, Roger. (2000) The Nuba People: Confronting Cultural Liquidation. In: Jay Spaulding and Stephanie Beswick, eds. *White Nile Black Blood: War, Leadership, and Ethnicity from Khartoum to Kampala*. Lawrenceville, NJ: The Red Sea Press, Inc.

Wojcicki, Janet, Ariane van der Straten and Nancy Padian. (2010) Bridewealth and Sexual and Reproductive Practices among Women in Harare, Zimbabwe. *AIDS Care: Psychological and Socio-medical Aspects of AIDS/HIV*, 22(6), pp. 705–710.

World Vision International (WVI). (2004a) *A Study of Customary Law in Southern Sudan*. Nairobi: WVI.

World Vision International (WVI). (2004b) *Promoting Peace and Justice for Sudanese Women and Children: A Report of the Conference on the Legal Status of Women and Children in Sudan*. Nairobi: WVI.

8 Gender, agency and peace negotiations in Africa

Aili Mari Tripp

Human security approaches to peacebuilding incorporate important agency-oriented, people-centered and bottom-up perspectives that are in many ways attractive to those adopting a gendered approach to security.[1] There are some approaches to human security, although not all, that even include an appreciation for the power dimensions of security, which is at the core of any analysis of gender (Hoogensen and Stuvoy, 2006; Grayson, 2008). However, there are many aspects of the human security approach relating to agency that need to be sharpened in order to make the concept workable from a gender studies perspective, especially when one looks at the concept from the point of view of women within conflict and post-conflict situations.

Gender relations within the context of conflict are one such set of social relations that reveal the complexities embedded within the notion of agency. Civil conflict breaks open, pathologizes, distorts and can even transform societal rifts, making it all the more important that we problematize the meaning of agency. First, we need to consider the agents themselves. What is meant by "people" in human security approaches needs to be clarified, especially where there are multiple and competing interests of different "people" that are embedded in power relations. Men and women do not always have the same motivations and objectives in processes like peacemaking. This chapter looks at differences between men and women in peacebuilding activities. It asks: Why have women's peacemaking activities differed so significantly from those of men in most African conflicts? Why have women been relegated primarily to localized peacemaking efforts? Why has it been so hard for them to participate in national peacekeeping negotiations and initiatives that are generally dominated by men?

Second, agency itself is not neutral and can serve multiple and competing purposes, both for ill and for good. One reality is that war and other forms of insecurity make people act in ways they would never dream of doing under normal circumstances in order to stay alive. Even peace activists—more than is often acknowledged—cut unholy deals and collaborate with "the enemy" in order to survive. Some women in Liberia accepted top positions within government ministries of the corrupt and autocratic Charles Taylor government in order to advance their careers personally, but also because they felt that this positioned them better to negotiate for peace and advance gender-related goals. Theft, corruption and deceit are rampant during conflict. Agency is often described in positive terms, but the realities of conflict may make agency a more ambiguous concept. During the Liberian women's peace movement, a few so-called peace activists associated with President Charles Taylor allegedly tried to ambush and kill the leaders of the movement during one effort to engage and disarm soldiers. To be clear, many women who had been associated with the Taylor government or who had supported Taylor belonged to the peace movement, but only a few resorted to such tactics.

Third, the more severe the circumstances, the more agency becomes problematic. How, for example, should one understand agency when the actions of one victimized group result in the suffering and misery of others? What is the meaning of agency when women use what little agency they have simply to survive through whatever brutal means is available to them? Kidnapped girl child soldiers in Sierra Leone found that the more violent and ruthless they were in their attacks on civilian populations, the more privileges they attained in the context where they themselves were victims of physical and other insecurities. Some girl soldiers used their fighting skills to defend themselves by killing combatants who tried to rape them.

Fourth, what is the meaning of agency when the solution is almost as bad as the problem, creating its own set of dilemmas? For example, women, girls and combatants sometimes use marriage and exchange sexual relations with fighters for survival and protection. Some scholars have described these survival strategies in terms of agency (Maclure and Denov, 2006; Denov and Gervais, 2007).

Fifth, human security approaches often tend to focus on the individual as both the means and the end of human security (Buzan, 2004: p. 37; Tadjbakhsh and Chenoy, 2007: p. 238). In practice, the way problems are framed have often resulted in statist solutions, e.g., by focusing on individual agency and the rights of the individual (Krause and Williams, 1997: p. 46; Richmond, 2007; Ambrosetti, 2008; Christie, 2010). This is premised on a liberal notion of rights as being located primarily with the individual. Yet agency is not only enacted by individuals. It often takes collective forms. Both individual and collective actors need to be accounted for. Women's demands to participate in peace negotiations were almost always made as a collective and were made in order to advance a women's rights agenda to benefit women as a collectivity because they were perceived as a group to be marginalized, particularly in context of war. In fact, conflict exacerbated the consequences of women's exclusions, making it all the more imperative to make demands as a collectivity.

Moreover, women's agency, like that of others, is largely defined or constrained by the broader gendered social structures within which women operate. Gender-based discrimination sets parameters on women's action. This chapter looks at why and how women seek to challenge those parameters and redefine agency collectively along more egalitarian lines in the context of war, with particular reference to Liberia. By "integrating a gender perspective into the concept of human security rather than *applying* human security to gender," as Hoogensen and Stuvoy (2006: p. 219) suggest, it becomes easier to adopt a more people-centered approach to security and appreciate the important ways in which women on the ground are collectively taking measures to address their vulnerabilities and claim a voice through political representation.

Although rarely acknowledged by the press, academics or policy makers, women and women's organizations in Africa—from Sierra Leone to Liberia, Somalia, Democratic Republic of Congo, Mozambique, Rwanda, Burundi and Uganda—have been actively engaged in peacebuilding activities at the local levels. Many of the most important and least recognized ways women engaged in peacemaking in Liberia, for example, involved a wide variety of peacemaking tactics, organizing rallies and boycotts, letter writing to international agencies, promoting small arms confiscation and negotiating with rebels to release abducted child soldiers. These activities gained virtually no recognition by national, regional and international bodies when it came to constructing peace negotiation delegations, which suggests that women's activities have often been relegated to the more informal, localized and private domains. This necessitates paying attention to the ways in which women have actually pursued peace, but also attending to the fact that women have been left out of the more formal peace negotiations.

The gendering of peacemaking

Although women peace activists had long been active in local initiatives for peace in many African countries, after the 1990s they began to seek a more active role in formal peace initiatives. Notably, when women's groups sought participation in these negotiations, they did so on the basis of unity with women of different ethnicities and political parties, which was strikingly different from the general starting point of male negotiators. This chapter suggests that the reason for this gender difference was not an essentialized "maternal politics of peace" (e.g., women pursuing peace because they are loving mothers), but rather because the common pursuit of a gender equality agenda formed a unifying platform for women from which to negotiate. One outcome of their involvement in peace initiatives can be seen in the fact that women's rights language was included in 86 percent of the peace agreements in Africa between 1989 and 2005, more often than in other regions of the world (Anderson, 2010).

This common agenda emerged for several reasons: It arose (1) within the context of women's peacemaking efforts and the expansion of women's movements in Africa after the 1990s, seeking to advance women's status and end their political marginalization. The outcomes of the movement are discussed only briefly in this chapter as they are elaborated elsewhere (Tripp et al., 2009). (2) These activities were supported by changing international norms regarding gender equality, by pressures from international organizations like the United Nations, regional bodies like Southern African Development Community (SADC), international donors, and by women's rights and women's peace networks. (3) The disruptions of war set the stage for the realignment of gender relations in a way that allowed women to mobilize for peace at the national level.

This chapter focuses on the Liberian case, which is situated within the broader African context.

One of the most common observations in the literature on gender and conflict/peace has to do with women's affinity to peacemaking and in particular their reluctance to endorse violence, especially state violence, to resolve conflicts. This is said by some to be related to women's inclination to support collective or consensual approaches to solving problems. Women's socialization presumably makes them less competitive than men, less interested in power struggles, more egalitarian and more collaborative in problem solving. Other studies have challenged such assumptions, showing that the attitudinal differences between women and men are minimal except for those women who identify with the women's movement (Conover, 1988) or with feminism (Cook and Wilcox, 1991; Conover and Sapiro, 1993), or who are supportive of gender equality (Tessler and Warriner, 1997; Caprioli, 2000: Caprioli and Boyer, 2001). My analysis of Afrobarometer[2] data in African post-conflict countries (Liberia, Mozambique, Namibia, Uganda, South Africa) shows similar patterns: men and women differ very little in attitudes regarding the use of violence to advance a political cause and on the question of whether they themselves would consider using violence to advance a political cause.[3] The patterns of response are similar in countries that have not gone through major conflict.

Perhaps the most common trope in popular discourse relies on connections between women's peacemaking and their essentialized roles as mothers. There are a number of arguments that link motherhood to peacemaking. For some, the gender gap regarding the use of force in international conflicts is based on gendered physiological differences, which for women is based on their natural reproductive ability (Daly, 1984). For others like Sara Ruddick (1995), it is the act of mothering that lies at the basis of the connection between women and peace, because it makes mothers more caring and empathetic of others. It is women's bodily experience of giving birth to life that gives them knowledge of the cost of life. However, Ruddick also argues that it is not only mothers who rear children and that mothering can be linked to women without children and to men and anyone else who has the experience of caring for others. Women tend to do most of the mothering, and therefore they are more inclined to adopt maternal thinking. Some have argued that women use motherhood strategically to give their movements greater leverage and credibility and to broaden their base of support (Swerdlow, 1993; Taylor, 1997).

In the early peace activist discourse in the US during World War I, women activists were drawn into organizations like the Women's International League for Peace and Freedom by claims that women had special insights and peaceful solutions based on their experiences in the private sphere which gave them a certain moral authority that set them apart from men. This notion of women as outsiders, untainted by war, corruption and human rights violations has also served women politically as they have sought a place at the negotiating table or in a post-war political order (Kelley and Eblen, 2002: pp. 198–199).

There is often a stereotypical belief that women are less threatening than men, thus allowing women greater room to maneuver in public spheres, and emboldening them to transform their private suffering into public protest (Giacaman and Johnson, 1989: p. 162; Sharoni, 2001: pp. 92–93). Wars break down the public and private spheres as homes become locations of raids by soldiers and sites of destruction, thus pushing women into public action (Aretxaga, 1997: pp. 54, 69). Still others see motherhood or women's potential for motherhood as a basis for women's engagement in politics and in peace activism (Rupp, 1997; Naples, 1998).

Variants of the maternal peace argument have come under criticism by others who find that it is not supported empirically in terms of mothers' and fathers' attitudes towards militarism and war. In the US, for example, mothers and fathers do not differ significantly from non-mothers and non-fathers in their views of war (Conover and Sapiro, 1993: p. 1087; Tripp *et al.*, 2009: p. 27).

Others criticize the conflation of women and motherhood with the idea that women are by nature peaceful by pointing out the many ways in which motherhood has been used to serve racist practices and sinister forms of nationalism, for example, in Nazi Germany (Koonz, 1997), among the Ku Klux Klan in the US (Blee, 1997) and within a conservative Italian housewives federation (Orleck, 1997). Women have been willing accomplices in nationalist or ethnic propaganda campaigns idealizing women and mothers of a particular group in ways that may serve to foment conflict (Waller and Rycenga, 2000). Motherhood, according to Cynthia Cockburn, thus skirts dangerously close to patriarchal definitions of women's role that can be co-opted by nationalisms propagating that very ideology (2004: p. 38).

Another common explanation for women's engagement in peace movements relates it to the upheaval in gender roles that occurs during times of conflict. For example, the *intifada* between Palestinians and Israelis (1987–93) was said to have eased restrictions on the movement of Palestinian women, allowing them to come into contact with other women, gain new confidence and broaden their political roles. Similarly, the absence of men in households gave women more leeway to engage in political activism, thus creating fluidity in social relations and roles (Sharoni, 2001: pp. 92–95). In Africa, some have argued that patriarchal gender relations are transformed as women assume male tasks and gain access to new public spaces. The absence of male household members may give women the space that they might not otherwise have to participate in civil society organizations and in peace initiatives. However, often this is accompanied by a backlash in the post-conflict context, where women are pushed back into their former roles after the conflict subsides (Meintjes, 2002: p. 72; Turshen, 2002: p. 80). While there is considerable evidence for the transformation of gender roles during conflict, the backlash phenomenon seems to have better described the earlier experiences of women in national liberation movements in Africa prior to the 1990s when women were told in countries like Zimbabwe that they needed to prioritize national developmental concerns and women's rights would eventually follow (Ranchod-Nilsson, 2008). It does not characterize the official stance of post-conflict governments in Namibia, South Africa, Mozambique, Uganda and Liberia, for example, after the 1990s regarding women's rights.

Yet another line of argumentation against essentializing motherhood draws on the experience of Women in Black in Kosovo in the 1990s where women's groups pressured their governments for effective international peacekeeping. Because women had not been subjected to male socialization and narrow constructions of masculinity, they were freer to pursue non-violent strategies in this context (Cockburn, 2004: p. 38). Similarly, because of the construction of masculinity in a country like Liberia, men, especially young men, had fewer options open to them, finding themselves making difficult choices about whether to go into exile (an option only for those who had resources), go into hiding or into the bush, or face abduction or forced conscription into the army. The alternative was being killed for not joining one of the armies or for being suspected of being with an enemy group. Women had greater leeway because the constructions of femininity in this context did not necessitate their participation in fighting, although some did fight.

In terms of conflict, norms of masculinity make war central to male identity (Enloe, 2000). Joshua Goldstein argues that war is highly gendered. For him the gendering of war is partially a result of "small innate biological gender differences in average size, strength, and roughness of play" coupled with "cultural molding of tough, brave men, who feminize their enemies to encode domination" (2001: p. 406). Goldstein sees women's involvement in peace movements as backfiring and unintentionally fostering greater male violence. Goldstein argues that conflict then becomes a test of manhood. In this view, male identity not only depends on women filling their roles as mothers, wives and girlfriends, but also on women actively opposing wars. Goldstein suggests that women peacemakers serve to reify peace as a feminine pursuit and war as a masculine one. He points out that generally more women than men act in the name of their gender to oppose wars and work for peace. At the local level they buffer inter-male violence in a wide variety of ways, from restraining men to playing roles as mediators. However, making peace feminine and associated with normal life thus reinforces militarized masculinity, enabling soldiers to "suspend social norms against killing and to withstand the hell of war" (Goldstein, 2001: pp. 331–332, p. 413).

While Goldstein is correct to highlight the gendered construction of warmaking and peacemaking, he probably goes too far in arguing that women's peacemaking exacerbates the male desire to kill, especially since more formal peacemaking initiatives are largely organized by men, not women. Moreover, a closer look at women's peacemaking activities, especially localized ones, shows them to be often very successful in disarming men, getting warring factions to talk to one another, and in demonstrating for peace. In the Liberian conflict, for example, male fighters listened to women because of their sheer audacity at times, their fearlessness and because many drew on the socially constructed maternal authority to get male combatants to listen to them in a society where mothers are highly respected. Women used every tactic they could think of, including laughing and joking about serious matters, to get faction leaders to listen to one another (AWPSG, 2004). Goldstein's argument is not borne out in the African examples discussed in this chapter.

The gendering of violence

As with peacemaking, the social and cultural construction of masculinity and femininity has generated scholarly debates about how men are more likely to engage in violence than women. However, it does not preclude men from peacemaking nor women from engaging in violence. Studies in the US (Conover and Sapiro, 1993) and the Middle East (Tessler, 1999) show that there are no attitudinal differences between men and women when it comes to violence. But what does differ radically is the inclination to act on those perceptions. Thus, women generally are not perpetrators of violence to the same degree as men, but they may be behind-the-scenes promoters of violence. Moreover, the way in which women and men are socialized as a collectivity creates different gendered cultures of violence.

Evidence from around the world and from different historical periods shows that women have often performed successfully in combat when they have fought (Goldstein, 2001). During the 1970s and 1980s women participated as fighters in armed liberation and guerrilla movements in countries like Mozambique, Zimbabwe, Guinea Bissau, Eritrea, Uganda and elsewhere, although generally in supporting positions rather than on the frontline. Women made up 25 percent of the Revolutionary United Front fighters in Sierra Leone (Cohen, 2010). Scott Straus reports that 2 percent of the *genocidaire* in Rwanda's 1994 genocide were women.[4] In the Afrobarometer survey in Liberia, of those who reported having been a fighter, 21 percent were women.

Ruth Jacobson also challenges the idealization of women as peacemakers, suggesting that some women in Northern Ireland, for example, took action to reduce violence, while others sought to reproduce divisions rather than challenge them. The majority of women, according to Ruth Jacobson, were neither peacemakers nor involved in paramilitaries. Women have engaged in a broad spectrum of activities, but, like men, were limited by gendered conditions and constraints (2000: pp. 181–182, 195). This is also true of women in African conflicts, of whom only a subsection were engaged either in peacemaking or in armed conflict. However, the ways they have engaged in these activities have been shaped by gendered societal norms, expectations and socialization.

Women and formal peacemaking strategies

One of the most important changes we have witnessed in Africa since the 1990s has been the rise of women's movements and the related efforts by women to gain greater political representation. In conflict situations women began to seek to influence formal peacemaking processes in ways not previously evident and to do so they had to seek greater representation in these processes. Those women who have mobilized for peace have done so primarily through women's organizations, in part, because this is one of the few ways society has allowed women to give expression to their pro-peace objectives.

Women have demanded a seat at the peace talks, in transitional governments and on constitutional commissions engaged in drafting new constitutions. They have pushed for increased representation in legislative bodies. It is still rare to find women leading official peace negotiations, although there are exceptions like Betty Bigombe, who until 2006 headed up the team negotiating a peaceful resolution to a conflict between the government and the Lord's Resistance Army rebels in northern Uganda. Women, however, did eventually gain entry into the negotiations in Burundi, Liberia and the Democratic Republic of Congo after protracted lobbying.

This heightened activity around peacebuilding is integrally tied to changing women's movements in Africa and the expansion of independent women's mobilization, which increased exponentially especially after the 1990s (Tripp, 2003). These new movements could be distinguished from earlier women's organizations by their autonomy from political parties and the government in terms of leadership, funding and agendas. This new wave of women's mobilization in Africa more generally arose as a result of the decline of the one-party state and the monopoly held by party/government-led women's organizations; new donor supports for independent associations; the influence of the international women's movement and expansion of rights-based discourse, especially after the UN conferences in Nairobi (1985) and Beijing (1995).

The new women's mobilization arose in conflict areas as a response to particular pressures women were facing. During times of conflict, women experienced sexual violence, often on a large scale. Men also suffered from sexual violence but not on the same scale as women. Women often shouldered the heavy burden of caring for family on their own because their husbands and other male family members fled to either escape or fight. In these instances, women's lack of access to land and other resources made land, property, inheritance issues and other such concerns of primary importance. Women's lack of political say over events that controlled them led to demands for political representation at the local and national levels. Thus, issues of gender-based violence, land rights, customary law and political representation rose to the fore and became part of women's rights agendas during and after conflict.

Men and women both suffered during conflict, but they responded very differently to their experiences. While it is almost impossible to compare suffering, it bears mentioning that more men than women died in conflicts. Based on Afrobarometer data, men reported being more likely to be involved in armed conflict than women. In Rwanda the change in the gender ratio from before to after the genocide in 1994 was as high as 2 percent as a result of the disproportionate deaths of men. During the two civil wars that occurred in Liberia between 1989 and 2003, four times more men responded affirmatively to the question: "Were you ever a fighter for or member of any faction involved in the conflicts, such as

AFL, LURD, MODEL, ULIMO, Government Troops or any other faction?" Some joined willingly, others were abducted. Of the 1,200 people surveyed by Afrobarometer, 540 people reported suffering bodily harm during the conflict. Men were four times more likely than women to have suffered such bodily harm. According to the 2008 Afrobarometer survey in Liberia, slightly more men than women reported that as a result of civil war they experienced a loss of personal property, destruction of and eviction from their home, a business closure, loss of a job, personal injury, loss of family member, or being forced to move or relocate to another part of Liberia, to the home of a relative, or abroad. In some cases the gender difference in responses was negligible.

The 2007 Demographic Health Survey showed that of 4,897 women surveyed, 44 percent had suffered some form of domestic violence. 90.5 percent suffered violence at the hands of a past or present boyfriend or husband, while 1.8 percent suffered violence at the hands of soldiers or police. 17.6 percent had suffered sexual violence at some point in their life. Half of the perpetrators were present or past husbands, or boyfriends. 8.2 percent were carried out by a soldier or police; 3.5 by a stranger.[5] These were some of the types of issues women sought to address through their mobilization around common concerns.

Women not only mobilized within their countries, they coordinated their activities across state boundaries. This networking among women, both on a sub-regional level and on a continent-wide basis, took place on an unprecedented scale. Peacemaking was a central concern of many of the networks like the African Women's Committee for Peace and Development (AWCPD) and the Federation of African Women's Peace Networks (FERFAP). Perhaps most significantly, the importance of women's participation in peace initiatives has gained recognition by African governments not previously evident in the post-independence era.

Cross-cutting interests

One of the most important differences between male and female peace negotiators has to do with the unity among women who came to the negotiating table across political, party, ethnic, clan and other lines—despite the fact that these cleavages had been violently contentious, differences generally kept male negotiators of these conflicts at opposite ends of the table. This was evident from Burundi to Somalia, Democratic Republic of Congo, Liberia and Sierra Leone.

In the Burundi peace talks the gendered differences in approach were palpable. One of the participants in the 1999 Arusha talks, Alice Ntwarante, was struck by how unity was the starting point for the women delegates in contrast to the men at this meeting:

> We [the women] were united in purpose, despite our ethnic split—three Hutus and three Tutsis. The various political parties to which we women belonged tried to split us up, but we resisted them. We said, no! We stand together with our sisters. We are here to represent women, not as members

of such-and-such a political party. Our unity spoke for us. We said to all Burundian women: "Come and join us! There is a place for you!" This was the big success of Arusha for women—that we remained united.

She contrasted the stance of the women to that of the male party negotiators:

I told myself, here are the men, the key players, who are going to negotiate, but right at the start of the conference they can't communicate with one another. Each was turning his back on his adversary. Each had brought his ideas to the peace table. They were partisan, even extremist.

(UNIFEM, 2001: p. 14)

This is not to say that the women did not have differing views or disagreements, but they started from the point of unity.

Women's unity was not based on a romantic idealized adherence to peace, but rather on a commonality of interest. There were two main reasons for this. First, since women's interests in advancing as women cut across ethnicity, clan, religion and other potential differences, they were able to give more salience to the gender agenda, and thus other differences were overcome.

For example, women held 10 percent of the seats in the National Assembly of the Somali Transitional National Government. They thought of themselves as the "sixth clan" of women rather than belonging to their respective clans since each of the major clans had a female representative (Hollier-Larousse, 2000). They voted as a bloc or "rainbow coalition" as they described it. "We are not here for decoration. Ten years of war and no government, that is enough. The women of Somalia are tired and will work to pressure the men to change the situation," as Asha Haji Elmi, a delegate to the 2000 reconciliation conference and the head of the Women's Association, put it.

Second, because women have generally been marginalized from most forms of power, women collectively have less at stake in preserving a status quo that has brought them considerable suffering. They are not likely to reap any material benefits from continued fighting either. They are therefore more likely than men to build alliances to de-escalate conflict and promote stability (Benderly, 2000).

Moreover, because of their exclusion from power, women tend to have a different relationship to power than men. Imelda Nzirorera observed from her experience in the Burundian peace negotiations:

What worries us most is that our Burundian brothers, who are members of political parties, are putting the division of the national pie first. In other words, they are thinking, at the end of the negotiations, what position and post will we get?

(Anderlini, 2000: p. 33)

The Liberian experience was very similar to the aforementioned cases with respect to the way in which women built cross-cutting ties.

Negotiating peace in Liberia

Liberia, a country that was founded in 1816 by freed slaves from the United States and the West Indies, became an independent republic in 1847. Americo-Liberians came to dominate the country politically and economically, even though they made up only 2.5 percent of the population. The country's history has been plagued by tensions between the Americo-Liberians and the local population, leading to a *coup d'état* in 1980 by Samuel Doe of African Krahn descent. His takeover as president thrust the country into years of rampant corruption, economic turmoil and violence. The conflict soon took on other ethnic dimensions, pitting the Mano and Gio against the Krahn and Mandingo.

In 1989, the Americo-Liberian warlord Charles Taylor and his National Patriotic Front of Liberia (NPFL) launched an invasion of the country with backing from Côte d'Ivoire and Burkina Faso. This sent the country spiraling into a conflict that was to continue until 1996. This period was marked by extreme violence that engaged the entire population. It involved the kidnapping of children, rape and violence against women, holding people hostage and torture. Women and family members were forced to take part in and witness the torture, rape and murder of their family members. While it is impossible to know how many were killed, United Nations estimates indicate that at least 250,000 were killed and a half-million were forced into exile in a population of 3.3 million and about half the country's population were displaced. For long periods, the capital city of Monrovia was without food. Large-scale massacres occurred at different times. In one instance in 29 July 1990, the Armed Forces of Liberia killed over 600 civilians, mainly women and children, in St. Peter's Lutheran Church (AWPSG, 2004).

For much of the conflict, the NPFL was based in Gbarnga, which was strategically situated to allow Taylor's forces to cut off much of the traffic throughout the interior of the country. Militia manned checkpoints, where they demanded goods or money, and could easily kill someone if they did not comply or if they spoke the "wrong language."

Various external efforts were made to bring an end to the fighting. The peace-keeping force, Economic Community of West African States Monitoring Group (ECOMOG), which was mainly made up of Nigerians and Ghanaians, arrived in 1990. Over 46 peace talks were held between 1989 and 1997, often under ECOWAS auspices. Over a dozen peace agreements were signed; however, they rarely lasted very long as conflict ensued. The Abuja peace agreement of 1996 set the stage for elections, which brought in the new government headed by President Charles Taylor in 1997.

The women's peace movement included Christian, Muslim, rural and urban women as well as women of different ethnicities from the outset. Women organized marches, petitions and prayer meetings held weekly in Christian and Muslim religions institutions throughout the country. Most women's organizations in Liberia had mobilized around relief until 1994, when Mary Brownell started a women's pressure group, the Liberian Women's Initiative (LWI), to speak out against the 1989–96 war. She ran an ad on national radio calling women together at the city hall in Monrovia. The organization was open to women of all ethnic, social, religious and political backgrounds. The Federation of Liberian Women had been banned in the 1980s because it had been deemed too political. It took until 1994 when women began to mobilize politically to deal directly with the conflict.

Historically, Liberians regarded women as the mediators and peacemakers within the family. Nevertheless, women's organizations had to fight every step of the way to be included in national peace negotiations and other peace processes. During the war, women were involved in keeping the households going, finding food, keeping their children safe, and hiding men, thus preventing them from being conscripted into the various armies. Market women risked their lives and bravely navigated dozens of checkpoints to bring food into Monrovia. At checkpoints, women faced intimidation, demands for bribery, sometimes even rape or death at the hands of the soldiers and militia. Women maintained communication across enemy lines. Groups like the Concerned Women of Liberia, Women in Action for Goodwill, the Muslim Women's Federation, Women's Development Association of Liberia, the Federation of Liberian Women and the National Women's Commission of Liberia worked together to support communities through food distribution, cater for internally displaced peoples and to provide trauma counseling, basic literacy programs, and healing and reconciliation workshops.

One of the primary aims of the women peace activists was to collect and confiscate small arms. Women's associations acted as monitors to see that promises were kept. LWI mobilizers also attended regional peace talks and engaged in letter writing campaigns with the Economic Community of West African States (ECOWAS), the United Nations and the Organization of African Unity (OAU). Groups like the Coalition of Political Parties Women in Liberia (COPPWIL) were formed to explicitly find a common agenda across party and ethnic lines around women's rights concerns.

Women's organizations also networked with Liberians in the diaspora and kept international women's organizations and international human rights organizations as well as United Nations agencies informed about what was going on. These organizations publicized their struggles and built links with women peacemakers around Africa and the world.

The initial focus of women's mobilization was disarmament and they opposed the holding of elections without disarmament. They formed the core of the Civic Disarmament Campaign chaired by the Interfaith Mediation Council that sought to stop the sale of guns to Liberia and promote disarmament. After the 1993 Cotonou Accord, a new Liberian national transition government was formed between the factions. The Liberian Women's Initiative met with various parties involved in setting up the government, including US and Nigerian ambassadors to Liberia, the Organization of African Unity representative to Liberia and various United Nations representatives to express their opposition to the installation of a new government before a disarmament agreement had been agreed upon. They then organized a public demonstration on 4 March 1994, to press for disarmament.

The first efforts by women to attend peace talks came in December 1994 when women's delegations tried to participate in the Accra Clarification Conference. They were initially kept out of the conference but as a result of wide coverage of this exclusion in the Ghanaian media, women's organizations were allowed to participate as official observers on the second day and by the third day they had official participant status. Encouraged by this initial victory, hundreds of women came together and drafted a position statement on the impact of the Liberian war on women and their communities. Women leaders used the statement as a mandate in order to gain access to the peace negotiations. They raised funds to travel to the various peace negotiations and were able to send a delegation of three women to the ECOWAS heads of state mediation committee in Abuja, Nigeria, in May 1995. President Jerry Rawlings of Ghana allowed the women to speak even though they were not officially on the program.

One important West African regional network that emerged in this period was the Mano River Union Women Peace Network (MARWOPNET) of women activists from Sierra Leone, Liberia and Guinea. Its leader Theresa Leigh-Sherman made a presentation in which she demanded representation of women in the peace negotiations:

Our lack of representation in the ongoing peace process is equivalent to the denial of one of our fundamental rights: the right to be seen, be heard, and be counted. This [denial] also deprives the country [of] access to the opinion of 51% of its human resources in solving the problems, which affect our lives as a people.

(AWPSG, 2004: p. 27)

Women's groups opposed UN-sponsored peace agreements that basically rewarded leaders of the armed factions with positions in the transitional government while doing little to disarm them. They challenged former US President Jimmy Carter and UN Special Envoy Trevor Gordon-Somers when they pursued a strategy of encouraging warring factions to meet separately with one another. They opposed all initiatives that lent credibility and power to armed factions (Moran and Pitcher, 2004).

Women were still not given a place at the Abuja meeting in July of 1995. From April to June of 1996, fighting intensified in Monrovia. Another conference was called in August of 1996 where Ruth Perry was selected to oversee the Liberian elections of 1997. Ruth Perry, who came to lead the National State Council of Liberia as the interim head of state in 1996, was a founding member of LWI. Perry's leadership of the transitional government was seen as a major achievement of the Liberian women peace movement.

Liberian women continued to mobilize across differences when fighting again flared in the 1999–2003 war. MAROWPNET mediated an intense conflict between Liberia and Guinea in 2001. In spite of minimal resources and of being excluded from the formal peace process, they were able to get the feuding heads of state to a regional peace summit. At one point President Conté of Guinea had been adamant about not meeting with Charles Taylor of Liberia. Mary Brownell, the LWI peace founder, was on the MARWOPNET delegation that met with Conté. As Brownell recounted to me:

> At the end of his political talk, I put up my hand and when he recognized me, I told him like I was talking to a little boy, "The fate of millions of people is in your hands. Women are delivering babies in the bushes. You men just gamble with our lives. You must meet with Taylor. When you meet I am going to be there. If you don't talk, I will take the keys to your room and lock you up and sit on them until you talk." He was shocked. No one had ever spoken to him like that before. Afterward he arranged for a meeting with Taylor in Morocco. Taylor heard about the incident and when he met with the women later on, he teased Brownell, saying: "You are ready to lock us up? Mother, only you could do something like that."[6]

Abibatu Kromah, a leader of United Muslim Women and Liberian Muslim Women for Peace, told me in an interview in October 2007 that at this time:

> We put the factions behind us. People fought for different reasons, some were forced to fight and some fought because of greed because at the time Taylor had a lot of money. People blamed one another. This is why we fought the war for 14 years, all because of blame. So we women [of all ethnicities] looked at this situation and said we have to put this behind us, God forbid we have another war: we will suffer, children will be killed, husbands will be killed, women will be raped. We need to put aside our differences and move ahead. We said why don't we embrace our Christian sisters and work together.

Kromah explained that the Muslim women's organizations got support from their religious leaders and went ahead to work closely with Christian women in 2002–2003 to bring an end to the conflict.

Women's associations took to the streets in 2003 when fighting between government forces and those of LURD and MODEL intensified. Multi-religious groups of women not only demonstrated in the streets, they also organized a sit-in at the airfield in Sinkor and went there on a daily basis to pray, sing, dance, cry and advocate for peace. Dressed in white T-shirts and headscarves to symbolize peace, they demanded a neutral peacekeeping force that would allow refugees to return home and called for free and fair elections. They also called for the strengthening of Monrovia's infrastructure since it was unable to accommodate the thousands of refugees who were returning home.

The Liberian chapter of MARWOPNET participated in the ECOWAS peace talks at Akosombo and Accra from June through August 2003. MARWOPNET was given accreditation to attend the Accra conference and had an eight-member delegation. Women's organizations on the outside of the talks had a strong ally in Ellen Johnson-Sirleaf, who kept them informed and consulted with them. In fact, Johnson-Sirleaf, who was to become Liberia's next elected president, was one of the most forceful negotiators. The women demanded greater civil society participation in the talks, 50 percent representation in the Transitional Government and voting rights in the peace talks. They called for an immediate ceasefire since violence had been escalating in Monrovia. MARWOPNET called on the UN Security Council to provide for a peacekeeping force and the establishment of a transition government that would "disarm, demobilize, reintegrate and resettle troops, prepare the way for elections, provide humanitarian relief, or for reconciliation and restructure the army and security forces" (AWPSG, 2004: p. 49).

As the talks continued, violence and rape escalated in Liberia at the start of August and women in turn stepped up their protests. Refugee women's groups based in Ghana protested outside the 2003 Accra talks. One of the more dramatic incidents that contributed to the peace settlement in Liberia involved a refugee women's organization, Women in Peace Building Network. At the talks, the women's refugee network locked negotiators in their meeting room and said they would not allow them out until they signed a comprehensive peace agreement. Drawing on funereal symbolism that has deep roots in West African history of women's protest, the women wept to protest the ongoing violations of a ceasefire on all sides and threatened to strip naked if the meeting did not produce a positive outcome. Nudity in protest in West Africa has traditionally been regarded as a shaming tactic and as a curse. Such transgressions of conventional gender expectations signify rejection of grave violations of women's and societal integrity and rights.

The protestors accused ECOWAS of pampering the negotiators and said the talks should have been held instead in Budumburam refugee camp on the Accra-Winneba road to help the negotiators understand the urgency for peace. The women complained that the negotiators had been housed in luxurious accommodations and were wearing expensive clothes and eating good food.[7] Eventually the "hostages" were freed, but the women had made their point. The women were motivated by a deep sense of economic justice combined with an understanding of how military might combined with gender to create a system of power and inequality that left them seemingly powerless in influencing the outcome of the conflict.

The Liberian Women's Initiative continue to put pressure on ECOWAS, the heads of state of Liberia, Sierra Leone and Côte d'Ivoire, as well as the president of the African Union and other involved parties. Over 45 women's groups that were attending the peace talks hammered out a position chapter at the Golden Tulip Hotel in Accra on 15 August 2003. They demanded that women had to be included in all proposed institutions within the new Liberian government and within all structures that would lead the post-conflict peacebuilding process. They also drew on the UN Security Council Resolution 1325 of 31 October 2000, which "calls on all actors involved, when negotiating and implementing peace agreements, to adopt a gender perspective."

Because of the important mediation role MARWOPNET had played between the various factions involved in the peace talks, the network became one of the signatories of a peace agreement as witness to the agreement signed on 18 August 2003 by the Government of Liberia, Liberians United for Democracy (LURD), Movement for Democracy in Liberia (MODEL) and all the 18 political parties. The talks resulted in the setting up of a transitional government that was installed 15 October 2003 and for the UN Mission in Liberia (UNMIL), which arrived two weeks before the transitional government of Gyude Bryant took over. Thus, women made modest gains in the peace negotiations, but more importantly they helped speed up the process that brought the talks to conclusion.

Gender, peace and power

What explains women's mobilization across lines of difference in the context of Liberia's war and peace negotiations? If peacefulness and collaboration across so-called "enemy" lines were an innate gendered trait based on women's motherly instincts, then women's response to conflict would be fairly uniform, but it was quite varied, with only about one-fifth of women fighting and another subset of women engaged in peacemaking activities. Similarly, men shared with women similar values regarding peace and concern for their children's future and well-being, but a much higher proportion ended up fighting and many less engaged in peacemaking.

I argue instead that women's common agenda around women's rights and political representation created a basis for unity across so-called "enemy lines," rather than an intrinsic gender-based love for peace. The difference lies not in an essentialized maternal politics, but rather with the goals certain women were pursuing as they formed cross-cutting organizations and coalitions. As Davidetta Brown, a radio producer, explained to me:

> Women came together to prevent the religious and ethnic dimension from becoming salient. Men stuck with their own ethnic group. Women sat down, regardless of whether they were Christian or Muslim and strove to go above religious affiliation to discuss the situation affecting women as a whole.
>
> The culture of male domination made it hard for women to have their voices heard. Women felt disadvantaged during war. Women during the war became heads of household. They became decision makers in their home. Men were sought to enlist in the fighting or they were killed, or hid under their beds or in the ceilings for security. Women wanted first to participate and then they wanted representation.... The women's agenda and peace agenda emerged at the same time and they were interwoven, not separated. The war reawakened women's interest in politics and decision making. It had been advancing all along but it was speeded up because of the war.

This connection between the demands for peace and power became even more evident with the 2005 elections, during which large numbers of women mobilized to get Ellen Johnson-Sirleaf elected as president because they believed she would be a fierce defender of women's rights. Ellen Johnson-Sirleaf, who was president of the Unity Party, served as head of the Governance Reform Commission in the transitional government. It is no accident that some of the biggest gains in women's political representation have occurred in post-conflict contexts in Africa. Over 17 countries have come out of major civil war in Africa since 2000. At the end of almost all these major conflicts, women's organizations pursuing a peace agenda have vigorously pressed for increased political representation, often in the form of legislative quotas.

Unlike the post-conflict situations prior to the 1990s, women were now able to realize their demands. International norms were changing, as evident in governmental commitments made at the 1995 Beijing UN Conference on Women to advance women's representation. Thus, women in post-conflict Rwanda, Angola, Burundi, Mozambique, Uganda and South Africa claim over 30 percent of their countries' parliamentary seats. Tanzania is the only non-post-conflict country with numbers that high. Moreover, Rwanda has the highest rate of representation for women in the world, with 56 percent of its parliamentary seats held by women. Angola follows with 37 percent. In African countries where conflicts ended after 1985, women hold, on average, 27 percent of legislative seats compared with countries that did not experience conflict, where women account for only 13 percent of the legislative seats.

In the case of Liberia, Ellen Johnson-Sirleaf became the first elected woman president in Africa in 2005. Women hold 32 percent of ministerial positions, many in key ministries of foreign affairs, justice, agriculture, commerce and industry. The police commissioner is a woman. Women are running for local office as well at higher rates. The mayor of Liberia's capital Monrovia is a woman and women head key counties.

Post-conflict countries are not only opening up possibilities for women's leadership in the legislature, executive and elsewhere in the government at rates that are faster than non-post-conflict countries, they are also adopting women's rights legislation and policies, and making constitutional changes at a faster pace. In Liberia, the Ministry of Gender launched a national campaign against sexual harassment with the slogan "No sex for help. No help for sex," making it clear that sex could no longer be used as a means of obtaining jobs, grades, medical treatment and other services.

Landmark legislation was passed in Liberia in 2003, allowing women to inherit property without interference from the family of the husband. Rape legislation was adopted in 2005. For example, the Law Reform Commission was formed to review national laws and one of their mandates was to review the laws for bias or discrimination against women. New initiatives had been set up to ensure that pregnant girls received an education and teachers who sexually harassed students were to be suspended without pay at a minimum for five years and possibly indefinitely depending on the circumstances. The Ministry of Gender is carrying out education programs through the radio and drama to educate people about women's rights. The Ministry of Justice installed Women and Children Protection Units in all of the country's 15 counties' police stations and each county had an attorney to prosecute cases. Various micro credit and other economic supports are being provided to women and girls throughout the country with the help of various donor partners. These are just a few examples of the kind of aggressive policy agenda the Liberian government has adopted to address the deficit in women's status.

Conclusions

This chapter showed how women built ties across ethnic, religious and other differences in promoting their collective peacebuilding agendas in a variety of contexts. The chapter explains why women were more engaged in peace activities than men and why women politicians and activists were able to forge coalitions more easily across ethnic and party differences than did male politicians. I suggest that existing human security understandings of individual notions of female agency in the context of conflict do not always fully capture the collective responses of women to the challenges they face during conflict. Women did not uniformly support peace initiatives and some women enlisted in the fighting, although male fighters still considerably outnumbered female fighters. Many women, like men, found that they had no choice but to back various warlords during the conflict. Some women believed that by occupying top positions in the Taylor government, they would be able to facilitate an end to the conflict. Nevertheless, women and men in general adopted different postures when it came to peacemaking. Formal peace negotiations were almost the exclusive domain of men, while women were relegated to the important yet often hidden localized peacemaking initiatives. Women's engagement with peace negotiations started from a position of unity across political divisions, whereas for male negotiators, the differences were what defined them from the outset. In Liberia, the face of peace activism was a female one.

This chapter has sought to explain these differences by looking at the common agenda women forged in the case of Liberia and in other countries in Africa plagued by civil war. Women activists mobilized not only for peace but also for greater political representation and around demands to advance women's status in society. They recognized that women's exclusions from political leadership had become the key obstacle in their attempts to bringing about peace. Therefore, the demands for peace and power became inseparable. Women's lack of education, their lack of access to land and inheritance rights, along with violence against women, were key obstacles to their political empowerment and their ability to shape the polity and influence peace negotiations. These demands cut across political and ethnic differences, allowing women to mobilize in ways that differed from those of men. Their common exclusion thus provided them with a basis for building broad coalitions and working across partisanship, ethnicity, religion or other factors.

Women's marginalization from politics and their outsider status, on the one hand, made them attractive contenders for power as the end of conflict opened up new political spaces. Often they were perceived as untainted by corruption and not linked as directly to the source of conflict. For this reason they often found it easier to lobby for quotas and for representation in post-conflict situations.

Many of women's strategies in peacemaking are shaped by and arise from their marginalization in society. The question remains, to what extent do these strategies simultaneously lock women into limited forms of peacemaking and keep them excluded from other roles? To what extent does women's participation in these gendered structures perpetuate institutions that marginalize women rather than challenge them? These are the kinds of questions women face as they seek to rebuild their societies.

Finally, the chapter demonstrates the importance of incorporating agency into discussions of gender and human security. But it also shows that agency is not an unproblematic concept, especially when considered within realities of conflict. Agency is not neutral. Under conditions of dire survival within the context of conflict agency can mean everything from uncommon bravery and principle to opportunism and even to the most nefarious forms of action. Human security approaches focus on the individual. This chapter shows the significance of paying attention to the importance of the collective, in this case, women in collective political groups pushing for change. The chapter also demonstrates the importance of human security approaches that view agency as a bottom up phenomenon. Such an approach should have led peace negotiators and international organizations to take more seriously the demands and protests of women, who had been operating primarily at the local level. However, this chapter also highlights how being relegated to the "grassroots" does not automatically translate into power at the national level.

Notes

1 Ramesh Thakur defines human security as

> concerned with the protection of people from critical and life-threatening dangers, regardless of whether the threats are rooted in anthropogenic activities or natural events, whether they lie within or outside states, and whether they are direct or structural. It is "human centred" in that its principal focus is on people both as individuals and as communal groups. It is "security oriented" in that the focus is on freedom from fear, danger and threat.
>
> (Thakur, 2004)

2 www.afrobarometer.org.
3 Response to questions: 1) "The use of violence is never justified in politics" and 2) "Here are a number of different actions people might take if government were to do something they thought was wrong or harmful. For each of these, please tell me whether you have engaged in this activity or not. D. Use force or violent methods." Mozambique, however, showed no gender difference in response to question 1 but there was some difference in question 2.
4 Personal communication, 9 August 2005.
5 Liberia Institute of Statistics and Geo-Information Services (LISGIS), Ministry of Health and Social Welfare [Liberia], National AIDS Control Program [Liberia], and Macro

International Inc. (2008) Liberia Demographic and Health Survey 2007. Monrovia, Liberia: Liberia Institute of Statistics and Geo-Information Services (LISGIS) and Macro International Inc. Available at: www.measuredhs.com/pubs/pdf/FR201/FR201.pdf [accessed 10 November2011].
6 Interview with author, 16 September 2007.
7 "Paper hails Liberian women for holding peace talks delegates hostage," BBC World-wide Monitoring, 24 July 2003, The Accra Mail website, Accra, Ghana.

Bibliography

African Women and Peace Support Group (AWPSG). (2004) *Liberian Women Peace-makers: Fighting for the Right to be Seen, Heard and Counted.* Trenton, NJ: Africa World Press.

Afrobarometer. (n.d.) Michigan State University, East Lansing. www.afrobarometer.org/.

Ambrosetti, David. (2008) Human Security as Political Resource. *Security Dialogue*, 39(4), pp. 439–445.

Anderlini, Sanam N. (2000) *Women at the Peace Table: Making a Difference.* New York: UNIFEM.

Anderson, Miriam. (2010) Considering Local Versus International Norms on Women's Rights in Contemporary Peace Processes. Presentation at "Gender, Peace and Security: Local Interpretations of International Norms," Davis Institute, Hebrew University, Israel, 10–11 May.

Aretxaga, Begona. (1997) *Shattering Silence: Women, Nationalism, and Political Sub-jectivity in Northern Ireland.* Princeton: Princeton University Press.

Benderly, Jill. (2000) A Women's Place Is at the Peace Table. *SAIS Review*, 20(2), pp. 79–83.

Blee, Kathleen. (1997) Mothers in Race-Hate Movements. In: Alexis Jetter, Annelisse Orleck and Diana Taylor, eds. *The Politics of Motherhood: Activist Voices from Left to Right.* Hanover, NH: University Press of New England, Dartmouth College, pp. 247–257.

Buzan, Barry. (2004) A Reductionist, Idealistic Notion That Adds Little Analytical Value. *Security Dialogue*, 35(3), pp. 369–370.

Caprioli, Mary. (2000) Gendered Conflict. *Journal of Peace Research*, 37(1), pp. 51–68.

Caprioli, Mary and Mark A. Boyer. (2001) Gender, Violence and International Crisis. *Journal of Conflict Resolution*, 45(4), pp. 503–518.

Christie, Ryerson. (2010) Critical Voices and Human Security: To Endure, To Engage or To Critique? *Security Dialogue*, 41(2), pp. 169–190.

Cockburn, Cynthia. (2004) The Continuum of Violence: A Gender Perspective on War & Peace. In: Wenona Giles and Jennifer Hyndman, eds. *Sites of Violence: Gender and Conflict Zones.* Berkeley: University of California Press, pp. 24–44.

Cohen, Dara Kay. (2010) Explaining Sexual Violence During Civil War: Evidence from the Sierra Leone War [1991–2002]. PhD dissertation. Stanford University.

Conover, Pamela J. (1988) Feminists and the Gender Gap. *Journal of Politics*, 50(4), pp. 985–1010.

Conover, Pamela J. and Virginia Sapiro. (1993) Gender, Feminist Consciousness, and War. *American Journal of Political Science*, 37(4), pp. 1079–1099.

Cook, Elizabeth A. and Clyde Wilcox. (1991) Feminism and the Gender Gap: A Second Look. *The Journal of Politics*, 53(4), pp. 1111–1112.

Daly, Mary. (1984) *Pure Lust: Elemental Feminist Philosophy.* Boston: Beacon.

Denov, Myriam, and Christine Gervais. (2007) Negotiating (In)Security: Agency,

Resistance, and Resourcefulness among Girls Formerly Associated with Sierra Leone's Revolutionary United Front. *Signs: Journal of Women in Culture and Society*, 32(4), pp. 885–910.

Enloe, Cynthia H. (2000) *Maneuvers: The International Politics of Militarizing Women's Lives*. Austin, TX: Women's International News Gathering Service.

Giacaman, Rita and Penny Johnson. (1989) Palestinian Women: Building Barricades and Breaking Barriers. In: Zachary Lockman and Joel Beinin, eds. *Intifada: The Palestinian Uprising Against Israeli Occupation*. Boston: South End Press and MERIP, pp. 155–170.

Goldstein, Joshua S. (2001) *War and Gender: How Gender Shapes The War System and Vice Versa*. Cambridge: Cambridge University Press.

Grayson, Kyle. (2008) Human Security as Power/Knowledge: The Biopolitics of a Definitional Debate. *Cambridge Review of International Affairs*, 21(3), pp. 383–401.

Hollier-Larousse, Juliette. (2000) Somali Women Win Political Emancipation with Parliamentary Quota. Arta, Djibouti: Agence France Presse.

Hoogensen, G. and K. Stuvoy. (2006) Gender, Resistance and Human Security. *Security Dialogue*, 37(2), pp. 207–228.

Jacobson, Ruth. (2000) Women and Peace in Northern Ireland: A Complicated Relationship. In: Susie Jacobs, Ruth Jacobson and Jennifer Marchbank, eds. *States of Conflict: Gender, Violence and Resistance*. London and New York: Zed Books, pp. 179–198.

Kelley, Colleen E. and Anna L. Eblen, eds. (2002) Conclusions. In: *Women Who Speak for Peace*, Lanham, MD: Rowman and Littlefield, pp. 193–213.

Koonz, Claudia. (1997) Motherhood and Politics on the Far Right. In: Alexis Jetter, Annelise Orleck and Diana Taylor, eds. *The Politics of Motherhood: Activist Voices from Left to Right*. Hanover, NH: University Press of New England, Dartmouth College, pp. 229–246.

Krause, Keith and Michael C. Williams. (1997) From Strategy to Security: Foundations of Critical Security Studies. In: Keith Krause and Michael C. Williams, eds. *Critical Security Studies: Concepts and Cases*. Minneapolis, MN: University of Minnesota Press, pp. 33–60.

Liberia Institute of Statistics and Geo-Information Services (LISGIS), Ministry of Health and Social Welfare [Liberia], National AIDS Control Program [Liberia], and Macro International Inc. (2008) Liberia Demographic and Health Survey 2007. Monrovia, Liberia: Liberia Institute of Statistics and Geo-Information Services (LISGIS) and Macro International Inc. Available at: www.measuredhs.com/pubs/pdf/FR201/FR201. pdf [accessed 10 November 2011].

Maclure, R. and M. Denov. (2006). "I Didn't Want to Die so I Joined Them": Structuration and the Process of Becoming Boy Soldiers in Sierra Leone. *Terrorism and Political Violence*, 18(1), pp. 119–135.

Meintjes, Sheila. (2002) War and Post-War Shifts in Gender Relations. In: Sheila Meintjes, Anu Pillay and Meredith Turshen, eds. *The Aftermath: Women in Post-conflict Transformation*. London: Zed Books, pp. 63–77.

Moran, Mary H. and M. Anne Pitcher. (2004) The "Basket Case" and the "Poster Child": Explaining the End of Civil Conflicts in Liberia and Mozambique. *Third World Quarterly*, 25(3), pp. 501–519.

Naples, Nancy. (1998) *Community Activism and Feminist Politics: Organizing Across Race, Class, and Gender*. New York and London: Routledge.

Orleck, Annelise. (1997) Housewives and Motherist Policies in the New Italy. In: Alexis Jetter, Annelisse Orleck and Diana Taylor, eds. *The Politics of Motherhood: Activist*

Voices from Left to Right. Hanover, NH: University Press of New England, Dartmouth College, pp. 268–284.

Ranchod-Nilsson, Sita. (2008) Gender Politics and Gender Backlash in Zimbabwe. *Politics & Gender*, 4(4), pp. 642–652.

Richmond, Oliver P. (2007) Emancipatory Forms of Peacebuilding. *International Journal*, 62(3), pp. 458–477.

Ruddick, Sara. (1995) *Maternal Thinking: Toward a Politics of Peace.* Boston: Beacon Press.

Rupp, Leila. (1997) *Worlds of Women: The Making of an International Women's Movement.* Princeton, NJ: Princeton University Press.

Sharoni, Simona. (2001) Rethinking Women's Struggles in Israel-Palestine and in the North of Ireland. In: Caroline Moser and Fiona Clark, eds. *Victims, Perpetrators or Actors: Gender, Armed Conflict and Political Violence*, London: Zed, pp. 85–98.

Straus, Scott. 9 August 2005. Personal communication.

Swerdlow, Amy. (1993) *Women Strike for Peace: Traditional Motherhood and Radical Politics in the 1960s.* Chicago: University of Chicago Press.

Tadjbakhsh, Shahrbanou and Anuradha M. Chenoy. (2007) *Human Security: Concepts and Implications.* New York: Routledge.

Taylor, Diana. (1997) Making a Spectacle: The Mothers of the Plaza de Mayo. In: Alexis Jetter, Annelisse Orleck and Diana Taylor, eds. *The Politics of Motherhood: Activist Voices from Left to Right.* Hanover, NH: University Press of New England, Dartmouth College, pp. 182–197.

Tessler, Mark. (1999) Further Tests of the Women and Peace Hypothesis: Evidence from Cross-National Survey Research in the Middle East. (senior author) *International Studies Quarterly*, 43(3), pp. 519–531.

Tessler, Mark and Ina Warriner. (1997) Gender Feminism, and Attitudes toward International Conflict: Exploring Relationships with Survey Data from the Middle East. *World Politics*, 49(2), pp. 250–281.

Thakur, Ramesh. (2004) A Political Worldview. *Security Dialogue*, 35(3), pp. 347–348.

Turshen, Meredith. (2002) Engendering Relations to State and Society in the Aftermath. In: Sheila Meintjes, Anu Pillay and Meredith Turshen, eds. *The Aftermath: Women in Post-conflict Transformation.* London: Zed Books, pp. 78–95.

Tripp, Aili M. (2003) Women in Movement: Transformations in African Political Landscapes. *International Feminist Journal of Politics*, 5(2), pp. 233–255.

Tripp, Aili Mari, Isabel Casimiro, Joy Kwesiga and Alice Mungwa. (2009) *African Women's Movements: Transforming Political Landscapes.* Cambridge; New York: Cambridge University Press.

UNIFEM. (2001) *Engendering Peace: Reflections on the Burundi Peace Process.* Nairobi, Kenya: UNIFEM.

Waller, Marguerite R. and Jennifer Rycenga, eds. (2000) *Frontline Feminisms: Women, War, and Resistance.* New York and London: Garland Publishing.

Index